# The Prince and the Monk

# The Prince and the Monk

*Shōtoku Worship in Shinran's Buddhism*

Kenneth Doo Young Lee

State University of New York Press

Published by
State University of New York Press, Albany

For information, address State University of New York Press,
194 Washington Avenue, Suite 305, Albany, NY 12210-2384

Production by Michel Haggett
Marketing by Anne. M. Valentine

Library of Congress Cataloging-in-Publication Data

Lee, Kenneth Doo Young, 1966–
    The Prince and the Monk : Shōtoku worship in Shinran's Buddhism / Kenneth
Doo Young Lee.
        p. cm.
    Includes bibliographical references and index.
    ISBN-13: 978-0-7914-7021-3 (hardcover : alk. paper)
    ISBM-13: 978-0-7914-7022-0 (pbk. : alk. paper)    1. Shinran, 1173–1263.
2. Shōtoku Taishi, 574?–622? — Cult.    I. Title.

BQ8749.S557L44    2007
294.3'926—dc22                                                        2006019064

*For my family*

# Contents

# Acknowledgments

It's 3:00 A.M. on February 9, 2006. I didn't think this time would ever come, but I'm thankful that it finally did. Like tonight, I've spent many long hours like a creature from another planet, immersed in this monumental project of writing my first book. Like a sculptor, I've been chiseling away bits and pieces of words and ideas, then pasting them back, then sanding them down so that the final product would somehow reflect the very image that I had in my mind from its original inception ten years ago, as a graduate student at Columbia University. Since then, I've moved back to Los Angeles, back to New York City, then to Orlando, and then back to Los Angeles. The last ten years flew by quickly, and my life has gone through different chapters of its own, but, like a jealous lover, this book project was always on my mind. Through all the long hours of research, brainstorming, writing, and editing, I've learned so much and have matured as a person and scholar. The satisfaction of finishing this project to the best of my ability is a personal reward, which I'll always be proud of. As I look back and remember the various faces during my ten-year journey of working on this project, I want to express my deep appreciation to those people whose guidance, encouragement, and support enabled me to complete this book.

First, I'd like to thank my teacher and mentor, Professor Ryūichi Abé, who introduced me to Shinran during my initial visit to Columbia University in the fall of 1991 and taught me all that I know about East Asian Buddhism. A man of extraordinary intelligence and gentle wisdom, Professor Abé was not only my advisor but also became my friend and bodhisattva, and compassionately helped me with this book and every aspect of my academic career. I'm also thankful to my other distinguished professors at Columbia, particularly those members on my dissertation committee—Professors Robert Thurman, Paul Anderer, David (Max) Moerman, and Alan Segal—who gave me invaluable feedback and constructive criticism to improve my manuscript for publication.

Next, I'd like to thank my colleagues at Stetson University—Mitchell Reddish, Donald Musser, Clyde Fant, Dixon Sutherland, Kandy Queen-Sutherland, and Phillip Lucas—for their encouragement and support. Also, I would like to thank my colleagues in the Religious Studies Department and the administrative staff in the College of Humanities at Cal State Northridge for their encouragement and support. I'd also like to acknowledge some key persons who took the time to read various sections of my manuscript and provided helpful feedback: Duncan Williams, William Bodiford, Kuwa Hitomi, Jayne Kim, Nae-seo Kim, Goro Shiraishi, Yukie Takimoto, Cyndy Brown, and Joyce Teague.

I'm also indebted to the constructive advice that I received from my reviewers at the State University of New York Press. I am deeply grateful for the time they took to read my manuscript carefully and offer helpful suggestions for revision. I also appreciate the editorial support provided by Michael Haggett, Allison Lee, and Nancy Ellegate. I'm sincerely grateful to the board members who voted to approve my book for publication, and the staff involved in its production.

Finally, I'd like to express my deep appreciation to my loving and supportive family—my mother Alice, sisters Anna and Grace, my brother Thomas, and my deceased father, Suk Chul Lee, and dear friends Steven Jhu, Michael Lim, Tim Boggess, Greg Sapp, Edward Kim, Billy Song, Hae Young Lee, Sil Kim, John Park, Peter Kim, Andy Choi, Jean-François Bouville, and Monica Ko. Thank you all.

K. LEE
Pasadena, CA

# Introduction

Shōtoku Taishi[1] (574–622), or Prince Shōtoku, was an imperial regent traditionally regarded as a cultural hero of Japan and the father of Japanese Buddhism. A member and representative of the Soga clan, the powerful Japanese court family that rose to prominence with the accession of the Emperor Kimmei in 531 C.E., Shōtoku, whose name means "sovereign moral power," is recognized for his pivotal role as the imperial regent (593–622) under Empress Suiko in the enhancement of Japanese politics and culture during the Asuka period (538–710). At this time, the Japanese government launched an exhaustive campaign to unify, reform, and modernize Japan by adopting Buddhism and instituting governmental and cultural reforms based on Chinese models. These included the promotion of the Confucian ideal of emperorship under the "mandate of heaven" concept,[2] establishment of the twelve official ranks at court, and implementation of the Chinese written language, the Chinese calendar, the practice of recording history, the use of coins, and the standardization of weights and measures. Although Japan was culturally backward and conservative at the time of Shōtoku's birth in 574, by the time of his death in 622 Japanese political, economic, and religious infrastructures had been drastically and fundamentally changed by the impact of Chinese and Korean culture. As a result of his significant contributions to the governance of the Japanese nation and the promotion of Japanese Buddhism, Shōtoku became a legendary figure over time, so much so that the character of the actual man had been lost. Following his death, Shōtoku continued to be so highly venerated by all Japanese people that he was worshiped as a *kami*[3] and an incarnation of the bodhisattva Kannon.[4] For centuries, imperial authorities and temple establishments have worked together to successfully promote the image of Prince Shōtoku as an ideal regent and Buddhist saint.

This book addresses the historical development of the political and religious myths surrounding the legend of Shōtoku Taishi and the role of faith in this figure for Shinran (1173–1262), the well-known founder of one of the Pure Land schools *(Jōdo Shinshū)* of Buddhism in the Kamakura period (1185–1333). This study examines the development of Shōtoku legends in

1

Japan and the importance of Shōtoku worship in Shinran's Buddhism, analyzing Shinran's liturgical text, his dream of Shōtoku's manifestation as the *guze* Kannon (world-saving bodhisattva of compassion), and other relevant events surrounding his life. Additionally, this study shows that Shinran's Buddhism was consistent with the *honji suijaku* culture—the synthesis of the Shintō and Buddhist pantheons—that existed in *kenmitsu* Buddhism,[5] the dominant Buddhist establishment during the medieval period.[6] In other words, Shinran's worship of Shōtoku as a manifestation of the bodhisattva Kannon was synonymous with devotion to Shōtoku as a powerful *kami*.

My thesis is that Shinran's thought has been misunderstood among nearly all the major branches of Buddhism he founded precisely because his heirs in the dharma failed to appreciate the central importance of his worship of this historical and legendary figure of Shōtoku. I believe that this is, in fact, the key element that helps us to better understand and appreciate the uniqueness of Shinran's religious views. Traditional understanding of Shinran's teaching by Western Shin scholars, such as the work by Dennis Hirota and Alfred Bloom, generally focuses on Shinran's doctrinal teachings regarding the practitioner's birth in the Pure Land through the primacy of *shinjin*[7] (sincere mind entrusting), and in reliance on Other-power *(tariki)* over self-power *(jiriki)*. However, there is hardly any mention of Shinran's worship of Shōtoku, which I believe needs further examination since Shōtoku figures prominently in the many liturgical hymns written by Shinran. Among the over 500 *wasan* (hymns) he composed, Shinran dedicated 190 of them in praise of Shōtoku after he experienced a revelatory event connected with Shōtoku that formed an important part of Shinran's religious identity. But since Shinran fails to discuss Shōtoku in any significant way in his doctrinal writings, the role of his reverence or devotion for Shōtoku is not clear.

The reasons why this problem has not been given much attention by Japanese scholars, and almost entirely ignored outside of Japan, center on two points. First, the cult of Shōtoku *(Taishi shinkō)* was quite widespread in Japan at the time, so Shinran's view does not seem particularly noteworthy. Second, one simply does not see faith in Shōtoku in the religious doctrines and social values professed or embodied in Shinran. Shinran was one of a great many disciples of his teacher Hōnen, and involved in the complex and often heated doctrinal debates that occurred at that time. These usually centered on issues raised by Hōnen, such as the importance of continuous recitation of nembutsu to assure one's birth in the Pure Land. The cult of Shōtoku was simply not relevant in these circles, and Shinran's own writings generally reflect this. Moreover, scholars may have ignored the importance of Shōtoku worship in Shinran's writings because of the subjective nature of Eshinni's account concerning Shinran's conversion experience at Rokkakudō. While there is no way of verifying

Shinran's dream accounts, I contend that the fact that Shinran himself expressed a deep devotion to Shōtoku in his hymns is significant evidence that Shōtoku worship was at the heart of his doctrine.

Some Western Shin scholars, like Alfred Bloom, have traditionally studied Shinran's Buddhism within the historical context of the tumultuous Kamakura period and focused on the rise and development of Pure Land Buddhism in relation to the older and traditional eight schools of Buddhism.[8] Their discussions often revolve around the comparison of "Old Buddhism" *(kyū bukkyō)*, referring to the eight schools of Buddhism from the Nara and Heian period, with "New Buddhism" *(shin bukkyō)*, the new schools of Buddhism that arose during the Kamakura period. Bloom and other modern scholars, such as Ueda Yoshifumi and Dennis Hirota—following the lead of early traditional Japanese sectarian scholars, such as Iyenaga Saburō, Sonoda Kōyū, and Inoue Mitsusada—study the lives and thoughts of the founders of the New Buddhist schools in medieval Japan, such as Hōnen, Eisai, and Shinran, as a central task to understand Kamakura Buddhism as a whole.[9] However, these studies, such as Bloom's analysis of Shinran's Buddhism, provide a rather simplified view of the religious developments that took place during the medieval period.[10] Other notable Japanese scholars, such as Akamatsu Toshihide, Shigematsu Akihisa, and Fujii Manabu also approach their study of Kamakura Buddhism from a sectarian textbook perspective,[11] engaging the traditional discussion that revolves around the distinction between Old and New Buddhism.

In response to the sectarian textbook approach to the study of Japanese Buddhist history, modern scholars such as Ishida Yoshito, Imai Masaharu, Takagi Yutaka, Ishimoda Tadashi, and Kuroda Toshio have offered a more comprehensive analysis that involves a closer examination of internal developments within the old schools that had begun in the late Heian period.[12] Among these revisionist scholars, Kuroda is unique. His study of monastic institutions during the medieval period helps us to better understand the uniqueness of Shinran's Buddhism as he redirects our attention to highly relevant internal events that took place within the sangha (Jpn. *sōgya*: Buddhist community). Kuroda's theory of *kenmitsu taisei*—the system of Buddhist doctrine and esoteric ritual that pervaded the Tendai, Shingon, and Nara schools—corrected the distinction between Old Buddhism and New Buddhism of the Kamakura period that had previously been drawn by sectarian textbook scholars and replaced it with the distinction between heresy and orthodoxy. Kuroda explains that New Buddhism of the Kamakura period—Pure Land, Zen, and Nichiren—were peripheral throughout medieval times and that Old Buddhism was the true representative of religious culture, as evidenced by the mentioning of old schools in most medieval documents. Therefore, Kuroda classified Pure Land Buddhism not as New Buddhism but as Old Buddhism, since it was integrated into the established religious order of the period. Kuroda regards that order, with its multiplicity of religious expressions and its variety of institutions, as the dominant religious motif of medieval Japan, and he views the new schools as divergent movements that became consequential only in late medieval times. For Kuroda, the importance of Shinran, Dōgen, and Nichiren rests not in their sanctified status as the founders of particular schools, but in their representing the break with and critique of the center, a dissension that provides rare insight into the nature of the hegemonic regime.[13] Thus, Kuroda considers Shinran's Buddhism as heresy *(itan)*, in accordance with the imperial decree that banned Shinran's teaching as heresy in 1207. Kuroda explains that Shinran began his career with the traditional study of Buddhism within *kenmitsu* Buddhism, but his struggles with the words, phrases, and logic of the orthodox scriptures raised doubts within him, and he ended up taking a stand against the orthodox view. Although Kuroda's *kenmitsu* theory offers a refreshing and comprehensive approach to the study of Japanese Buddhist history during the Kamakura period, I argue that his reinterpretation of the New Kamakura Buddhism under the orthodoxy-heresy distinction incorrectly casts Shinran's Buddhism and the 'exclusive nembutsu' *(senju nenbutsu)*[14] teaching as heresy.

In support of Kuroda, Satō Hiroo and Taira Masayuki have closely examined Buddhism's involvement in medieval Japanese statecraft and the religious role of the emperors of the late Heian period and of the Kamakura shogunate in maintaining the *kenmitsu* regime.[15] I will reexamine their observations since they shine light on the internal court politics that were involved in the persecution of *senju nenbutsu* teachers. Satō's study on the *honji suijaku* culture in his *Shinbutsu ōken no chūsei* (The Theory of Divine Rights of Shintō Deities and Buddhas in the Medieval Period) is particularly important because it highlights the synthesis of the Shintō-Buddhist pantheon during the medieval period.[16] Specifically, Shinran's worship of Shōtoku as a manifestation of Kannon was synonymous with his devotion to Shōtoku as a powerful *kami* who appeared during *mappō* (the age of degenerating dharma).[17] Moreover, the Shōtoku worship that is integral to Shinran's Buddhism provides a challenge to modern Shin school proponents, who have suppressed the element of *kami* worship in Shin Buddhism in their effort to present their school as free of native religious cults.

This study argues that Shinran's Buddhism cannot be considered as heresy because it contained the common aspect of *kami* worship prevalent in *kenmitsu* Buddhism in the context of the *honji suijaku* culture of the medieval period. In fact, the core of Shōtoku worship in Shinran's Buddhism most likely originated from Shinran's rigorous religious discipline within *kenmitsu* Buddhism. By incorporating the aspect of Shōtoku worship in his teachings, Shinran simply participated in the prevailing and widely accepted practice of promoting and legitimizing his innovative teachings through the worship of Shōtoku as a *kami* and manifestation of the bodhisattva Kannon. In other words, the *honji suijaku* culture remained influential throughout the medieval period because it was the ideology that legitimized the claims of ruling authorities. I contend that Shinran's innovative teaching is legitimate because of its roots in the medieval Shōtoku cult—the same way that the *kenmitsu* establishment, consisting of the Fujiwara court, Kamakura shogunate, and powerful temples, legitimized its power within the fabric of *honji suijaku*.

This book has five chapters. In chapter 1, I discuss the importance of Shōtoku worship for Shinran. How and why did Shōtoku come to be an important figure for Shinran? To begin, I analyze two main areas in which we can clearly see Shinran's personal devotion to Shōtoku Taishi: the liturgical tradition represented by his many hymns composed in praise and worship of Prince Shōtoku, and his dream about Prince Shōtoku as manifestation of the bodhisattva Kannon. Eshinni's account of Shinran's dream of Shōtoku may seem speculative due to its subjective nature and in light of the popular trend of Shōtoku worship during the medieval period, but for this study it serves as an important piece of evidence from Shinran's wife, who was simply recounting her husband's devotion to Prince Shōtoku, a devotion revealed in his own writings. Shinran's description of Shōtoku as 'guze Kannon' or 'the world-saving bodhisattva of compassion' of Japan confirms that Shōtoku, for Shinran, was more than a historical and legendary figure—Shōtoku was his personal savior.

In chapter 2, I investigate the historical and legendary status of Shōtoku Taishi. Did Shōtoku truly exist as a historical figure? How and why was he promoted to such legendary status? Although some scholars have debated these issues, I believe that examining the second question in particular will help us better understand the reasons behind the evolutionary process of Shōtoku deification. In this chapter, I examine the life of Shōtoku Taishi by taking a closer look at his regency, his Buddhist outlook, and his contributions to promote Buddhism through the building of many temples. For instance, a closer examination of the Seventeen-Article Constitution (*Jūshichijō kenpō*, 604) reveals that Shōtoku attempted to restore the notion of the absolute authority of the emperor and promote Buddhism as the official religion. In later periods, the Seventeen-Article Constitution became an important source among ruling authorities, the shōgun, court, aristocracy, and temple establishments who promoted Shōtoku worship to legitimize their claims to authority. During his regency, Prince Shōtoku instituted important reforms that laid the ideological foundations for a Chinese-style centralized state under the authority of the emperor. In particular, an in-depth analysis of the Constitution discloses ideologies that served to legitimize the ruling class's claims to authority in medieval Japan. For instance, in Article II, Shōtoku's injunction to rely on the Three

Treasures was especially significant because it officially promoted Buddhism in Japan and honored Shōtoku as the father of Japanese Buddhism.[18]

In chapter 3, I discuss the provenance of Shōtoku legends in early Japan. Who encouraged Shōtoku worship in early Japan and why? Earliest sources indicate that the promotion of Shōtoku worship was initiated by the imperial family, particularly through two significant historical books, the *Kojiki* (Record of Ancient Matters, 712) and the *Nihon shoki* (Chronicles of Japan, 720), and was sanctioned by imperial command. Through the prevalent Shintō mythology linking the imperial descent from the goddess Amaterasu and simply elevating the charismatic Prince Shōtoku as patron, ideal regent, and *kami* status, the imperial court successfully promoted Shōtoku as imperial ancestor and national hero. Shōtoku served as an ideal figure, particularly because not only did he represent the imperial family through his regency, but he was also regarded as the father of Japanese Buddhism in his role as progenitor of Buddhism in Japan. The uniqueness of Shōtoku's dual role and significant contributions to the Japanese nation and Japanese Buddhism naturally and quite easily elevated Shōtoku as more than a historical figure; by virtue of his charisma and popular influence he rose to the level of *kami*. The effort to promote Shōtoku to a legendary status was effectively conducted, given the fact that the state and Buddhism enjoyed a close and interdependent relationship in early Japan, as evidenced by the many state-sponsored temples and saturation of Buddhism at the capital of Nara. Interestingly, hardly any early accounts of Buddhist sources on Shōtoku worship exist because the imperial authorities were also serving in the dual capacity as religious authorities, or, at the least, regulated or censored Buddhism to support the interests of the state. Not surprisingly, when we examine sources in early Japan regarding Shōtoku, we see Shōtoku portrayed primarily as an imperial ancestor and *kami*, rather than as a Buddhist divinity; that status would follow later during the medieval period when Buddhist institutions began to assert their independence from the imperial court.

In chapter 4, I examine the medieval Japanese cult of Shōtoku worship and the continual evolutionary process of deification of Shōtoku. How did Shōtoku worship continue to evolve during medieval Japan? How did the changing climate of the medieval period affect the promotion of Shōtoku worship through the effort of imperial and religious authorities? During the volatile medieval period and changing of ruling powers, the imperial court and Buddhist institutions did not enjoy as close a relationship as they did in the early period of Japan. The Fujiwara family was more concerned about survival than in finding ways to strengthen their strong rule through their royal Shintō mythology based on Shōtoku worship as a *kami* and imperial ancestor. *Daimyōs* (local warlords) waging war and vying for control were not interested in such mythology so long as they were able to wield power for themselves. Meanwhile, as Buddhist institutions gained more independence as a result of the weakening ties with the imperial court, as evidenced by various *engis*—the quasihistorical accounts of miraculous events of distinctions that surrounded them—they began to promote Shōtoku in different ways, according to their own interpretations and elevation of Shōtoku primarily as a Buddhist saint or deity. A key element that helped to effectively facilitate the promotion of Shōtoku not only as a *kami* but also as a Buddhist figure was easily accomplished through the *honji suijaku* context of the medieval period. During medieval Japan, the unique phenomenon of *honji suijaku* enabled a smooth proliferation of Shōtoku worship as a Buddhist figure. Within the fabric of *honji suijaku* culture, Shōtoku worship continued to evolve through the gradual development of legends that now portrayed Shōtoku not only as a powerful *kami*, but also as a reincarnation of Tendai Eshi,[19] as a manifestation of bodhisattva Kannon, and later, as Amida Buddha and even Shinran himself. Interestingly, while the men were at war and involved themselves in political affairs, women in the court played a significant role in promoting Shōtoku worship, as we will examine in the case of the Hōryūji temple.

Finally, in chapter 5, I examine Shinran's appropriation of Shōtoku worship in his Buddhism within the fabric of the *honji suijaku* society. How and why did Shinran emphasize Shōtoku worship in his writings? How did Shinran successfully promote his innovative teaching by using Shōtoku? Like most people in medieval Japan, Shinran revered Shōtoku Taishi as a cultural and religious icon, but as a result of his conversion experience at Rokkakudō, his worship of Shōtoku went beyond the religious and political role of Shōtoku. Shinran worshiped Shōtoku as his personal savior, as evidenced by his devotional hymns in praise of Shōtoku following his Rokkakudō experience. After twenty years of religious training at Mount Hiei, Shinran left the establishment and shortly met his master Hōnen, who took him as his apprentice to learn the *senju nenbutsu* teaching. When both Hōnen and Shinran were exiled after the execution of two nembutsu proponents, Gyōku and Junsai,[20] Shinran became "neither monk nor layman" *(sō ni arazu zoku ni arazu)* and took on a wife, Eshinni, who was a daughter of the provincial governor in Echigo. Although the practice of a monk living with a woman was not new, Shinran was the first Buddhist monk who openly married and had children. On the surface, it may seem as though Shinran apostasized when he rejected his clerical vows of celibacy, but closer examination of Eshinni's account of Shinran's dream reveals his rationale for marrying Eshinni and his profound worship for Shōtoku. In his dream, Shōtoku, who appeared to Shinran as a manifestation of Kannon, assured Shinran that "she" would incarnate herself as Eshinni, thereby permitting Shinran to marry Eshinni with the implication that he would actually be marrying Kannon.

In conclusion, Shinran's Buddhism may be understood as one of the many expressions of Buddhist practice that incorporated and participated in the rich *honji suijaku* culture, and not as the single path advocated by the Shin school. Thus, instead of ignoring the aspect of Shōtoku worship in Shinran's Buddhism, Shin scholars should take a closer look at Shinran's writings in order to better appreciate the profound nature of Shinran's teachings within the cultural context of the medieval period. Consequently, by showing an openness toward a fuller understanding of Shinran's teachings in this way, Shin proponents do not necessarily have to commit a total surrender of their strong, exclusive, and conservative doctrinal position. Rather, traditional Shin scholars may come to better appreciate other expressions of Buddhist practice that emerged during the same period within the same *honji suijaku* cultural context, particularly those expressions found in Zen and Nichiren Buddhism, by incorporating a sophisticated understanding based on the acknowledgment of the importance of Shōtoku worship in their master's writings. Consequently, I hope that this study will encourage further "digging," as my own work relies and builds on the works of nonsectarian scholars such as Kuroda Toshio and Satō Hiroo, to provide a more in-depth and comprehensive understanding of the unique and rich historical context of the medieval period in Japan.

# Chapter 1

---

## Shinran and Shōtoku

Revered as the founder of *Jōdo Shinshū* Buddhism, Shinran is one of the most interesting and controversial figures in medieval Japan because his version of Buddhism appears to represent a qualitative departure from the traditional teachings of Buddhism. Buddhist teaching in general does not aspire to a belief in a deity or worship of a god, but Shinran's Buddhism is clearly marked by the veneration of Amida Buddha. When Buddhism entered Japan via Korea in the sixth century, about 1,000 years after its inception in India, the Japanese people inherited a developed form of Mahāyāna Buddhism, which included the worship of the Buddha in various forms. In particular, the Mahāyāna Buddhist interpretation of the 'three bodies of the Buddha' (Sk. *trikāya*; Jpn. *sanshin*) included the practice of chanting the name of Amida Buddha—viewed as one of the "bodies of bliss" (Sk. *sambhōgakāya*) of the Buddha—in Pure Land Buddhism. Because the Amida Buddha and other Buddhist deities, such as the bodhisattva Kannon, were associated with the attribute of compassion and played a salvific role in assisting practitioners toward enlightenment, these Buddhist figures naturally became objects of veneration over time. Moreover, in Pure Land Buddhism, the salvific role of Amida Buddha and the bodhisattva Kannon was further strengthened with the notion that Japan entered *mappō* (the age of degenerating dharma). I focus on Shinran because his brand of Buddhism contains a worship element that seems to contradict the traditional Buddhist teaching, yet is regarded as an orthodox branch of Buddhism. Previous patriarchs, including Shinran's master, Hōnen, did not emphasize a worship component in their practice. Even among Indian and Chinese masters of

9

the Pure Land Buddhist tradition, Pure Land Buddhist practice focused on techniques, such as visualizations and chanting nembutsu, rather than a worship of a Buddhist figure, whether Amida Buddha or Prince Shōtoku as a manifestation of Kannon. In this chapter, I examine how and why Shōtoku come to be an important figure for Shinran through a closer examination of Shinran's liturgical text, his dream of Shōtoku's manifestation as the bodhisattava Kannon, and other relevant events surrounding his life.

## SHINRAN'S LIFE

Born in 1173, Shinran (1173–1263)[1] was the son of Hino Arinori, a middle-rank nobleman.[2] According to tradition, in 1182, at the age of nine, Shinran was taken by his foster father Hino Noritsuna to Shōren'in, a branch temple of Enryakuji, where he was initiated into the monkhood by Jien.[3] After he had diligently studied the major Buddhist sutras and practiced the traditional forms of nembutsu for twenty years, Shinran voluntarily left Mount Hiei because he was dissatisfied with the growing corruption of the *sangha* due to the promotion of state Buddhism. He left in search of an alternative way toward enlightenment.

Upon leaving Mount Hiei, Shinran undertook a one-hundred-day seclusion at Rokkakudō, a hexagonal temple in Kyoto containing an image of Kannon and supposedly founded by Shōtoku Taishi. During his seclusion, he prayed for divine inspiration and guidance. After ninety-five days, Shinran had a vision of Prince Shōtoku, who appeared to him in a dream as a manifestation of bodhisattva Kannon and told him that he would meet a great person. Soon after, Shinran met his master, Hōnen, and became his disciple.[4] From 1201 to 1207, Shinran studied under Hōnen. The fact that, in 1205, he was allowed to copy Hōnen's *Senjakushū* (Collection of Passages Concerning the Nembutsu of the Selected Original Vow, 1198) along with a portrait of the master indicates Hōnen's recognition and approval of Shinran's grasp of the *senju nenbutsu* teaching that was based on simply invoking the name of Amida for individual salvation.[5] Together, Hōnen and Shinran actively and successfully spread the *senju nenbutsu* teaching to people in the countryside, especially to poor farmers in nearby villages.

When news of the popularity of *senju nenbutsu* teaching reached the mainstream Buddhist leaders at Mount Hiei, Jōkei drafted a petition, the *Kōfukuji sōjō*, to ban its teaching on the grounds of heresy and its threat to the status quo of the nation. Leaders of mainstream Buddhism appealed to the retired emperor, who was regarded as the official representative of the sangha, and the imperial and political authorities subsequently approved the petition to ban *senju nenbutsu* teaching and exiled Hōnen, Shinran, and some of their active disciples. In 1207, Shinran was sent to Echigo, a distant province near the sea, where he quietly spent the next seven years practicing Buddhism and reaching out to the peasants there.[6]

After the exile was lifted in 1214, instead of returning to the aristocratic lifestyle of the Kyoto capital and reuniting with his master Hōnen, Shinran moved to another rural region, the Kanto area in the Hitachi province, and continued to teach among the simple folk of Japan. Shinran had a genuine desire to meet the needs of the poor farmers. Hirota remarks that the common people of Japan were one of the strongest inspirations in Shinran's life, and he sought "to deepen his own self-awareness and his insight into the dharma by sharing it with the people of the countryside."[7] In Kanto, Shinran established *dōjōs*, places where all people could gather to hear him preach the dharma. These were different from the traditional temples' *dōjōs*, which were intended primarily for use by monks. As a well-educated monk who was fluent in classical Chinese, Shinran wrote and translated many works on Buddhism into simple Japanese for the benefit of the commoners, who were mostly illiterate. In these ways, Shinran tried to bring the message of Buddhism to those who had been traditionally shut out.

The message of Buddhism that Shinran taught was radically different from the traditional one in that he preached the possibility of Buddhahood for all believers. Shinran taught that the key to enlightenment was *shinjin*.[8] He preached that one did not need to become a monk, build grandly ornamental stupas (shrines housing Buddha's relics), or say the nembutsu one thousand times to attain salvation. Shinran explained that when Amida Buddha took his Eighteenth Vow,[9] he promised access to the Pure Land to all sentient beings who placed their faith in him. Since money and education were not necessary for Buddhahood, "people of the countryside, who did not know the meanings of characters and who were painfully and hopelessly ignorant . . . easily grasped the essential meaning."[10]

For the next seventeen years, Shinran devoted much of his time to completing the *Kyōgyōshinshō* and other writings, including various hymns *(wasan)* and personal letters. He continued to teach among the villagers and steadily gained followers in the Kanto area. Then, in 1231, with the imminent threat of persecution due to the issue of another official decree to ban *senju nenbutsu* teaching in the countryside, Shinran returned to Kyoto. There he lived the rest of his life, writing a series of *wasan* and apologetic letters while being cared for by his youngest daughter, Kakushinni.[11] He died in 1263 at the age of ninety.

## SHINRAN'S DREAMS

Dreams played an important role in Shinran's religious development. However, due to the subjective nature of dream accounts, most traditional *Jōdo Shinshū* scholarship from both English and Japanese writers tends to overlook the significant part that dreams had in Shinran's life and religious development, particularly after his one hundred days of seclusion at Rokkakudō. These dream accounts may have been ignored because of the mistrust of sectarian theorists who use mythical anomalies to establish Shinran as the charismatic founder of the *Jōdo Shinshū* Buddhism. Although sources may not draw attention from skeptical scholars, they may help us to understand certain meaningful motifs that seem to emerge from Shinran's teachings and writings. After examining Shinran's life path before as well as after the time of his one-hundred-day seclusion at Rokkakudō, I conclude that there is no doubt that Shinran experienced a paradigm shift, a "conversion experience," that played a meaningful role in shaping Shinran's Buddhism.

For the twenty years prior to the time of his retreat at Rokkakudō, a temple dedicated to the bodhisattva Kannon in Kyoto city, Shinran was engaged in *dōsō*[12] practice at Mount Hiei and consequently reached some degree of spiritual attainment. However, he did not undergo the climax of his profound awakening of faith.[13] Moreover, the development of Pure Land thought in Shinran teaching focuses on the important notion of faith; therefore, a "conversion" to a central belief in the Pure Land path would have had to happen at some point. If Shinran were exposed to Pure Land sutras on Mount Hiei, then he would have been motivated to seek Hōnen's teaching, based on his philosophical identification with the Buddhist values of Shōtoku Taishi and his interest in the Pure Land path.[14] Shinran's conversion experience to the Pure Land faith must have taken place either before he met Hōnen or during his discipleship. In this context, the Rokkakudō dream assumes its importance in the course of Shinran's spiritual development.

Also, in the dream, the bodhisattva Kannon gave Shinran permission to marry Eshinni, claiming that Kannon would incarnate herself as Eshinni. Through the dream and the truth of the prophecies, according to Eshinni, Shinran came to believe that Shōtoku was his personal savior. After receiving divine inspiration at Rokkakudō, Shinran soon met Hōnen by way of fate, according to the dream account, and set out on an active campaign to spread the Buddhist message of salvation in the name of the Amida Buddha among the countryside masses. Although we may not be able to ever verify the authenticity of Shinran's dream account due to its subjective nature, the fact that Shinran took a different approach toward life and Buddhism from that point on speaks for itself as evidence that the inspiration he received from the dream spurred his religious metamorphosis. For instance, with a closer examination of Shinran's dream at Rokkakudō, we gain an insight into his personal worship of Prince Shōtoku as a manifestation of the bodhisattva Kannon. The significance of his dream was that he personally received the word from Shōtoku Taishi, whom he considered the bodhisattva Kannon. In his dream, the bodhisattva Kannon says, "I will adorn your life and guide you to attain birth in the Pure Land."[15] These words of reassurance became an important source of legitimization for Shinran's innovative teaching, which emphasized Shōtoku worship. Moreover, Shinran also believed that Amida Buddha himself authorized his marriage to Eshinni and that she was an incarnation of the bodhisattva Kannon.

The account of Shinran's dream at Rokkakudō is found in several places: in his *Kyōgyōshinshō* (Teaching, Practice, Faith and Enlightenment), Eshinni's letters, Kakunyo's *Honganji no Shōnin Shinran denne* (Illustrated Biography of the Master Shinran of the Honganji Temple), and in the *Shinran muki* (Shinran's Dreams).[16] In his dream, Prince Shōtoku appeared before Shinran as bodhisattva Kannon and conveyed a message to him in verse form.[17] Significantly, in a verse entitled *Taishi byōkutsu-ge* in his *Jōgū Taishi gyoki* (The Record Honoring the Prince of the Higher Palace),[18] Shinran describes the words of Shōtoku, which appear in a slightly varied form in Shinran's *Kōtaishi Shōtoku hōsan* (Hymns of Respect to Imperial Prince Shōtoku; see Appendix B for my translation):[19]

1

Give reverence to Prince Shōtoku of the country of Japan!
Out of his deep compassion,
Prince Shōtoku brought the profound Buddhist teachings to the
    people
And was responsible for the spread of Buddhism in Japan.

2

After he ordered the construction of the four sub-temples of
    Shitennōji,
Prince Shōtoku went into the mountainous forest
In Ōtagi (Kyoto) and made a proclamation.

3

Prince Shōtoku stated that the imperial capital
Would surely be established there sometime in the future.
To commemorate the event,
A hexagonal platform was built on that land.

4

Inside the hexagonal temple (Rokkakudō),
A three-inch-tall, Jambūnada[20] golden statue of the world-saving
Bodhisattva of compassion (*guze* Kannon),
Was placed there for security and protection.

5

After spending several decades in the imperial capital
Of Nanba in the Settsu province,
Prince Shōtoku moved to Tachibana,
Where he built the Hōryūji.

6

From the capital of Tachibana, Prince Shōtoku moved again to Nara,
Where he built many more temples
And continued to spread the Buddha's teaching.

7

After the reign of four emperors in Nara,
The capital was moved to Nagaoka for fifty years
And then moved again to Ōtagi.

8

During the reign of Emperor Kammu, in Enryaku 6 (787),
When the capital was being built,
The world-saving bodhisattva of compassion (*guze* Kannon),
Performed miraculous signs for people to behold.

9

The Hōryūji was constructed on the first site,
Which marked the spread of Buddhism in Japan and
Prince Shōtoku's building of many temples and pagodas in various
    places.

10

In observance of Prince Shōtoku's orders,
The people, along with the imperial family and court officials,
Gave homage and paid their respects at the hexagonal temple.

The above ten hymns recount, in Shinran's own words, the place where Prince Shōtoku visited him in a dream as a manifestation of *guze* Kannon. This appearance gave him the inspiration to build many Buddhist temples as an expression of the immense gratitude for the proclamation of the Buddhist teaching in Japan. Additionally, as hymns 3–7 indicate, Shinran claims that Prince Shōtoku possessed divine powers, namely, the ability to predict the future, in accordance with his portrayal in the *Nihon shoki* when Prince Shōtoku predicted the moving of the capital from Nara to Heian.

The Chinese characters of the title *Taishi byōkutsu-ge* also expressed special devotion to Prince Shōtoku and were often written on his portrait as a devotional practice by Shōtoku worshipers. In various writings, Shinran associates the *Taishi byōkutsu-ge* with the following description of Shōtoku Taishi: "I am the reincarnation of the Bodhisattva *Avalokiteśvara* (Kannon) in this world and my wife is the reincarnation of the Bodhisattva *Mahāsthāmaprāpta* (Seishi). The mother who nurtured and looked after me is the reincarnation of the Amida Buddha, one who is filled with great compassion. These reincarnations exist to save people during *mappō* (age of degenerating dharma)."[21] The major symbol in this hymn is the Pure Land or Amida triad, which consists of the Amida Buddha with his two attendants, bodhisattvas *Avalokiteśvara* and *Mahāsthāmaprāpta*, identified as a family consisting of mother, husband, and wife. The compassionate response (of the Amida triad) to save all people during *mappō* exemplifies a prevalent theme from Shinran's reinterpretation of Prince Shōtoku's ideals.

Consequently, Rokkakudō was the place where Shinran attained birth in the Pure Land. Located in the southeast of the intersection of Karasuma and Sanjo streets in central Kyoto, Rokkakudō was originally founded by Prince Shōtoku to enshrine *guze* Kannon near a pond *(ike)* where he bathed; the small hut *(bo)* of succeeding generations of Buddhist priests gave rise to the name "Ikebo." During Shinran's time, statues of the Buddha, temples, and unusual land features were considered to have certain mystical powers that could be directed toward one's spiritual benefit. Villagers used Rokkakudō as a gathering spot, at which times flower arrangements were usually placed at the temple. A detailed description of the interior and exterior design of Shitennōji in Shinran's *Kōtaishi Shōtoku hōsan* informs us about Prince Shōtoku's typical design for a temple dedicated to the world-saving bodhisattva of compassion:

17

In 593, after moving to the eastern section of the Kōryō region,
Prince Shōtoku built the Shitennōji
And spread the Buddhist teaching everywhere.

18

At this place, it was believed that the Tathāgata[22] came in the past
And declared that he would turn the wheel of dharma
In order to spread the Buddhist teaching.

19

At that time, the honorable Prince Shōtoku
Made offerings to the Tathāgata.
Out of his devotion, he built the temple and pagoda
To honor the Tathāgata.

20

Constructing the statues of the Four Guardian Deities
And spreading the Buddhist teaching,
Prince Shōtoku built the Kyōden-in temple
As a place where enlightenment could be realized.

21

At this place, there is a body of pure water, which is called Kōryō
    pond.
An auspicious dragon lives there
And protects the Buddhist teaching.

22

In 597, Prince Shōtoku performed rituals for the dragon
On the banks of Tamatsukuri
To propagate the Buddha's teaching.

23

The place is adorned with the seven precious materials;
The dragon is always there.
The pure water, flowing to the east,
Is called "flowering water of white jade."

24

For those who drink the pure water with a heart of compassion,
It becomes a medicine of dharma.
Those who obey the words of Prince Shōtoku humbly draw from
    its flow.

25

The main hall and the pagoda stand in the center,
Facing the eastern gate of the Paradise.
All who make a pilgrimage there once
Will surely attain birth in the Pure Land.

26

Prince Shōtoku placed six grains of relics of the Buddha inside the
    pillar,
Which is erected in the center of the pagoda;
By doing this, Prince Shōtoku was bestowing benefits
To sentient beings of the six courses.

27

A gilt bronze statue of *guze* Kannon
Is enshrined in the Kyōden-in temple.
After the death of Prince Shōtoku, King Seong Myong of Paekche

28

Built the sacred image to express his love and devotion,
And instructed Prince Ajwa, as a royal envoy,
To deliver it to Japan to be used as a memorial.

29

With his own hand, Prince Shōtoku laid gold on the base of the
    pagoda,
To symbolize the spread
And influence of Śākyamuni's teaching in Japan.[23]

In Eshinni's letter to her daughter Kakushinni—a letter discovered by Washio
Kyōdo in 1921 (Taishō 11)—the detailed explanation of her husband Shinran's
dream at Rokkakudō confirms that his worship of Prince Shōtoku played an
important role in his conversion to the *senju nenbutsu* teaching:

Shinran left Mount Hiei and remained in seclusion for one hundred
days at Rokkakudō, and prayed for the salvation of all people. On the
dawn of the ninety-fifth day, Shōtoku Taishi appeared to him in a
dream, revealing the path to enlightenment in verse form. Immediately after Shinran left Rokkakudō and, seeking a karmic link that
would lead him to salvation, he met his master Hōnen, who would
show him the way of salvation. Just as he confined himself for a
hundred days at Rokkakudō, Shinran visited Hōnen daily for a hundred days, rain or shine, regardless of obstacles. He heard the Master
teach that in order to be saved in the afterlife, regardless of whether
one was good or evil, only the recitation of the nembutsu was necessary. Since he carefully kept this teaching in his heart, Shinran would

say the following when people talked about the nembutsu: "I shall follow Hōnen wherever he goes, even if others may say that I would go to hell, because I have wandered since the beginningless beginning and I have nothing to lose.[24]

Here, Eshinni's dream account also reveals Shinran's motivation to begin religious training under Hōnen: to be saved in the afterlife. Following Shinran's dream, it is said that Shinran studied so diligently under his master that he was allowed to paint Hōnen's portrait and later changed his name to "Zenshin," which is the name that Prince Shōtoku gave to him in the revelation.

A copy of the *Shinran muki* (Record of Shinran's Dreams) by Shinran's disciple Shinbutsu (1209–1261)[25] and another version recently discovered by Hiramatsu Reizo, which has been authenticated to be in Shinran's handwriting, provide further evidence of the profound impact that Shinran's dream encounter with Shōtoku had on his life:[26]

> *Guze* Kannon appeared as a righteous monk at Rokkakudō. Dressed in simple white robes and seated on a large white lotus, he said to Shinran: "If a practitioner is driven by sexual desire because of his past karma, then I shall take on the body of a holy woman *(gyokunyo)* to be ravished by him. Throughout his entire life I will adorn him, and at death I will lead him to birth in Pure Land." After saying these words, *guze* Kannon proclaimed to Zenshin [Shinran]: "This is my vow. Expound it to all people." Based on this proclamation, I realized that I needed to tell this message to millions of people, and then I awoke from my dream.[27]

The following is Kakunyo's account of the appearance of the bodhisattva Kannon in Shinran's dream, taken from the *Honganji shōnin Shinran denne* (An Illustrated Biography of Shinran):

> On the fifth day of the fourth month in the third year of Kennin (1203), Shōnin had a vision at night in the hour of the Tiger. According to records, the world-saving bodhisattva of compassion [*guze* Kannon] of the Rokkakudō manifested himself in the form of a holy monk of dignified appearance, wearing a white robe and sitting in a proper posture on the pedestal of a huge lotus flower. He said to Zenshin: "If you are obliged to have sexual contact with a woman through some past karma, I will transform myself into a beautiful woman and become your partner. I will adorn you with virtues throughout your life, and at your death I will guide you to the Land of Utmost Bliss.[28]

Particularly interesting in this passage is the sexual transformation of bod-hisattva Kannon, who has been traditionally worshiped as a male figure in Bud-dhism.[29] Scholars remain uncertain about the beginning of female worship of Kannon in Japan, but this account provides one logical rationale for its origin and development. Many writers have interpreted this part of Shinran's dream in modern terms, suggesting that Shinran left Mount Hiei because he desired to have sexual relations—Shinran's subsequent marriage to Eshinni and birth of his children are consistent with this interpretation. Although monks typi-cally took vows not to eat meat and abstain from sexual relations, during Shin-ran's time it was widely known that many monks lived with women who bore them children; they simply pretended to remain celibate by not legally marry-ing the women they lived with. Unwilling to be hypocritical like his peers, Shinran was the first monk who openly and legally married a woman. More-over, according to *Jōdo Shinshū* scholar, Hattori Shisō, Shinran had at least two, perhaps three wives, and a total of seven children.[30] In any case, in view of his master Hōnen's teaching of complete reliance on the Other-power, Shinran's decision to publicly break the Buddhist precept of celibacy was based on his belief that marriage did not hinder one's birth in the Pure Land.[31]

Interestingly, in the *Honganji Shōnin Shinran denne*, Kakunyo claims that it was the bodhisattva Kannon who appeared before Shinran, while Eshinni's account claims that it actually was Prince Shōtoku:

> In the third year of Kennin (1203) on the fifth day of the fourth month, during the hour of the Tiger (3:00–5:00 A.M.), it is recorded that the statue of the Bodhisattva Kannon assumed a human form with a calm appearance and wearing a white robe. Sitting on a lotus blossom, he said to Zenshin: "You are destined to know women so I shall transform myself into the woman you will make love to. I shall be by your side all your life to purify this act. When you leave this world, I shall lead you to the Pure Land." The Bodhisattva Kannon said to Zenshin [Shinran], "This is my vow to you." Zenshin under-stood the vow and proclaimed it to the masses.

The following is Kakunyo's[32] account of Shinran's inspiration received from Kannon of the Rokkakudō Temple:

> In the first year of Kennin (1201), Shōnin [The Master; Shinran] received an inspiration from Avalokiteśvara of the Rokkakudō Temple. According to his instruction, Shōnin proclaimed Avalokiteśvara's mes-sage to the multitude of men and women who gathered in Higashiyama. One of the three people resting in the hall is Shōnin, who was attempting a 100-day confinement. Shōnin worshiped

Avalokiteśvara with his palms joined together. The white-robed world-saving bodhisattva of compassion Kannon is seated on a white lotus seat. Shōnin proclaimed Kannon's message to the multitude of people who gathered in Higashiyama.

Kakunyo also includes an account of Ren'i's dream:

> In the eighth year of Kencho (1256), Ren'i, who constantly attended Shōnin, had a dream in the hermitage at Nishino toin, Gojo, Kyoto that Prince Shōtoku worshiped Shōnin as Amida's incarnation.
>     Shōnin is wearing a black robe, aged eighty-four. Prince Shōtoku worshiped Shōnin with his palms joined together.
>     Ren'i-bo was lying in bed dreaming.
>     On the ninth day of the second month in the eighth year of Kencho (1256), at night at the hour of the Tiger, Shaku Ren'i had a vision in a dream: Prince Shōtoku bowed in worship to Shinran Shōnin and said in verse,
>
>> Adoration to Amida Buddha of Great Compassion!
>> You have appeared in this world (as Shinran Shōnin) to
>>     spread the excellent teaching;
>> You lead people of the evil world in the evil period of the five
>>     defilements
>> To definitely attain the supreme enlightenment.
>
> Hence, it is clear that Shōnin, the Patriarchal Master, was an incarnation of Amida Tathāgata.

Although this is a slight variation from Eshinni's dream account, we may deduce that Eshinni's recollection is likely to be more accurate than Kakunyo's because she probably heard it firsthand from Shinran. Also, it is highly likely that Kakunyo had Eshinni's letters as reference when he wrote the *Honganji Shōnin Shinran denne*. Why, then, did Kakunyo change which person spoke to Shinran? Despite the fact that there is no conclusive evidence for this change, if one considers the purpose of Kakunyo's version—to unify and strengthen *Jōdo Shinshū* followers at Honganji—there is a more dramatic effect of bodhisattva Kannon appearing before Shinran rather than Prince Shōtoku.

In the Higashi Honganji copy of the *Honganji Shōnin Shinran denne*, Ren'i, a disciple of Shinran's later years, described a vision in which Shōtoku Taishi supplicated himself before Shinran and said: "He who bows to Amida Buddha (Skt. Amitābha, 'He of Immeasurable Light'), the Tathāgata of Great Compassion whose purpose in coming into this world is to transmit the holy teaching, will be enlightened even if he is born when the five unpardonable transgressions are commonplace." It is thus clear that Shinran is the manifestation of Amida Buddha.

According to this Honganji record, Shinran is elevated to a deified status as Amida Buddha; it is no longer Shinran bowing to Shōtoku Taishi, but rather Shōtoku Taishi bowing to Shinran. In fact, Eshinni had a dream in which she saw Shinran as a manifestation of bodhisattva Kannon:

> In front of the temple, images of the Buddha were hung on something that looked like a *torii* (a Shintō shrine archway). One image, which I could not clearly see, seemed to emanate a bright light from the head of the Buddha. There was another image that clearly showed the face of the Buddha. When I asked which Buddha it was, someone replied that the one that emanates a bright light is Hōnen Shōnin, who is none other than Seishi (*Mahāsthāmaprāpta* Bodhisattva). Then when I asked about the other image, the voice replied that the one with the face of the Buddha was Bodhisattva Kannon, who is none other than Zenshin (Shinran Shōnin). After I heard these words, I awakened and realized that it was all a dream.[33]

Ever since that dream, Eshinni regarded her husband Shinran as the manifestation of bodhisattva Kannon. Needless to say, such distortion of facts served to promote the interests of *Jōdo Shinshū* leaders at Honganji but obviously went far beyond the limits of historical reality. Although the subjectivity of Eshinni's dream account may cause us to doubt the reasons involved in Shinran's life change, a closer examination of Shinran's subsequent compositions of hymns in praise of Shōtoku reflects that he did indeed experience some profound change, one in which he emphatically incorporated the worship of Prince Shōtoku in his version of Buddhist teaching. From that point on, Shinran's life took a new course as he began his discipleship under Hōnen and, later, as a family man.

## Hymns Dedicated to Shōtoku

It is evident from the numerous hymns that Shinran dedicated to Shōtoku as a manifestation of bodhisattva Kannon that Shōtoku's revelation at Rokkakudō had a profound effect on Shinran.[34] To understand Shinran's unique doctrine, it is essential to understand the importance of that revelation. Shinran wrote over 500 hymns during his lifetime: 307 are dedicated to eight specific individuals; 190 are about Shōtoku Taishi. The other 117 are dedicated to the seven patriarchs of the Pure Land movement: Nāgārjuna (10), Vasubandhu (10), T'an-luan (34), Tao-ch'o (7), Shan-tao (26), Genshin (10), and Hōnen (20).[35] In the *Shōzōmatsu wasan* (Hymns of the Dharma-Ages, 1258), Shinran dedicated eleven hymns to Prince Shōtoku, whom Shinran regarded as responsible for the introduction of the dharma into the country. Prince Shōtoku's importance in the *Shōzōmatsu wasan* (Hymns of the Dharma-Ages, 1258) and *Kōtaishi Shōtoku hōsan* (Hymns in Praise of Prince Shōtoku) stems from Shinran's view of him as a manifestation of bodhisattva Kannon, who compassionately appeared in Japan to deliver the nembutsu teaching during *mappō*.[36]

In the Appendix of *Kōsō wasan* (Hymns of the Pure Land Masters, 1248), Shinran found special significance in the timing of Prince Shōtoku's birth: "Born on the first day of the first month in the first year of Emperor Bidatsu, 1521 years after the passing of the Buddha."[37] According to a widely accepted belief, the world entered the last dharma-age (*mappō*—the final period in the decline of the dharma in the world) 1,500 years after Śākyamuni's death. Thus, Prince Shōtoku's life corresponded to the onset of the last age, and Shinran regarded him as a manifestation of the bodhisattva Kannon, who appeared in Japan precisely at this time to guide beings to the Pure Land path.[38]

### 83

Entrusting ourselves to the vow of the inconceivable wisdom of
    the Buddha through the kindness of Prince Shōtoku
We have entered the true stage of the settled mind
And have become like Maitreya (Jpn. Miroku), the Buddha-
    to-come.

### 84

The world-saving bodhisattva of compassion, *guze* Kannon, who
    appeared
And announced himself as Prince Shōtoku
Is like a father, never deserting us,
And like a mother, always looking after us.

### 85

From the beginningless past to the world of present,
Prince Shōtoku has compassionately looked after us like a father
And stayed close to us like a mother.

### 86

Prince Shōtoku has compassionately recommended and led us to
    believe
In the vow of inconceivable wisdom of the Buddha,
So that we are now able to enter the true stage of the settled mind.

87

May all those who entrust themselves in *tariki* (Other-power) to
    fulfill the
Benevolence of the Buddha,
Spread the two aspects of the Buddha Tathāgata's virtue
Throughout the ten quarters.

88

The world-saving Prince Shōtoku of great love
Stays in our heart like he is our father;
The world-saving bodhisattva of compassion, *guze* Kannon,
Stays in our heart like she is our mother.

89

From the incalculable aeons of the past to this present world,
Out of Prince Shōtoku's great compassion, we have now entered the
Inconceivable wisdom of the Buddha,
Which is beyond the notion of good and evil, pure and impure.

90

Prince Shōtoku, the religious founder of Japan:
We are profoundly indebted and grateful to him.
Trust him wholeheartedly and praise him always.

91

Out of deep concern for the people of Japan,
Prince Shōtoku came to enlighten people
By proclaiming the compassionate vow of Tathagata.
Let us rejoice and praise him always!

92

Through countless lives and incalculable aeons
Of the past to this present world,
Every one of us has received his profound compassion.
Trust him wholeheartedly and praise him always.

93

With his compassionate care, Prince Shōtoku always provides for us
And protects us and encourages us
To receive the two aspects of Buddha Tathāgata's virtue.

We can clearly see from these *wasan* that Shinran worshiped Prince Shōtoku as the incarnation of Kannon and the manifestation of the Buddha's virtue of love and compassion.

In his *Kōtaishi Shōtoku hōsan* (Hymns in Praise of Prince Shōtoku), Shinran again describes Prince Shōtoku, with his significant achievements and contributions to the promotion of Buddhism in Japan, as the incarnation of bodhisattva Kannon who appeared in Japan during *mappō*. In support of his belief that Shōtoku was an incarnation of bodhisattva Kannon, Shinran traces Shōtoku's karmic connections to previous dharma masters in India and China:

11

Prince Shōtoku was born
As Queen Śrīmālā in India
And appeared as Master Hui-ssu (Jpn. Eshi) in China.

12

He appeared in China to help people;
He was reborn as both man
And woman five hundred times.

13

He appeared in the Hunan province at Mount Heng
In order to spread the Buddhist teaching;
Having experienced tens of incarnations,
He proclaimed Śākyamuni Tathāgata's teaching.

14

He appeared as Master Hui-ssu to help people in attaining
    liberation;
He was referred to as Master of Southern Mountain
At the Mount Heng temple where the Wisdom sutras were pro-
    claimed.[39]

According to Shinran, in this hymn Prince Shōtoku was born as Queen Śrīmālā, who renounced her imperial duties to become a devoted nun and disciple of Buddha. In other words, Shinran is essentially claiming that Prince Shōtoku received the dharma directly from Śākyamuni Buddha. Consequently, Shinran's vision of Shōtoku incarnated as a woman has special significance. Because Kannon was understood to be feminine, Shinran obviously had a positive view of femininity. Shinran's explanation of Shōtoku's incarnation as

Queen Śrīmālā in India confirms that Shinran identified with Shōtoku's idea of salvation for all sentient beings, including and especially women, who were considered inferior by older and traditional schools of Buddhism.

Shinran explains that Shōtoku was reborn in China as Master Hui-ssu, who spread Śākyamuni Tathāgata's teaching. Shinran describes how Shōtoku was responsible for transmitting and spreading the teaching of Śākyamuni Buddha in China through the incarnation of Master Hui-ssu. Shinran also explains that Prince Shōtoku was reborn in Korea to spread the dharma to all sentient beings there. Without making any specific references to a certain Buddhist monk in Korea, Shinran explains that Prince Shōtoku, working together with King Seong Myong and Prince Ajwa of the land of Paekche, "sent Buddhist statues, collections of sutras, *vinaya* texts, and treatises, robes, monks, and nuns to Japan."[40] After tracing the transmission of the dharma through Shōtoku's rebirths in India, China, and Korea, Shinran explains that Prince Shōtoku was born in the imperial family in Japan to spread Śākyamuni Tathāgata's teaching and to save all sentient beings:

33

Prince Shōtoku was born in the imperial family;
His edict was declared throughout the provinces.
He instructed the people to build many temples, pagodas, and
    images,
In reverence of the Buddha.

34

Prince Shōtoku, a child of Emperor Yōmei,
Composed three major Mahāyāna commentaries:
The Lotus Sutra, the Śrīmālā Sutra, and the Vimalakīrti Sutra.

35

After Prince Shōtoku died, those who desire
To spread the teaching of Śākyamuni Tathāgata
And help others toward enlightenment
Are to be regarded as manifestations of Prince Shōtoku.

36

Honoring the teachings of the six schools,
Prince Shōtoku helped people incessantly.
Always observing the five precepts, Prince Shōtoku was called
    Śrīmālā.

37

When this queen was alive long ago,
Śākyamuni Tathāgata compassionately preached
The Śrīmālā Sutra.

38

Subsequently, Prince Shōtoku gave lectures on this sutra
And also wrote a commentary, which marked the beginning of
The propagation of the Buddhist teaching in Japan
For the sake of all the Japanese people.[41]

Interestingly, in these verses, Shinran describes the former incarnations of Prince Shōtoku rather than the former incarnations of bodhisattva Kannon. For instance, instead of saying that the bodhisattva Kannon was born as Queen Śrīmālā or Master Hui-ssu, Shinran says that "Prince Shōtoku was born as Queen Śrīmālā and appeared as Master Hui-ssu in China."[42] Shinran identifies bodhisattva Kannon with Prince Shōtoku and points to Prince Shōtoku as the embodiment of the Amida Buddha:

41

The gilt bronze *guze* Kannon
Was delivered to Japan by Prince Ajwa, as a royal envoy,
And was enshrined in the Kyōden-in temple.

42

Always take refuge in this statue, which is the body of Prince
　　Shōtoku!
Give reverence to this statue,
Which is the transformed body of Amida Tathāgata!

43

Queen Śrīmālā, a child of the Buddha,
Gave homage to the buddhas of the ten quarters;
"May Brahma, Indra, the Four Guardian Deities, the Dragon-god,
And other guardians protect the dharma!"

44

Ilra of Silla proclaimed, "Give reverence to *guze* Kannon,
The king of millet-scattered islands
Who transmits the light of dharma to the east,"
And prostrated before the Prince of eight ears.

45

Prince Ajwa of Paekche bowed down and declared:
"Give reverence to the most compassionate *guze* Kannon,
Who has spread the wonderful teaching eastward to Japan,
Transmitting and explicating the light of dharma for forty-nine
    years!"

46

In China, Prince Shōtoku's teachers
Were Master Hui-ssu and Master Hui-wen.
When Prince Shōtoku was incarnated as the nun Śrīmālā,
Master Hui-ssu was his teacher.[43]

The last part of the *Kōtaishi Shōtoku hōsan* describes Shōtoku's victorious
defeat of Moriya no Mononobe, who, in Shinran words, "sought to destroy the
Buddhist teaching."[44] Interestingly, Shinran interprets this historical event as a
spiritual battle between Prince Shōtoku, who sought to spread the dharma, and
Moriya, who sought to destroy the dharma in Japan:

62

In order to spread the Buddhist teaching and help people,
Prince Shōtoku left Mount Heng
And appeared here in Japan where the sun rises.

63

Emerging victorious from the wrong views of Moriya,
Prince Shōtoku bestowed the gracious merits of the dharma.
The Buddhist teaching will soon spread all over
And many people will attain birth in the Land of Peace.

64

All those who doubt and reject the teaching given by the Tathāgata
And try to destroy it by using ill tactics
Are reincarnations of Moriya no Mononobe.
Do not be kind and become close to such people!

65

As Prince Shōtoku was proclaiming the Buddha's dharma
To teach and guide people,
Moriya no Mononobe, being the destructive enemy,
Followed him like his shadow.

66

Rebels of Moriya no Mononobe's clan harbored deep malice,
Attempted to destroy the Buddhist teaching by
Burning temples and pagodas.

67

In painful grief during the destruction of the dharma,
Prince asked the emperor with respect
To dispatch soldiers

68

Joining the soldiers with his bow of meditation and arrow of
    wisdom,
Prince Shōtoku subdued the rebel Moriya
For the sake of all people.

69

There are people who seek to destroy temples, pagodas,
Buddha's dharma and bring disaster and ruin to the nation and
    people;
Those people are reincarnations of Moriya;
They should be rejected and cast aside.

70

The rebel Moriya no Mononobe,
Having gone through innumerable rebirths in the many realms
    of samsara,
Follows the Prince like his shadow
And is determined to destroy the dharma.

71

Those people who constantly slander the Buddha's dharma,
Lead people astray with their wrong views,
And seek to destroy the teaching of sudden attainment
Are reincarnations of the rebel Moriya.[45]

These verses show that Shinran interpreted the historical battle of Shōtoku and
Moriya through his Buddhist worldview. Shinran's description of Moriya, for
instance, "having gone through innumerable rebirths in the many realms of
samsara," emphasizes the karmic connections in Moriya's attempt to stop the
spread of the dharma in Japan.

## OTHER WRITINGS ON SHŌTOKU

Shinran left two other writings on Shōtoku Taishi: *Jōgū Taishi gyōki* (Account of Prince Shōtoku of the Upper Palace) and *Dai Nihon koku zokusan ō Shōtoku Taishi hōsan* (Hymns in Praise of Shōtoku Taishi, Minor Ruler of the Great Country of Japan). The first two books contain the *Byōkutsu-ge* ([Shōtoku Taishi's] epitaph verse), allegedly written by Prince Shōtoku, in which he describes himself as the incarnation of the bodhisattva Kannon, his mother as the incarnation of the Amida Buddha, and his wife Kashiwade no hikikimi no iratsume as the incarnation of the bodhisattva Seishi—Seishi stands next to Amida Buddha and shines on everything with the power of *chie* (to bring the truth to light and realize enlightenment) in order to dispel people's illusion *(mayoi)* and help them toward the actualization of enlightenment. According to Kenshin 1, *Byōkutsu-ge* was dedicated to the *Zenkōji Nyorai* 2 by Shōtoku Taishi. In the *Kōtaishi Shōtoku hōsan*, Shinran used the following titles to describe Shōtoku Taishi: (1) *guze* Kannon—the world-saving bodhisattva of compassion, Kannon; (2) *Daiji guze* Shōtoku—the great world-saving Prince Shōtoku; and (3) *Daihi guze* Kannon—the great world-saving bodhisattva Kannon with a great merciful heart; and (4) *Wa-koku no kyōsyu* Shōtoku—the world-saving Shōtoku, leader of Japan.

These hymns clearly reveal that Shinran had a profound worship of Prince Shōtoku, whom he believed to be more than an imperial regent who was responsible for the promotion of Buddhism in Japan and more than a charismatic figure that was regarded as a *kami*. What is particularly important to note is Shinran's use of the same adjective, *guze* (world-saving), in describing both Kannon and Prince Shōtoku. Shinran's use of *guze* refers to his significant role as the founder of Buddhism and also as a manifestation of the bodhisattva Kannon. This constitutes the most remarkable difference between Hōnen's Jōdoshū and Shinran's *Jōdo Shinshū*. The Jōdoshū does not have this level of veneration of Prince Shōtoku, but it is a salient feature in the *Jōdo Shinshū*. Thus, to truly appreciate the uniqueness and profound depth of Shinran's Buddhism, one cannot overlook the importance of Shinran's worship of Prince Shōtoku as *guze* Kannon. In the next chapter, we will examine more closely the figure of Prince Shōtoku and how he evolved into a deified entity from early to medieval Japan.

# Chapter 2

## The Legends of Shōtoku

According to historical Japanese works, Shōtoku Taishi, the second son of Emperor Yōmei (585–587),[1] was appointed prince regent at the age of nineteen and given administrative control over the government during the reign (592–628) of his aunt, Empress Suiko.[2] During his regency (593–622), Prince Shōtoku made significant contributions to Japanese unification by adopting many features of Chinese civilization. He sent governmental envoys to the Chinese court, which brought back valuable ideas for centralized government ultimately leading to the *ritsuryō*[3] reform movement. These reform measures included the reorganization of the court and etiquette based on Chinese models, the adoption of the Chinese calendar, the opening of formal diplomatic relations with China, and the promotion of Buddhism as the official religion in Japan. These envoys also played an important role in the development of Japanese Buddhism, as their encounter with the purer forms of Chinese Buddhism led to a deeper understanding of the sutras and the importation of Chinese schools, such as T'ien T'ai (Jpn. Tendai), to Japan.

Perhaps the most significant contribution of Prince Shōtoku was the formulation of the Seventeen-Article Constitution *(Jūshichijō kenpō)*[4] that provided the philosophical and religious principles on which the Japanese imperial government came to be based. Fundamentally Confucian in character, the Seventeen-Article Constitution represented a set of moral and administrative injunctions rather than a body of law. Insofar as it supported a centralized government and bureaucracy based on merit rather than heredity, the Seventeen-Article Constitution represented a radical innovation for Japan.

With the adoption of the Chinese model ruler as "Son of Heaven," Shōtoku sought to centralize the government and unify the autonomous clans *(uji)*. In early Japan, society was divided into autonomous clans; each clan was headed by a chieftain *(uji no kami)* and worshiped a divinity, a *kami*[5] that was associated with the clan. The chieftain's responsibility was to ensure that proper ceremonies were performed for the clan's *kami*. If one clan defeated another, the *kami* of the conquered clan was made subject to the *kami* of the victorious clan; each clan still worshiped their respective divinities, but the hierarchy of those divinities shifted. In the Seventeen-Article Constitution, Shōtoku devised a political theory that legitimized imperial authority through the symbolic authority of the emperor over the autonomous clans by adapting the Shintō mythology and the concept of subordinating one clan's *kami* to another. This legitimization of authority reached its fullest expression in the *Taika* reforms (645–694) in a doctrine that can be described as "tennōism" (Jpn. *tennōsei*: emperorship),[6] which reflected Shōtoku's assimilation of the Chinese cultural–political system.

Shōtoku's Seventeen-Article Constitution became an important source for the continual development of the Shōtoku legend during the medieval period. In the turmoil of this era, both traditional and new ruling authorities advocated and promoted Shōtoku worship to legitimize their rule. For instance, the Seventeen-Article Constitution was an important source for the Fujiwara court's promotion of the symbolic authority of the emperor, whose political power had been significantly undermined by the onset of military rule of the shōgunate in Kamakura. Article III stated: "The lord is Heaven, the vassal is Earth. Heaven overspreads, and Earth upbears. When this is so, the four seasons follow their due course, and the powers of Nature obtain their efficacy." According to the theory of sovereignty that Shōtoku adopted from China, rulership derives from Heaven, symbolizing the natural, moral order.[7] The ruler, as Son of Heaven, established this model for men through his ordering of the ritual and regulating of his own conduct. The ruler established clear standards and a universal pattern for his subjects to follow and be nourished by, as the world of nature followed the sun and its seasons, giving life to all things according to their natures. Individual and social morality, likewise, came from Heaven and natural social relationships. Thus, one of the main objectives of the Seventeen-Article Constitution was to establish a single hierarchy of authority, which defined the responsibilities and duties of all under Heaven, culminating in the Japanese emperor, the Son of Heaven. This promotion of the divine and symbolic authority of the emperor in Shōtoku's Seventeen-Article Constitution was one of the main reasons why emperors advocated and promoted Shōtoku worship in the medieval period, after losing political power to the military rule of the shōgun.

The Seventeen-Article Constitution was also an important source for the temple establishments' veneration and promotion of Shōtoku as the ideal Buddhist king *(cakravartin)*, who instituted societal reform by subscribing to Buddhism as a means of achieving the ideal of social harmony:

> Sincerely revere the Three Treasures. The Three Treasures, Buddha, Dharma, and Sangha are the final refuge of the four generated beings and the supreme objects of faith in all countries. Few men are utterly bad. They may be taught to follow it. But if they do not take refuge in the Three Treasures, how shall their crookedness be made straight?[8]

Along with his construction of many state-sponsored temples, Shōtoku's official promotion of Buddhism through the Seventeen-Article Constitution paved the way for Buddhism's strong presence in Japan, and for the Fujiwara court, the aristocracy, and the temple establishments to establish close ties. Since the Fujiwara court, the aristocracy, and the temple establishments mutually benefited from various aspects of Shōtoku's Seventeen-Article Constitution, they worked together to promote the worship of Shōtoku. Consequently, Buddhism played an important role in promoting Shōtoku worship in medieval Japan, as mythological images and supernatural allusions in Buddhism, such as those found in *jātaka* tales ( Jpn. *honjō-wa*: birth stories),[9] served to develop the Shōtoku legends that went far beyond his historical achievements. Within temple establishments, Shōtoku worship evolved over time. Initially, Shōtoku was seen as an ideal Buddhist king; eventually, however, he was regarded as a powerful *kami* and protector of Buddhism, a reincarnation of Tendai Eshi (Ch. Hui-ssu), and an incarnation of bodhisattva Kannon and Amida Buddha as well. The development of Shōtoku worship was a practical ideology for both traditional and new authorities that sought to legitimize their rule in ancient and medieval Japan.[10]

The second article of the Seventeen-Article Constitution, which urges citizens to "revere the three treasures of Buddhism," marked the beginning of the official promotion of Buddhism as the state religion in Japan. Particularly notable was Shōtoku's reputation as a devout Buddhist. By the age of nineteen, Shōtoku had received considerable education in Buddhism and was able to explicate some of the major Buddhist sutras, which were written in Chinese. His studies of the Buddhist scriptures resulted in his writing commentaries on three major Buddhist sutras: the *Shōmangyō* (True Lion's Roar of Queen Śrīmalā; Sk. *Śrīmālā simhanada sutra*), *Yuimagyō* (Sk. *Vimalakīrti nirdesa sutra*), and *Hokekyō* (Lotus Sutra; Sk. *Saddhama pundarika sutra*).[11] These three works demonstrate Shōtoku's considerable knowledge of Buddhist philosophy. His understanding of the transitory and illusory nature of the present world was a conviction derived from contemplation of Buddhist sutras and teachings. On his deathbed, Shōtoku's statement, "*Seken-koke-yuibutsu-zeshin*" or "this world [for the unenlightened] is illusion, the Buddha alone is true," displayed a profound understanding of Buddhism.[12] The idea that the world might be an illusion did not enter Japanese thought until generations later, in the Heian period.

During his regency, Shōtoku built forty-six state-sponsored temples, including Shitennōji and Hōryūji. According to legend, Shōtoku spent many hours in meditation at these temples. These state-sponsored temples facilitated the development of Buddhism in Japan and became important pilgrimage sites for Shōtoku worshipers, especially among ruling authorities, following the prince's death. The Shitennōji, for instance, was built to fulfill Shōtoku's vow to the *Four Guardian Deities*, protectors of Buddhism, made during the Soga victory over the Mononobe in 587. In medieval Japan, shōgun, emperors, and leaders of temple establishments ritually visited the Shitennōji and other temples related to Shōtoku to worship Shōtoku as the ideal general, ideal regent, and ideal Buddhist king. These visits enabled ruling authorities to use Shōtoku worship to legitimize their claims of power. In turn, these temples furthered the perpetuation of Shōtoku legends in order to assert their superiority over other temples.

In tribute to Shōtoku's monumental role in spreading Buddhism and building temples, each of the temples formulated an official record, called *engi*,[13] which included various narratives and *jātaka* tales describing Shōtoku as a manifestation of the bodhisattva Kannon.[14] Quite often, these temples would borrow certain legends of Shōtoku's achievements that were recorded in official chronological sources such as the *Nihon shoki*, but they also formulated their own embellished versions that described Shōtoku's role in the founding of their temple. For example, the *Gangōji engi*[15] account describes the emergence of Prince Shōtoku as the victor in the war between two political factions with different religious understandings of the spiritual forces that affect worldly events. The deities are identified in opposition to each other, the one Buddhist and the other Shintō. Since powerful, unseen forces identified as deities directly affect the temporal world, the violent struggle between the two factions is also a battle of the *kamis*, and the Buddhist deities proved themselves the greater masters of war. Grateful for the support of the buddhas and bodhisattvas, Prince Shōtoku became an influential supporter of Buddhism and sponsored the building of the Gangōji temple, among others.

## LEGENDARY SHŌTOKU

Mystery and mystique surround the legends of Shōtoku. Western scholars have questioned whether Shōtoku Taishi was indeed a historical or legendary person in Japanese history. Given the fact that there are only scant sources available on

Shōtoku Taishi's biography, all of which were composed by imperial command, and given his evolvement into a legendary figure through years of deification, an astute reader may seriously doubt his actual existence. We may examine some areas of Shōtoku's life, such as his Buddhist background. According to *Nihon shoki*, Shōtoku was a devout Buddhist, one who understood the dharma intrinsically to the point that he even wrote commentaries on sutras. Here we explore some reasons why the imperial authorities may have wanted to deify Shōtoku. During the Asuka period, Japanese society was quite unstable due to the many disparate clans *(uji)* vying for control of Japan so there was a need for a centralizing figure to unify the country. Shōtoku represented the perfect unifying figure. He was the ideal archetype, in the Weberian sense, of a *cakravartin* (dharma-emperor), joining both the state and religion in Japan during his day. The Japanese imperial government instituted reforms based on the Chinese form of government from the glorious T'ang dynasty in China. However, in order to deemphasize their reliance on the more highly civilized Chinese culture, the Japanese imperial authorities promoted Shōtoku as the father of the Japanese nation. But in the process and over time, the historical and the legendary figure became so intertwined and elaborated on that one cannot separate what was fact from fiction. Essentially, it really does not matter.

What is centrally important is not proving the truth of Shōtoku's miraculous exploits or other stretched truths, but understanding how Shōtoku was worshiped during the early and medieval period in Japan. In this sense, Western scholars are missing the point when they focus on the true existence or actual contributions that Shōtoku made in Japan. Their work essentially implies that the Japanese spun a long web of exaggerated lies to promote Shōtoku. Just as after World War II America attempted to demystify the emperor to modest human status, Western scholars may be too fixated on cutting the legs off of Shōtoku's deified status. In doing so, Western scholars fall short of appreciating the mystery and mystique that surround not only the emperor, with all its Shintō mythology of divine descent, but also the Japanese people as a whole. In essence, the mystery and mystique about Shōtoku reflect the Japanese society and people as a whole, especially given the underlying Shintō mythology, which describes the people of Japan as *kami ko* or "children of *kami*." Mootonori defines *kami* as something that inspires awe, such as Mount Fuji. It can occur in nature, but also in humans, especially charismatic leaders or important figures in Japanese history. These people seem to be endowed with an extra *kami* nature, inspiring others toward realizing the *kami* nature from within, just as heroes do in Western culture.

Hero, genius, and great person are examples of descriptions of charismatic historical figures who have been adored for hundreds, even thousands, of years in history. Regardless of whether a historical figure was actually an outstanding person in real life, their image can be inflated due to people's demands. From this assumption, knowing the truth can change people's perspective on their beliefs. In his book, *Shōtoku Taishi no denshō* (The Legend of Shōtoku Taishi), Fujii Yukiko states, "Shōtoku Taishi is a good example of an overrated Japanese historical person who is considered as one of the Japanese representative legends. Ages of accumulation of demand and worship for a historical hero can distort and reform the actual personal career due to the Japanese religious background in which Shōtoku Taishi, for instance, had to be the symbol of all Japanese people."[16]

Although the Japanese have been worshiping Shōtoku Taishi as a legend for years, the stories about his life before the Edo era seem unbelievable. It was said that Shōtoku's mother saw the gold priest (*guze bosatsu*: world-saving bodhisattva) entering her womb in her dream just before she gave birth to him in a stable. When Shōtoku was two years old, he joined his hands together toward the east and said, "nam-butsu" (I call upon the Buddha) on the fifteenth of February, the anniversary of the Buddha's death. When Shōtoku became an adult, he was capable of understanding ten people complaining simultaneously. He also had the ability to prophesy, and was considered a prophet during his time. These stories seem implausible to the average reader. In an effort to conduct a thorough investigation on this matter, Japanese scholars devoted many years researching the truth or falsity of Shōtoku Taishi's existence in Japanese history. In addition to addressing this debate, I will concentrate on elucidating the background and understanding the reasons behind the invention of these legends that captured the minds of the Japanese people.

## HISTORICAL SHŌTOKU

In his *Nihon koten no kenkyū* (Research of Japanese Classical Literature), Tsuda Sōkichi (1873–1961),[17] a noted scholar of *Kojiki* and *Nihon shoki*, expressed his doubts about the existence of Shōtoku Taishi. Referring to the account of Prince Shōtoku's birth in a stable, his ability to speak soon after his birth, and his power to predict the future, Tsuda stated, "I have serious doubts about the existence of Shōtoku Taishi during the era of Empress Suiko."[18] Tsuda believes that such descriptions were intentionally created to portray Shōtoku as a holy man so that people would come to admire him as a god. Moreover, he denies that Shōtoku wrote the Seventeen-Article Constitution in the *Nihon shoki*. Based on a closer examination of the Constitution, Tsuda points out that the Constitution could not have been composed in 604.[19] Tsuda explains that the expression, *kokushi kokuzō* [or *kokushi kuni no miyatsuko*] did not even exist in 604, but was established after the seventh century. The term *kokushi* means "a government official" under the *ritsuryō* system, which was the system of the old Japanese administration established in 701. On the other hand, *kuni no miyatsuko* [*kokuzō*] is also "a government official," but under the imperial court of Yamato. Tsuda Sōkichi argues that it is questionable that the two terms would be used together in the twelfth Constitution. He concludes that this awkward expression must have been formulated after the end of the seventh century.

In addition to doubts about the authorship of the Seventeen-Article Constitution by Shōtoku Taishi, Tsuda Sōkichi insists that the central ideology behind the Constitution closely resemble the movement to create a system of centralized power and bureaucracy, instituted after the Taika Reforms in 645 C.E. Tsuda states that it is more probable that the Constitution was composed during the *shisei* (municipal organization) system, used during the Suiko era when a special political name was given to a government official who was recognized as a Tennō officer. Furthermore, Tsuda points out that some of the words and expression used in the Constitution are difficult to understand. Although many classical Chinese characters and expressions were used, they were extremely similar to those in the *Nihon shoki*, which was compiled in 720 C.E., one hundred years later. Tsuda's conclusions have cast serious doubts about Shōtoku's authorship of the Seventeen-Article Constitution among Shōtoku scholars. Based on Sōkichi's persuasive arguments, most Japanese scholars today believe that the Constitution was composed sometime between the end of the seventh century and the beginning of the eighth century, a time corresponding to the enactment of the *ritsuryō* system in Japanese history.

After extensive investigation, Japanese medieval historian Ōyama Seiichi claims that Shōtoku Taishi was actually a fictitious person, but points out that the creation of this myth was very well done.[20] Even Shinran believed in Shōtoku's existence after 500 years. Moreover, Ōyama claims that "Shinran was not even Hōnen's disciple, but was simply a Shoki *shinshū* founder who attracted many poor people to his teachings." Ōyama adds that "Shinran did not have anything to do with Honganji; Honganji was built by the person who claimed to be Shinran's descendant."[21] Ōyama deduces that the *Nihon shoki* and Kojiki must have been very influential. Visual effects from Hōryūji also added to the Shōtoku mystique, which caused the emergence of Hakuho culture based on the beautiful Taishi arts and culture. Hence, *Jōdo Shinshū* gradually ascended to become the most dominant Buddhist sect in Japan. Ōyama explains that traditional studies on Shōtoku tend to focus on the fictitious history, but one cannot overlook how such creative narratives have strongly influenced the Japanese culture and philosophical development.

Ōyama believes that Shōtoku Taishi was a fictitious figure included in the *Nihon shoki*, which was edited between Tenbu 10th (681) and Yōrō 4th (720) by many Japanese scholars.[22] He explains that during the editing process, which took more than forty years, Japanese scholars gathered and incorporated various sources in their attempt to portray him as a true historical figure. Beyond the question of whether Shōtoku Taishi was a real or fictitious character lies the more important question: why did scholars try to establish Shōtoku Taishi as a historical person in the *Nihon shoki*? Although this is a difficult question to answer since the *Nihon shoki* is an extremely complex and old book, we must explain the underlying reasons behind the conspiracy that originated with the imperial court.

Ōyama explains that the court created Shōtoku Taishi to promote the emperorship in the new *ritsuryō* system of government, which was modeled after the Chinese form of government in the late seventh century.[23] In the *ritsuryō* system, the emperor or *tennō* is the pivotal figure regarded as the head of the country. Just as the emperor in China had absolute authority to rule the country, the imperial authorities attempted to establish an oligarchy, following the model of the Chinese government by promoting the status of the emperor. However, since the idea of emperorship was new in Japan, the imperial authorities wanted to promote the image of the emperor not only as a political figure, but also as one who held absolute authority over all people in Japan. As a result, the imperial authorities sanctioned the writing of the *Nihon shoki*. Ōyama explains the primary responsibility for the editors of the *Nihon shoki*: "For scholars, it was more important for them to prove the greatest power of the current emperor rather than leave records of the true account of Japanese history for later historians and generations."[24] Thus, in order to establish the new political system based on the *ritsuryō* codes, Japanese scholars created the mystique of Shōtoku Taishi in the *Nihon shoki*.

In Taihō 2nd (702), the Japanese government selected several people, such as Shinjin Kurita, as emissaries to China for the first time in forty years. These emissaries returned to Japan with the news that the *ritsuryō* system, established by the imperial Fujiwara and based on the Chinese model, was starkly different from the one that they witnessed firsthand in China. One of the clear differences resided in the perception of the emperor. In China, the emperor was a very powerful figure who reigned over all politics, culture, and society, unlike the Japanese emperor who primarily held symbolic, not political, authority. Therefore, the imperial authorities decided to elevate the Japanese emperor to possess not only absolute political power but also religious power and influence. However, since it was impossible to instantly instill such a belief in the minds of the Japanese people, Ōyama claims that the imperial authorities had to create a figure like the powerful Chinese emperor to be inserted into the history of the imperial family so that the present Japanese emperor could claim his lineage for the sake of legitimizing his emperorship.[25]

Ōyama explains that the only person in Japan who could have been elevated to such a powerful status was Soga no Umako (551?–626), the strongest member of the powerful Soga clan and one who built the Asuka temple and controlled the town of Asuka during Yamato Japan. According to Ōyama, in Yōrō 2nd (718), when the emissary Dōji returned from China after his meetings with the Chinese emperor, Japanese governors, such as Fujiwara Huhito, asked him to write a book. The work was to center on a powerful charismatic figure who could be identified as the Fujiwara's imperial ancestor, who ruled in Soga's place during the Asuka period. Hence, Shōtoku Taishi was born with the completion of the *Nihon shoki* in Yōrō 4th (720).

In fact, the term "*guze* Kannon" was never used as a name or description of the bodhisattva Kannon prior to this time; it was created by the compilers of the Heian era to describe the symbolic and spiritual role of Shōtoku Taishi, who came to be regarded as Kannon's incarnation, especially among Buddhist circles. Ōyama explains that during the spreading of Mahayana Buddhism in East Asia, Japan needed a symbolic person who was highly educated and had a strong spirit and will to embody the new universal thought to help Japan. Fujii Yukiko notes that during the waning of the *ritsuryō* system and the time of changing structure in Japan, Buddhist priests promoted Shōtoku Taishi as the incarnation of Kannon in order to maintain the Buddhist faith.[26]

## THE CULT OF SHŌTOKU

The main source that clearly asserts Shōtoku Taishi to be the incarnation of *guze* Kannon is *Shōtoku Taishi denryaku* (The Biography of Shōtoku Taishi), which was compiled in the tenth century. This book describes not only Shōtoku Taishi's achievements in chronological order, but also discusses *Taishi shinkō* (Shōtoku Taishi worship; Shōtoku cult), including miracles that Shōtoku performed as the incarnation of Kannon. In contrast to other fictitious biographies on Shōtoku, such as the *Nihon shoki*, the *Denryaku* had a unique intention to be used as a source that affirmed the historical existence of Shōtoku Taishi and recorded his miraculous feats as the incarnation of the bodhisattva Kannon. In later compilations on Shōtoku Taishi, the reader may begin to notice an increasing deification of Shōtoku as more than a holy person. For instance, one of the recurring images of Shōtoku is the description of his continuous rebirth and mission to help people out of his infinite compassion. In another account, the *Denryaku* recounts how Shōtoku was born after his mother had a dream of a golden-hued Buddhist priest who claimed to be *guze* Kannon and entered the side of her womb, an obvious reference to Siddharta's birth. Fujii Yukiko states that this ideology can be traced to the predominant teaching in the *Hokekyō* (Lotus Sutra), which describes how a bodhisattva undergoes continuous rebirth to help people out of compassion.[27] Since the *Hokekyō* was already acknowledged as a classical teaching in Buddhism, it did not require too much imagination for people to relate to Shōtoku as the incarnation of Kannon, given the obvious and intentional connections made to Kannon—and even to Shakaymuni Buddha, by the compilers of the *Denryaku*. Fujii explains that the image of Shōtoku Taishi and promotion of *Taishi shinkō* were a powerful and effective ideology that penetrated many people at the time of its origination.

During the Heian period, before *Shōtoku Taishi denryaku* was written, Japanese historians compared another book, *Jōgū Shōtoku Taishi den hoketsuki* (Supplementary Note on Shōtoku Taishi's Biography), to the *Denryaku*. Although there are not as many references made to Shōtoku Taishi in the *Hoketsuki* as there are in the *Denryaku*, the presence of many common themes indicates a high probability that the *Hoketsuki* was clearly influenced by the *Denryaku*. For instance, in the beginning of the *Hoketsuki*, the story that Shōtoku Taishi's mother became pregnant after seeing the golden-hued Buddhist priest in her dream is exactly the same as the birth narrative in the *Denryaku*. The only difference in the two accounts is that in the *Denryaku* the golden-hued Buddhist priest identifies himself as "the hope of world-saving bodhisattva," whereas in the *Hoketsuki* the golden-hued Buddhist priest is *guze* Kannon. Fujii Yukiko postulates that the compilers of the *Denryaku* added their own redactionary interpretations to *Hoketsuki* to strengthen the meaning of the incarnation of the bodhisattva Kannon.[28] Consequently, the *Hoketsuki* did not take the opportunity to promote Shōtoku Taishi as the bodhisattva Kannon as the *Denryaku* did. Fujii deduced that the *Denryaku* is a book clearly different from other Mahāyāna Buddhist sutras due to the presence of a changing image of Shōtoku Taishi.

*Shitennōji engi* (Record of the Temple of Four Guardian Deities) is considered an autobiography of Shōtoku Taishi and preserved with great care in Shitennō Temple as a treasure of Japanese history. However, the authenticity of Shōtoku's authorship has been questioned by several noted Japanese historians such as Ekisai Kariya in his book *Awaharaji rohanmei* (Awahara Temple's Archives); and in the *Kokyō ibun* (The Old Capital's [Kyoto] Recording) in 1818, which is preserved in *Kokuritsu kokkai toshokan shozōbon* (Possession of the Japanese National Assembly's Library) and published by the Hōbundō in 1893, Sōkichi Tsuda (1873–1961) in his *Nihon jōdaishi no kenkyū* (1930); and Akamatsu Toshihide in his book *Shitennōji no shoseki* (Recordings of Shitennō Temple), which is a part of the *Hihō* (A Hidden Treasure) volume 3 *Shitennōji* published by Kodansha in 1968. Based on their in-depth research, these Japanese historians arrive at the same conclusion—that Shōtoku Taishi was not the author of *Shitennōji engi*, but it was made to appear that he was.

The suspicion regarding Shōtoku's authorship of the *Shitennōji engi* is confirmed by the fact that Sōshō, who devoted himself to studying the religious climate at the Tōdaiji during the Kamakura period in 1270, apparently made a copy of the actual *Shitennōji engi* in his book, which is entitled *Shitennōji goshuin engi* (Record of the History of the Shitennōji). According to Sōshō's *Shitennōji goshuin engi*, a man named Jiun found the *Shitennōji engi* at Shitennōji on August 1, 1007, and noted that the whole *engi* was written in one person's handwriting. The suspicious part of the *engi* was the signature and date that appear at the end as "Kōtaishi Busshi shōman, January 8, 575."[29] Sōshō explains that although "Kōtaishi Busshi shōman" was one of the Buddhist names for Shōtoku Taishi, the *engi* was actually written by a different person after Shōtoku's death. Due to the fact that no traces from any sources or books were ever found to prove that Kōtaishi Busshi shōman was another name for Shōtoku Taishi, Sōshō pointed out the awkwardness of such a notation at the end of the book.

Closer examination of the *Shitennōji engi* reveals that there are inconsistent reports about the building of the Shitennō temple, which lead us to believe that Shōtoku Taishi had nothing to do with the temple's establishment or the writing of the records. Japanese scholar Kariya Ekisai explains that although the *Shitennōji engi* discusses the design and gives information about the temple compound, the *engi* does not mention any contextual information about the Asuka era when Shōtoku Taishi was living. Excavations of the temple conducted from 1955 to 1957 and further comparisons made with historical records also confirmed the discrepancy that existed between what was written in the *engi* and the actual events that occurred in the temple. For instance, according to the *Maizō bunkazai hakkutsuchōsa hōkoku* volume 6 *Shitennōji* (The Report of Excavation for Japanese National and Cultural Buried Things Volume Six Shitennō Temple) stored by the Japanese National Cultural Committee in 1967, the *engi* reports that "parts of the Shitennō Temple were lost to fire in the year 960 so the middle gate and the south gate of the temple were rebuilt, which expanded the temple compound."[30] However, the investigation committee reported the discrepancy that the expansion of the temple took place before the fire, which did not occur in the Asuka period.

Japanese scholar Akamatsu Toshihide explains that the compilers of the *Shitennōji engi* most likely attributed the authorship to Shōtoku in order to promote the temple and thereby increase its revenue from frequent visitors. The *engi* was also written for a broader base of people from different social classes, not just for the wealthy and powerful, so that the temple could be financially supported by all people.[31] Akamatsu contends that the real author of the *Shitennōji engi* cleverly and effectively promoted the idea that the author of the *engi* was Shōtoku Taishi, who was already venerated by the general populous as a holy man or superman, as described in the *Nihon shoki*. The true authors of the Shitennōji, most likely selected members associated with the Imperial court, used Shōtoku as a way to legitimize the temple as a central place of Shōtoku worship, thereby attracting many visitors and sponsors. To further strengthen their legitimization, the compilers of the *engi* included miraculous accounts performed by Shōtoku, such as his famous prophecy regarding his promise to build the Shitennōji after a successful military campaign against his enemy, Moriya, and further adorned with descriptions of the Pure Land and promises to all adherents who donated to the temple. As a result, the Shitennōji came to be regarded as one of the most holy places for Shōtoku worship.

Returning to discussion of the *Nihon shoki*, this work was written in 720 C.E. by Fujiwara-no-Fuhito, an active member of the imperial court, under the direction of Nagayao, Emperor Temmu's grandson, and with guidance by Dōji, a monk who had recently returned from T'ang China. In the *Nihon shoki*, Fuhito portrayed Shōtoku as a godlike saint of the Asuka period who later was described as the reincarnation of the noble Chinese monk, Hui-ssu. After the *Nihon shoki*, there was a continual proliferation of Shōtoku Taishi's glorious accomplishments that was passed down from generation to generation through the writings of various monks and aristocrats. In fact, the legacy of Shōtoku Taishi established Japanese Buddhism and built the base of the Hakuho culture. However, as we have seen, recent study by Japanese historians seem to indicate that Shōtoku Taishi was a fictitious person, one who was fabricated in the *Nihon shoki*, a book that was written during the rapidly changing society and politics of the Tenpyo era (720–794). Further investigation purports that works attributed to the authorship of Shōtoku Taishi are now considered to have been written by others following Shōtoku's death. Moreover, circumstantial evidence seems to indicate that none of Shōtoku's achievements can be confirmed.

One of the areas of discrepancy can be seen in the *Gangōji garan engi narabini ruki shizaichō* (Records of the Gangō Temple and Its Accumulated Treasures), a book from the Daigo temple that was found during the Meiji era (1868–1912) by the art historian Takurei Hirako. Located in Kyoto and considered the head temple of the Daigo Shingon sect, the Daigōji houses eighteen volumes of *engi*. The *Gangōji garan engi narabini ruki shizaichō* is the second volume, and contains important chapters about the reign of Empress Suiko. The inconsistencies occur in the dating that is found in the second volume, which was supposedly written by Shōtoku to Empress Suiko as a dedication for her 100-year-old anniversary. In the beginning of the chapter, it is written that Shōtoku wrote the dedication "in 613," which clearly contradicts the dating of the dedication at the end of the chapter, "747." Moreover, Japanese historian Yoshida Kazuhiko contends that not only the time conflict but also the discourse in the *Gangōji garan engi narabini ruki shizaichō* made it unbelievable.[32]

Another prominent Japanese historian from the Meiji period, Kita Sada-kichi, in his *Daigōji bon shoji engishū shoshū Gangōji engi ni tsuite* claimed that the *Gangōji engi* was a counterfeit book. Based on his meticulous study of its content and form, Kita concluded that the *engi* could not possibly have been written during the Tenpyo era. Kita's finding was further supported by a renowned historian of Japanese architecture, Fukuyama Toshio, who stated in his *Nihon kenchikushi kenkyū* that most of the contents in the *Gangōji engi* were written at the end of the Nara period. Fukuyama concluded that *Gangōji engi* was a "blundering product, full of false claims and inconsistencies."[33]

If closer examination of such historical records reveals that Shōtoku Taishi was a fictitious person, then why was there a need to create such a figure? Fujii Yukiko states in her *Guze Kannon no seiritsu* (The Formation of the World-saving Bodhisattva of Compassion) that during the waning of the *ritsuryō* system, Buddhist monks needed to secure a new patronage for Buddhism through the deification of Shōtoku Taishi as the incarnation of *guze* Kannon. Hence, Fujii points out that "sometimes these things are created to meet the demands of the people." With the spread of Daijō Buddhism in East Asia, Fujii explains that the Japanese people were seeking to promote a spiritual and highly educated personage in their own country, coupled with the idea of the need for a savior figure (i.e., *guze* Kannon) during the time of *mappō*.

## THE SHŌTOKU CONSPIRACY THEORY

Efforts to unravel the conspiracy concerning the existence of Shōtoku Taishi are quite complex and daunting. The truth behind Shōtoku Taishi has been buried under many layers and hundreds of years of fabricated stories in the *Nihon shoki*. Japanese historians propose other viable reasons for the great historical fabrication of Shōtoku Taishi. We must first examine the writings of the Hakuho culture, one known for its Buddhist arts, which begins in 672 C.E. to the early part of the eighth century. Consequently, the Hakuho culture was strongly influenced by the T'ang dynasty in China as the Japanese tried to centralize the government by establishing a model similar to that successfully designed in T'ang China.

If Shōtoku Taishi was indeed an imaginary person, then one has to also question the existence of Empress Suiko, who appointed Shōtoku to serve as her regent. Given the fact that all the information about Suiko's emperorship is found in books related to Shōtoku, Ōyama believes that in actuality Suiko was only led to believe that she was the empress in order to support the imaginary existence of Shōtoku Taishi.[34] Ōyama explains that the person most affected by the fictitious existence of Shōtoku Taishi is Empress Suiko, which in turn casts doubt on the true emperorship of Yōmei and Sushon, also emperors during this time.

Before conducting a more in-depth investigation of the emperors of Shōtoku's era, we must take into consideration other interesting findings. To begin with, in the *Tenjukoku shuchō*, a work written during the time of Empress Suiko, emperors were posthumously given Buddhist names with a distinct Korean pronunciation (e.g., ko kan on). For example, the Emperor Kimmei's name is pronounced as "A me ku ni o shi ha ra ki hi ro ni ha"; Yōmei's name as "Ta chi ba na to yo hi"; and Suiko's as "To yo mi ke ka shi ki ya hi me." Japanese historian and linguist Sema Masayuki points out that "some parts of the Korean syllables, called 'ko kan on' in the names were brought by the Korean people in the late seventh century, so these names could not have been used during Empress Suiko's time."[35] In his *Inariyama tekkenmei to accent* and *Wakatakeru daiō to sono jidai*, another Japanese historian and linguist, Mori Hiromichi, argues that Kimmei's pronunciation of "A me ku ni o shi ha ra ki" is a unique and only part that corresponds with the intonation of the original pronunciation *(gen on seichō)* with a Heian accent, citing that the accent used during the fifth- through sixth-century Yamato period was very close to that used in the Yamashiro area during the Heian period. Thus, Mori concludes that the *Tenjukoku shuchō* was not written during the era of Empress Suiko, but during the editing of the *Nihon shoki*. Given these findings, there is no confirmation that Empress Suiko or the other emperors ever ruled.

Moreover, Ōyama postulates that Emperor Yōmei's reign (585–587) was also created because of the need to provide legitimacy for the regency of his son "Umayado no ōji" (i.e., Shōtoku Taishi), who was described as a holy man in the *Nihon shoki*. In support of his theory of Emperor Yōmei's invented reign, Ōyama points to the discrepancy that exists in the *Nihon shoki*'s description of the enthronement of Emperor Yōmei, who ascended to the throne *during* the mourning period of the previous Emperor Bidatsu (572–585) and the customary practice of enthronement, which was traditionally held *after* the mourning period of the previous emperor. As for the Emperor Sushun, he ascended to the throne (587-592) after Soga no Umako's victorious defeat over Mononobe no Moriya. However, during his reign, Soga no Umako assumed hegemony and began to build the Asuka temple and later killed the Emperor Sushun in 592 C.E.

Ōyama also cites a trustworthy Chinese source from the Sui dynasty, *Zui shō*, which further supports the conspiracy theory surrounding the false existence of Empress Suiko. According to *Zui shō*, "an envoy *(kenzuishi)* from Sui China named Hai Seisei arrived in Japan in 608 and met with the Emperor who had a wife," a statement that is confirmed by many accounts. The phrase "the Emperor had a wife" obviously refers to the Emperor as a male figure, contradicting the account in the *Nihon shoki* that identifies Suiko as the empress during that time.

Another peculiar and suspicious aspect of the *Nihon shoki* was that it did not contain any detailed accounts of the three emperors during the Asuka period. Ōyama explains that we do not have detailed accounts because they did not exist. According to Ōyama, the true emperor was Soga no Umako, who held the actual political power in Asuka and was treated as such, given the strong evidence we find in reference to the customary practice of burying emperors near the city. Ōyama points to the fact that Soga no Umako's tomb, which is the famous *Ishibutai kofun*, is located in Asuka, inside the *Mise Maruyama kofun*, which belonged to his father, Soga no Iname, in the Yamato region.[36] Further archaeological investigations revealed that the tombs of Soga no Umako's son and grandson, Emishi and Iruka, were also near the city, confirming the fact that the royal family's tombs were all located in the Asuka capital. Ōyama adds that the main street pointing northeast from the Nara basin (i.e., Asuka) was built around 613 C.E., which marks the start of Soga no Iname's tomb. In other words, Ōyama concludes that "Soga no Umako decided that his tomb would be facing the direction of Yamato, using his father's tomb as its starting point." On the other hand, the tombs of Emperor Bidatsu, Emperor Yōmei, Empress Suiko, and Prince Shōtoku are located in the Kawachi area, over a mountain and much further west of the Asuka capital. This archaeological evidence gives a compelling reason to refute the accounts of the emperorship found in the *Nihon shoki* and strongly supports the theory that Soga no Umako was the real emperor during the Asuka period.

One may question the cogency of this argument, particularly since Emperor Kimmei's tomb, called *Umeyama kofun*, is located south of Soga no Iname's tomb, outside the Asuka capital. However, there is a good explanation for such an exception. Ōyama explains that the Soga family actually intended to place Kimmei within the compounds of the Soga territory, although he was technically not a member of the Soga family by blood but only through marriage to Soga no Iname's daughter, Kitashihime.[37] Ōyama points out that Kitashihime was originally buried with her father, but was moved to her husband Kimmei's tomb and explains that this move was a way to declare Soga no Umako's inheritance of royal authority from Kimmei. As Ōyama notes, "By acknowledging Kimmei as Soga no Umako's son-in-law by burying Kitashihime at the same location, the Soga family was essentially trying to merge Kimmei's spirit with the spirit of Soga family's ancestor. As a result, the Soga no Umako declared that he and the Soga family inherited Kimmei's sovereign power through his daughter's marriage to Kimmei." Hence, the joining of the tombs must have been done intentionally to validate Soga no Umako's status as the "great emperor" *(daiō)*.[38] Japanese historian Masajiro Ōta remarks that there is a sentence in the *Settsu koku fudoki* that says "there were two historical systems, the one that was centered on the Imperial family and the one that was centered on the Soga family."[39]

Instilling the new concept of emperorship based on the Chinese model proved challenging for Japanese historians, and required the editing of historical books to explain the origins of the emperorship. To promote the idea of emperorship, the imperial court tried to manipulate the political, social, and religious spheres, following the example of China. In order to discuss the basic foundation of the emperorship in Japan, the imperial court told Japanese historians to create basic laws, later called Taihō *ritsuryō* and completed in 689 C.E., and to compile two historical books, the *Kojiki* (712) and the *Nihon shoki* (720), that offered an explanation of the divine origins of the emperorship.

The main purpose of *Kojiki* and *Nihon shoki* was to provide the historical legitimacy of the emperor's existence. *Kojiki* begins with the origins of the emperorship that are traced back to the Shintō mythology based on the emperor's lineage to Amaterasu and ends with the enthronement of Empress Suiko. Conveniently, Shōtoku Taishi appears as "Umayado-ō" at the end of *Kojiki*, but without any mention of his identity, most likely because the writers did not know how to formulate a false biography around a fictitious character. In any case, the editors' main goal was to introduce Shōtoku Taishi without being too concerned about leaving accurate historical records regarding his lineage and more concerned about providing the legitimacy for the present imperial rule. In contrast, the *Nihon shoki* ends with Emperor Jitō's abdication of the throne and the ascendancy of Emperor Bunbu. Ōyama points out that the ultimate purpose of the *Nihon shoki* was to prove the legitimacy of Emperor Bunbu's enthronement. Thus, the editors created a fictitious character, Shōtoku Taishi, to be used as a source for this legitimacy.

Ōyama explains that the editors of *Nihon shoki* cleverly established a lineage of the emperor that originated from the Shintō mythology. Through the idea of "Takamagahara, tenson kōrin, bansei ikkei," which means that "The Sun Goddess, Amaterasu, dwells in the Takamagahara, which is a sky that is higher than heaven; Amaterasu's grandson, Ninigi, came down to Earth *(Tenson kōrin)*, brought rice to the people, and governed the land; and, the notion that the present emperor is a direct descendant and legitimate successor from Ninigi's paternal line *(Bansei ikkei)*." This concept established the deification of the emperor. Interestingly, the same relationship of Amaterasu and Ninigi strongly implied that Emperor Jitō represents Amaterasu and his grandson, the Emperor Bunbu, represents Ninigi. Therefore, the "Takamagahara, Tenson kōrin, bansei ikkei" theory proposed that the authority of the emperor was essentially granted by the *kami* goddess Amaterasu. For this reason, emperors frequently visited the Ise Shrine, where Amaterasu is believed to reside, to foster the perception that the emperor was a direct descendant of Amaterasu.[40]

Ōyama explains that Shōtoku Taishi was also created to diminish, even eradicate, the existence of Soga no Umako. The editors of *Kojiki* and *Nihon shoki* were faced with a very serious problem of denying the true emperorship of Soga no Umako, who held the actual political power. Since it was impossible to include Soga no Umako in the lineage of the Fujiwara family, the editors created the Shintō mythology based on the emperor's descendancy from Amaterasu. Then, by inventing and promoting the unique figure of Shōtoku Taishi as a holy person who had performed miraculous acts, the editors tried to take the attention away from Soga no Umako's significant achievements, such as the building of the Asuka temple, establishment of the Buddhist culture, and governing of the nation.

The oldest scroll of Shōtoku Taishi by Jitsunyo was found in the Shiga prefecture. Shōtoku Taishi is standing on a *raiban* (a step in front of the Buddha statue that monks stand on during the service) holding an *ekoro* (an incense burner with a long stem), and his hair is tied in a Mizura style. This style of the image of Shōtoku Taishi is called *kyōyō zō* (educated version), a typical scroll style that was circulated in *kenmitsu* Buddhism after the Kamakura period; the *Jōdo Shinshū* center at Honganji chose this style of Shōtoku Taishi over the Shoki *shinshū* version that ordinary people often used to venerate Shōtoku Taishi. Why did the Honganji center decide to use the *kyōyō zō* rather than the Shoki shinshū version? Another style that was made and used by the Shoki shinshū followers is called the *kōmyō honzon*. On the *kōmyō honzon* the Buddha stands on the right side and the Amida Buddha is on the left side. Above the Amida Buddha, three Indian bodhisattvas, Seishi, Ryūki, and Sesshin, appear. Above the Buddha, one can see Shōtoku Taishi with long hair. Finally, above Shōtoku Taishi, there are three Japanese patriarchs of Jōdoshū: Genshin, Hōnen, and Shinran. From the positioning of the figures, one can clearly note that Shōtoku Taishi is placed on a higher plane than the Jōdoshū patriarchs, indicating that Shōtoku Taishi is or should be worshiped on the same level as the bodhisattvas. What this means is that, in Shoki Shinshū circles, Shōtoku Taishi is a bodhisattva, not just an ordinary person.

Followers of Shinran at the Honganji center, however, did not appreciate the fact that their patriarch was drawn significantly smaller and placed at the corner of the scroll, compared to Shōtoku Taishi's portrayal as a bodhisattva. Realizing the hidden danger of such comparisons, Jōdo Shinshū followers of Shinran decided to use the *kyōzō zō* version of Shōtoku Taishi as their official scroll since the *kyōyō zō* version did not portray Shōtoku Taishi's status as a bodhisattva but merely regarded him as one of the founders of Buddhism. Japanese historian Shinya Seko describes this shift toward the Honganji's emphasis on Shinran worship over Shōtoku worship as a change from "Shōtoku Taishism" to "Shinranism."

Ōyama explains that it was necessary to use Shōtoku Taishi images as Honganji's official scrolls in order to attract Shoki Shinshū people; however, it was not necessary to position Shōtoku on a higher plane than Shinran. During the Sengoku period, Shinran's portrait was used to indicate the official status for branch temples. Ōyama points out that members of the Shoki Shinshū consisted of "wandering people from the mountains and the rivers," as Japanese scholar Inoue Toshio described.

In summary, in his *Nihon shoki no kōsō*, Ōyama Seiichi reinterprets the timeline of Japanese history beginning with the completion of the *Asuka kiyomihara ryō*, laws that were established by Emperor Temmu in 681. Then, in 694, the capital was moved to Fujiwarakyō; in 697, Emperor Jitō abdicated the throne to Emperor Bunbu; in 701, Taihō *ritsuryō* was completed, thus establishing the Japanese *ritsuryō kokka* (state based on the *ritsuryō* system). During that time, Ōyama claims that the Takamagahara and Tenson kōrin myth was completed in the *Nihon shoki*. In 702, due to the battle at Hakusonkō, the imperial court discontinued the practice of sending *kentōshi* (envoys to T'ang China). Based on witnessing the strong emperorship existent in China, the *kentōshi* proposed on their return that the imperial court create a similar system to strengthen the power and legitimacy of the newly established emperorship in Japan. At the time, only Soga no Umako wielded the power and authority on a par with the Chinese emperor. By the end of the seventh century, Japan had successfully built the Japanese *ritsuryō kokka* modeled after T'ang China. To strengthen the political and spiritual power of the Japanese emperor, the imperial court asked the editors to create a charismatic figure, Shōtoku Taishi, who could legitimize their rule. Thus, Shōtoku Taishi came into the world in the *Nihon shoki* in 720.[41]

Ōyama Seiichi's study seems to offer convincing evidence that Shōtoku Taishi was indeed a fictitious figure. An in-depth investigation of the existing historical sources reveals a lack of evidence or inconsistencies pointing to Shōtoku's existence in Japanese history. Instead, his presence is mainly found in creative stories composed by the compilers of historical documents, namely, the *Nihon shoki* and the *Kojiki*, both of which were sanctioned by imperial authorities. Like the layers of an onion, there is no real Shōtoku to be found. Instead of a historical account of his life from childhood to regency, we have only miraculous birth narratives—oddly similar to the Buddha's birth—and stories demonstrating his extraordinary powers. No reliable historical sources or genealogies regarding his existence can be found; instead, Shōtoku simply appears as a ghost and in timely fashion to unite the nation and become the central figure of worship and Japanese identity. I agree with Ōyama's stance that Shōtoku Taishi was created because the Japanese people needed a central figure that had the fluid capability to achieve various objectives of the ruling class. In an effort to unify the Japanese nation's disparate makeup of contending *uji* clans during the Yamato period, following the Chinese model of centralized government through the figure of an emperor, Shōtoku Taishi served the purpose of providing a bridge and "glue" for the imperial court to initiate and promote the notion of emperorship in Japan, a new concept for the Japanese people. To strengthen the image of the emperor, thereby strengthening the legitimization of their own rule, the imperial court initiated an aggressive campaign toward centralizing the nation through the promotion of the emperor. However, since Japan did not have a history of emperorship, the imperial court had to create a narrative history, based on mythological proportions, that would explain the origin of the emperor and his descendants. Through the backdrop of the belief in the *kami* in the prevailing indigenous religion of Shintō, the Japanese imperial authorities were able to successfully develop a mythological account that explained not only the birth of the first emperor, but also the creation of Japan through such mythological accounts, which is the reason why the *Nihon shoki* begins with the creation of the islands of Onogoro by the two primordial Shintō deities, Izanami and Izanagi. Moreover, a closer examination of the term "taishi" may reveal a more fundamental level of meaning underlying the cult of Shōtoku Taishi. According to ancient Japanese belief, taishi (also read ōko or ōiko) denoted a child of the *kami* who every year traveled from one village to another in accordance with the seasons. This taishi generally appeared at harvest time or at the end of the year "to instill new power in rice seeds and human beings in order to insure vigorous germination in the approaching spring." Moreover, the term is also associated with traditional Japanese notions of rulership since the rites of accession of a new emperor, called Daijō-sai, are celebrated at harvest time.[42] These two connotations seem to explain fittingly why emperors and retired emperors were especially mindful to partake in accession rituals at Shōtoku-centered temples, such as Shitennōji.

In their efforts to establish the exact duplicate of the T'ang capital in the Nara capital, the imperial court also needed to promote a new and foreign religion of China, which was Buddhism. Through the Seventeen-Article Constitution, the imperial court was able to accomplish three key goals: promoting the notion of the emperor through the Confucian-based ideology that is evident in the undeniable character of the Constitution; officially sponsoring Buddhism by including an explicit clause calling people to follow Buddhism; and acknowledging Shōtoku Taishi as the progenitor of the Constitution, which legitimized Shōtoku's existence and his significant contribution to Japan. Then, in order to offer further documentation of Shōtoku's existence, and in particular for the sake of legitimizing the imperial rule and divine descendancy of the emperor, the imperial authorities ordered the compilation of *Nihon shoki* and *Kojiki*. Over time, Shōtoku's legend continued to evolve through the various miraculous accounts in the *Nihon shoki* and *Kojiki*. But as Buddhism continued to spread, the image of Shōtoku also developed and he was worshiped first as more than a real person, even as a *kami*, but later as an incarnation of Buddhist founders, of the bodhisattva Kannon, and even of Buddha himself. In other words, the evolution of Shōtoku worship gained monumental proportions in later Japanese history.

In the end, the truth or falsity of Shōtoku Taishi's actual existence in Japanese history is not the central issue, since there is no denying that people worshiped and continue to worship Shōtoku in this way. My study examines how Shōtoku worship was promoted, and discusses the motivation of individuals and groups who benefited from such promotion during early and medieval Japan. Another concern is to explain the complex nature of the formation of Japanese Buddhism, one that took on its own interpretations and was indigenized to fit the needs of the Japanese people. Shōtoku was a central figure in helping not only the imperial authorities, but also the Buddhist institutions, which particularly needed a source of legitimacy to meet their need to find a sponsor and continue imperial support during this volatile period in medieval Japan. Moreover, this study also critiques the Shin sect that tends to elevate their founder Shinran and, in their efforts to preserve pure doctrine, ignores indigenous aspects of native Shintō religion and also denies other forms of Buddhist expression. As we will see, Shōtoku, though fabricated, was worshiped in the foundational practice of Pure Land Buddhism, which stems from the Tendai center at Mount Hiei. Shinran included the worship of Shōtoku to legitimize his innovative teaching, but this was common practice during the medieval period.

# Chapter 3

## Images of Shōtoku in Early Japan

During a time when Japan was engaged in civil wars and political strife, Shōtoku played a pivotal role in formulating a national identity and providing stability for the Japanese nation. The Nara period (709–795) witnessed the active promotion of state Buddhism by imperial and political authorities. After the fall of the Soga by the successful coup d'état of 645, otherwise known as the Taika Reform, the Fujiwara family attempted to create a central government based on Chinese models. As previously mentioned, Prince Shōtoku's Seventeen-Article Constitution was an important source for the Fujiwara court's promotion of the symbolic authority of the emperor and Shōtoku worship to legitimize their power. For instance, Emperor Kammu (781–806), great-grandson of Tenchi,[1] promoted Shōtoku worship to validate his claim to the throne. Although Emperor Kammu was primarily a Confucian and somewhat anti-Buddhist because of his disregard for priests who had secular ambitions, he realized that he needed Buddhist support for the political reforms that he attempted to effect. In order to control Buddhist institutions, which were growing rapidly in Nara, Emperor Kammu implemented two significant measures that would change the course of Buddhism in Japan. First, with the support of the Fujiwara and certain other important families that had traditionally been opposed to Buddhism, Emperor Kammu decided to move the capital away from Nara, stronghold of the Six Schools of Buddhism (*Kusha*, *Jōjitsu*, *Ritsu*, *Sanron*, *Hossō*, and *Kegon*), to Heian, thirty miles north of Nara, in order to restore to the sovereign his full prerogatives.[2] Second, Emperor Kammu sponsored Saichō in the establishment of a new Buddhist center at Mount Hiei, which was to become the new site of the capital.

Following Shōtoku's practice of sending *kenzuishi* (Sui embassies) to China in 607, Emperor Kammu sent Saichō to China in 804 to study the T'ien-t'ai (Jpn. Tendai) teachings and gain spiritual sanction for the new Buddhist foundation on Mount Hiei.[3] Since Chinese Buddhism was considered to be authoritative at this time, imperial authorities sent Saichō to China as a way to establish a sense of orthodox transmission. When we consider that Saichō only spent a total of nine and a half months in China, we have to presume that his was a token trip, primarily taken for the purpose of establishing proper transmission and collecting necessary texts. More significantly, in the effort to legitimize the founding of a new Buddhist center at Mount Hiei, the imperial authorities cleverly linked the founding of the new sect with an endorsement from Shōtoku. Saichō picked up on this and claimed the Tendai center's legitimacy by promoting the notion of Shōtoku as the manifestation of Tendai Eshi (Ch. Hui-ssu). According to the fragments of the *Hokkeshū-fuho-engi*, Saichō lists Prince Shōtoku as the first promulgator of Tendai thought in Japan in order to provide the newly established Tendai sect with an advantage over the traditional schools: a link to a cultural icon.[4] This claim was substantiated by the popular belief that Shōtoku Taishi was the legendary Hui-ssu of Nangaku Zenji (Jpn. Eshi), the second patriarch of the Chinese T'ien-t'ai sect.[5] Accordingly, in *Shōtoku Taishi denryaku*, it is written that Shōtoku Taishi had five previous lives as Chinese monks (two of whom lived on Mount Heng) before his present life.[6] Because of the association of Mount Heng with Hui-ssu, the theory that Prince Shōtoku was himself a reincarnation of Hui-ssu became popular.

With the moving of the capital to Heian and the establishment of the new Buddhist center at Mount Hiei, Buddhist leaders of traditional schools vehemently opposed Saichō, an appointed official emissary of Japanese Buddhism, who claimed religious authority at Mount Hiei. Obviously this was an attempt by the Fujiwara court to promote state Buddhism by establishing a unified, religiopolitical bureaucracy at Mount Hiei. To validate his claim of religious authority, Saichō called upon the veneration of Shōtoku as an incarnation of Kannon, along with his claim that he was the legitimate receiver of the Tendai teachings, which he acquired during his travels to China. Yuki Yoshifumi confirms that the worship of Shōtoku Taishi as the incarnation of *Jūichimen* ("Eleven-face" Kannon) and family member of the Tennō (emperor) played a significant role in promoting state Buddhism at the Tendai center at Mount Hiei. In contrast, according to Yoshifumi, the growing worship of Shōtoku Taishi is evidence that the situation of Tendai Buddhism was worsening.[7] Thus, during the Nara period, Shōtoku worship was jointly promoted by the imperial authorities, who attempted to establish state Buddhism, and by those founders or consolidators of different Buddhist schools, such as Saichō, who were able to legitimize their claim of religious authority through their own veneration of Shōtoku.

## MYTHIC IMAGES OF SHŌTOKU IN THE *NIHON SHOKI*

Some of the earliest legends of Shōtoku, in addition to those in the *engis*, are recorded in the *Nihon shoki* and the *Jōgū Shōtoku hōō teisetsu*.[8] Written by imperial command, these two official historical documents reveal a clever scheme, devised by the Fujiwara court and the aristocracy, to compose an "ahistorical account" of Shōtoku's mythic origins and miraculous powers. For instance, in the *Nihon shoki* (Suiko, 1st year, 4th month, 10th day), Shōtoku is described as being able to speak the moment he was born and having such wisdom that he could attend to the claims of ten men at once and decide them all without error:

> Shōtoku was the second child of Emperor Yōmei. His mother, the empress, was Anahobe no Hashihito. On the day Shōtoku was born, she went around the Imperial palace inspecting each of the government offices. When she came to the Bureau of Horses she entered as far as the stable door. Suddenly, and without any pain, she gave birth. Shōtoku was able to speak at birth and possessed the wisdom of a holy person. When he reached adulthood, he could listen to the lawsuits of ten people at the same time and judge them without error. He was also able to know things that were going to happen before they occurred. He learned Buddhism from the Korean monk Eji and studied the Confucian Classics with the scholar Kakuka. He diligently studied both areas. The emperor loved his son and prepared a residence for him in the south upper hall of the palace. Thus, he was praised as the Prince Born before the Stable Door, Residing in the Upper Hall, and Gifted with the Power of Great Discernment.[9]

A shortened version of Shōtoku's auspicious birth and miraculous powers is recorded in the *Jōgū Shōtoku hōō teisetsu*:

> When Anahobe no Hashihito, the emperess of Emperor Yōmei, went out to the stable door, she suddenly gave birth to Shōtoku Taishi. Prince Shōtoku was wise from a very young age. When he became an adult, he was able to listen to the statements of eight people simultaneously, and to differentiate their points. He heard one thing and understood many. Accordingly, he was called Prince Stable Door, Gifted with the Power of Great Discernment, and Eight Ears.[10]

The *Jōgū Shōtoku hōō teisetsu* also describes Shōtoku's mastery of the classical Buddhist sutras, alluding to his inherent Buddhahood and suggesting that Shōtoku was an incarnation of the Buddha:

> Shōtoku was able to understand the principle that nirvana is immutable and unchanging, and that there are five kinds of buddha-nature. He also clearly discerned the meaning of the Lotus Sutra teaching concerning the three vehicles and the two kinds of wisdom. He perceived the meaning of the Vimalakīrti Sutra's teaching of the wondrous nirvana. Moreover, Shōtoku knew the *Hinayāna* teachings known as the *Sautrāntikas* and the *Sarvāstivāda*. He also knew the meaning of the three profound Chinese teachings and the five Chinese Classics. At the same time, he also studied astronomy and geography. He wrote seven volumes of commentary on the Lotus Sutra and other sutras. These are called the 'Upper Palace Commentaries.' Once, Shōtoku asked a question his teacher could not answer. That evening, Shōtoku dreamed that a gold-colored person appeared and taught him the meaning of what he did not understand. After he awoke, Shōtoku was able to explain the point. When he explained it to his teacher, he, too, was able to understand it. This kind of thing occurred several times.[11]

Furthermore, not only did he display great wisdom, characteristic of the bodhisattva Seishi, Shōtoku practiced infinite compassion, strongly suggesting that he was the incarnation of bodhisattva Kannon. The *Nihon shoki* describes an episode of Shōtoku's sympathetically reaching out to a starving man:

> Suiko 21 (613) 12th month, 1st day. Prince Shōtoku traveled to Kataoka. At that time, a starving man was lying by the side of the road. Accordingly, the crown prince asked him his name, but the man did not respond. Shōtoku, observing this situation, provided the man with food and water and removed the coat he was wearing and covered the starving man with it. He said to him, "Lie there in peace." Shōtoku then sang this verse:
>
> > On the sunny hill of Mount Kataoki,
> > Look! There lies a poor traveler
> > Starving for food.
> > Were you born without parents?
> > Without a lord prosperous as a bamboo?
> > Look! There lies a poor traveler
> > Starving for food.

Prince Shōtoku dispatched a messenger to check on the starving man. The messenger returned, saying: "The starving man has already died." The crown prince was extremely saddened by this. Accordingly, he immediately had the starving man buried at the place by the side of the road. The grave was firmly sealed. Several days later, Shōtoku summoned his attendants and said to them, "The starving man who was lying by the side of the road the other day was no ordinary man. He must surely have been a holy person *(hijiri)*."[12] Shōtoku dispatched a messenger to investigate. When he returned, the messenger said, "When I went to see the grave the earth covering it had not been moved, but when I opened the grave and looked inside the corpse was not there. Only your coat was there, folded and placed on top of the coffin." At this, Shōtoku sent the messenger back to retrieve his coat. The crown prince then wore the coat again as before. People at this time thought these events most strange and remarked, "It is true that only a holy person *(hijiri)* knows a holy person *(hijiri)*." They were all the more awed by this situation.[13]

Here Shōtoku expresses his compassion for the condition of the starving man and, by extension, for the universal condition of suffering humankind. In its context, the song integrates the events and creates the emotional climax in the first half of the episode. Shōtoku's benevolent character is portrayed, a character fully in keeping with the qualities required of an exceptional leader. Thus, the story reveals the intention of the compilers of *Nihon shoki*, acclaiming Prince Shōtoku as a person of outstanding administrative and cultural accomplishments, endowed with superior intelligence from birth, and dedicated to the propagation of Buddhism in Japan.

The promotion of Shōtoku in this legend became the basis for the continual evolution of Shōtoku worship in later versions.[14] For instance, the most striking development of the story occurs in the person of the dying traveler. The early version found in *Nihon shoki* already suggests that Shōtoku was no ordinary human being, mysteriously attracting the prince's attention and then disappearing from a sealed tomb, leaving only the robe on the coffin. In the *shijiexian*, or "dissolved body of the sage" legend, the corpse often disappears from its tomb, leaving behind robes or other belongings on the coffin.[15] A familiar example is that of Bodhidharma (Jpn. Daruma), the founder of the Ch'an (Jpn. Zen) school of Buddhism. After his death, his body disappeared from its coffin, which had been securely placed within a sealed tomb on Mount Xionger in southern China, and only a single shoe was left in its place.[16] The beginning of the association between the Bodhidharma legend and Shōtoku is found in *Ihon Jōgū Taishiden*, written by Keimei around 771, which asks, "Could that starving man have been Bodhidharma?"[17] This speculation became fact in *Den-jutsu Isshin Kaimon*, composed in 834 by Kōjō, when it was turned into: "That starving man was after all Bodhidharma."[18]

The association between Shōtoku and the Bodhidharma legend was established and further elaborated in Kashima Mondo, 1337, a Buddhist-Shintō work that discusses the lineage of Shintō deities of the Kashima Shrine. The author Ryoyo postulates that Prince Shōtoku had been, in a previous existence, a Zen monk named Keishi, a disciple of Bodhidharma.[19] A simple description had now developed into a medium of veneration of Prince Shōtoku. One notices that the story attempts to provide a heightened significance of Shōtoku's achievements to show that the importance of the episode was greater than it first appeared. Yet, along with its profound message, it was still a true story, relating an objective, historical event. The final and most elaborate form of the story is found in Shinran's *Dai Nihon zokusan-o Shōtoku Taishi hōsan*:

> Close by the hill of Kataoka, there was a starving man lying beside the road. The prince stopped and dismounted from his black horse. Moved by compassion, the prince took off his purple robe, covered him with it, and sang a song, "On the sunny Hill of Kataoka, there lies a man, hungry for food. Look! He has no parents." The starving man raised his head, and replied with a moving song of his own, song in reply. "Only if Tomi Brook of Ikaruga village runs dry, will I forget my lord's name." The prince returned to the capital, and the starving man died. After some time of mourning, the prince prepared a burial ceremony. After the funeral, the prince took back his purple robe that he had given to the man, and wore it every day. His seven ministers were confused. So the prince told them, "Go and see the Hill of Kataoka." They went there but did not find the dead man's body. However, the coffin was still filled with fragrance. Amazed, they said, "Indeed, the Prince is no ordinary man."[20]

The medium in which the story was nurtured was the mind and imagination of audiences, storytellers, writers, and editors. As the story persisted over time, it developed and changed, acquiring further embellishment, finally becoming a complex and extraordinary message in order to keep the memory of Prince Shōtoku fresh in the minds of the Japanese people.[21] Finally, the events surrounding his death were described with the addition of the veneration of Shōtoku as a *kami*, as recorded in the *Jōgū Shōtoku hōō teisetsu*:

> In the twelfth month of the first year of *Hoko gansei* (621), the Empress Anahobe no Hashihito, Shōtoku Taishi's mother, died. On the

twenty-second day of the first month of the following year (622), Shōtoku Taishi became gravely ill. On account of this, the Empress Kashiwade, Shōtoku's wife, became ill as well. Both were bedridden. At this time, queens, princes, and various retainers—Dharma friends—with great sadness made the following vow: "Because of our reverence for the Three Treasures, we will make an image of Śākyamuni with the body proportions of Shōtoku Taishi. With the power of this vow, we hope that Shōtoku will heal from his illness, his life prolonged, and that he will live peacefully in the world. If he dies because of karmic consequence, we hope that he will be born in the Pure Land and quickly ascend to the realm of enlightenment." On the twenty-first day of the second month, the empress Kashiwade died. The following day, Shōtoku Taishi also died. In the middle of the third month of the thirty-first day of Suiko's reign (623), Dharma friends reverently followed the empress, Shōtoku Taishi, and the Empress Kashiwade, even after their death. They promoted the Three Jewels, desiring to attain enlightenment together. Also, they hoped that all deluded people living in the samsaric world would become liberated from the painful retributions from their past karma and seek enlightenment. The image of Śākyamuni was made by Shiba Kuratsukuri no Tori [Tori Busshi]. The above is similar to the account on the inscription on the back of the halo of the Śākyamuni image enshrined in the Golden Hall of the Hōryūji.[22]

Sakamoto Tarō, in his *Zadankai Shōtoku Taishi kenkyū no kaiko to tenbō*,[23] constructed a history of Shōtoku worship divided into three periods: the period between the medieval ages and the Edo period, the period between the Meiji period and the end of World War II, and the postwar period. According to Sakamoto, during the first period, Prince Shōtoku was mainly venerated by monks but criticized by Confucian scholars in the Edo period. During the second period, Shōtoku's reputed contributions to Japanese history were steadily reported, but without challenging the validity of such claims. In the third, or postwar, period, legendary accounts of Shōtoku's accomplishments were viewed with more skepticism and suspicions were raised as to the reliability of the *Nihon shoki*.

In the Meiji period, both Sonoda and Kumei Kunitake critically dealt with the influence of the veneration of Prince Shōtoku on historical data and set out to draw a purely historical picture of Prince Shōtoku in *Shōtoku Taishi*[24] and *Jōgū Taishi jitsuroku*.[25] At the same time, in part because the tenth year of the Taishō period (1921) marked the 1,300th anniversary of his death, the prewar study of Prince Shōtoku involved a historical approach imbued with the veneration of the prince. However, criticism with regard to the possible embellishment of the compilers of *Nihon shoki* was put forth by Karitani and Tsuda Sayukichi in *Nihon jōdaishi kenkyū*,[26] and these in turn developed into postwar criticisms of *Nihon shoki* in all aspects. It is worth noting that in the postwar period historical materials on Prince Shōtoku underwent critical examinations that led to an increasing number of historically reliable texts, archeological findings, and the emergence of more objective historical perspectives that focused on the reformation of the Taika era.

Iyenaga Saburō, in his *Asukachō ni okeru sesshō seiji no honshitsu* in *Shakai keizaishigaku* (1938), treated the description of the regency of Prince Shōtoku in *Nihon shoki* as its compilers' embellishment, and put forth his theory that the prince's actual authority was no more than auxiliary in nature. Later scholars, such as Naoki Kojirō and Inoue Kaoru, supported Iyenaga's theory. They argued that alternative readings of Empress Suiko's words recorded in *Roku sessei* should be provided.[27] In response, Sakamoto Tarō, in his *Nihon zenshi*, and Ishio Yoshihisa, in his *Nihon kodai no tennōsei to dajokan seido*, both objected to the theory of the co-presence of the crown prince or ministerial, auxiliary power. Tamura Enchō, too, judged, in his *Asuka bukkyō shi kenkyū*, that Prince Shōtoku's political position was an administrative position, newly and temporarily established to relieve Empress Suiko of her administrative duties.[28] Moreover, Tanaka Tsuguhito, in his *Shōtoku Taishi shinkō no seiritsu*, presented his interpretation that the designation of Prince Shōtoku as the crown prince was made possible by Soga no Umako's recommendation.[29]

On the other hand, Hayashi, in his *Jōgū oke* in *Nihon rekishi* (1982), characterized Umayado's (i.e., Prince Shōtoku's) basic activities as passive in nature. He also held that the prince's political participation in no way constituted full-fledged regency. Hayashi developed the theory that Prince Shōtoku, though he had become more active after gaining confidence through his association with Hata no Kawakatsu, retired to Ikaruga to devote himself to religious activities after Empress Suiko's demise. As for the relationship between Prince Shōtoku and surrounding clan members, Yokota Kenichi, in his *Shōtoku Taishi no oitachi to jinbutsuzō* in *Rekishi kōron* (1979), pointed out that the Hata clan was involved in the fundamental management of the prince's life. Kato Kenkichi, however, states in his *Jōgū oke to kashiwade uji ni tsuite* in *Shōtoku nihongi kinko* (1977) that the Kashiwade clan, whose members were related to Prince Shōtoku's family by marriage, was in close association with the family to the extent that they resided in the same territory. Jindō Atsushi, in his *Ikaruga no miya ni tsuite* in *Nihon rekishi* (1985) and *Ikaruga no miya no keizai kiban* in *Hisutoria* (1987), asserted that the imperial family resided in different parts of Ikaruga to ensure the land development of Ikaruga and their control over its people.

As for the imperial family, though mention was made of Prince Shōtoku's children in certain works, such as *Jōgū Shōtoku hōō teisetsu*, *Joguki* (incomplete verses, in *Shōtoku Taishi heiji denzatsukanbun*), *Jōgū Shōtoku Taishi denpō kekki*, and *Shōtoku Taishi denreki*, their contents differ somewhat. Mayuzumi Hiromichi, in his *Jōgū ni tsuite* in *Shin teizō hōkokushi taikei geppō* (1966), and *Jōgū ōke no Hitobito*, in his *Rekishi kōron* (1979), pointed out that the total number of Prince Shōtoku's children should be thirteen, as opposed to fourteen recorded in the *Jōgū Shōtoku hōō teisetsu*.

As for the *kan'i junikai* (i.e., cap-ranks in twelve grades) system, because it is mentioned in the description of Empress Suiko's enactment of laws in the year 603, in *Nihon shoki* and in *Zuishō* (an account of the country of Yamato), its factuality is indubitable. Consequently, the *kan'i junikai* system has been examined in comparison with the later *ritsuryō* court-rank system by scholars such as Sakamoto Tarō in his *Taika no kaishin no kenkyū* and *Kōdai ikai seido nidai*.[30] At the beginning, *taitoku*, the highest of the twelve grades, was simply regarded as equivalent to the highest rank established under the *ritsuryō* system. However, Mayuzumi Hiromichi revealed that *taitoku* corresponds to the fourth rank; he also speculated that the minister Soga no Umako was not eligible to receive the cap-rank *taitoku*. Inoue, in his *Kan'i junikai to sono shiteki igi* in *Nihon rekishi* (1963), provided evidence of Mayuzumi's speculation and asserted that ministers were given purple caps while other nobilities were bestowed the cap-ranks in twelve grades. He also agreed with Mayuzumi's assertion that both Prince Shōtoku and Soga headed the political system under the empress's reign. As for the origin of *kan'i junikai*, Inoue argued, in his *Kan'i junikai to sono shiteki igi*, that *kan'i junikai* was founded on the systems of two of the three main Korean countries, namely, Kudara (Kor. Paekche) and Kokuri (Kor. Koguryŏ), with principal focus on the former's system. Sakamoto, however, stressed in his *Shōtoku Taishi*[31] that *kan'i junikai* was Prince Shōtoku's creation based on the neighboring countries' respective systems because it was not identical to any of those systems.

The time of Prince Shōtoku's execution of the Seventeen-Article Constitution is identified as the fourth month of the twelfth year of Empress Suiko's reign, or the year 604, in *Nihon shoki*; in *Hōō teisetsu*, it is identified as the seventh month of the thirteenth year. Ōkada Masada, in his *Kenpō jūshichijō ni tsuite*[32] and *Ōmi narachō no kanbungaku*, believing that the idea of *kasshi kakurei*,[33] derived from the ancient Chinese theory of *shini* prophecy, had influenced the making of the Constitution, held that the Constitution was executed in the twelfth year, the year of *kasshi*. This has been the commonly accepted view. Furthermore, Kojima, in his *Kanbun gaku* in *Zusetsu nihon bunkashi taikei*,[34] identified the written style of the Constitution recorded in *Nihon shoki* as the style prevalent during Empress Suiko's reign (i.e., the style called *ibun*).

Today, since it has been established that the system of officialdom was already being organized at the time of Empress Suiko's reign, the view that the system of *shisei* (i.e., honorific clan titles) was prevalent prior to the Taika period has been rejected in most cases. However, Naoki Kojirō, in his *Nihon no rekishi*,[35] reexamined the view that the Constitution was indeed Prince Shōtoku's creation and asserted that what is known today as the Constitution of Prince Shōtoku was recreated after the actual Constitution that he developed had been lost.

Ōkada, in his *Kenpō jūshichijō ni tsuite*, and Takigawa, in his *Ritsuryō kakushiki no kenkyū*,[36] regarded the Six-Article Declaration put forth by the Chinese, Hokushū dynastic system as the basis of the Seventeen-Article Constitution. However, Sakamoto, in his *Shōtoku Taishi*, expressed his doubt as to the validity of this theory because he believed that the Six-Article Declaration was compiled subsequent to the time of Prince Shōtoku. Moreover, among different versions of the Seventeen-Article Constitution, the version produced in the Katei period was designated as an important cultural asset in 1949. However, Tada Shojirō, in his *Jūyō bunkazai kateibon jūshichijō kenpō wa nisemono de aru*, in *Tōkyō daigaku shiryō hensan jōhō* (1974), judged it to be a forgery because of the manner in which years were recorded in *okushō*. As for the Japanese readings of the Chinese characters that appear in the Seventeen-Articles, different theories were put forth in Kojima's essay, *Kenpō jūshichijō no kundoku ō megutte*;[37] Shōtoku Taishi hōsankai's *Kenpō jūshichijō*, Sakamoto's *Shōtoku Taishi*;[38] and also in *Shōtoku Taishi shū*, a history of Japanese thought. English, German, and French translations can also be found in Anezaki Masashi's *Jōgū Taishi Shōtoku ō mon*.[39]

*Hokke gisho*, which was supposedly written by Prince Shōtoku himself and is kept at the Hōryūji Temple, has been handed down from generation to generation and has been designated a national treasure. Accounts of how Prince Shōtoku annotated *Shōmangyō* (Queen Śrīmālā Sutra), *Hokekyō* (Lotus Sutra), and *Yuimagyō* (Vimalakīrti Sutra) can be found in such texts as *Hōō teisetsu*, *Hōryūji garan engi heiryuki shizaichō*, and *Hōryūji tōin shizaichō*. *Jōgū Shōtoku Taishi denpō kekki* also comments on the period of *sanshō senjutsu*, the time during which Prince Shōtoku wrote the three sets of annotations. Their contents, however, do not exactly accord with one another. Moreover, *Nihon shoki* offers descriptions of Prince Shōtoku's preaching of *Shōmangyō* and *Hokekyō* alone, without referring to *seisō* (the prince's production of the annotations). In addition, based on the view that those descriptions in *Nihon shoki* were tainted with its compilers' embellishment under the influence of their veneration of Prince Shōtoku, some doubts about the authorship of the annotations on the three sutras have been expressed since prewar days.

Tsuda Sayukichi criticized the contents of a series of works on *Nihon shoki*, such as *Nihon jōdaishi kenkyū*[40] and the second volume of *Nihon koten no kenkyū*,[41] and asserted that he doubts that Prince Shōtoku was able to write in such a highly specialized manner. He also found discrepancies among the contents of *Hōō teisetsu*, *Hōryūji garan engi heiryuki shizaichō*, and *Hōryūji tōin shizaichō*, which he claimed came about due to historical modifications of the story about the prince's preaching of the sutras.

Hanayama Nobukatsu, however, examined the annotations on *Shōmangyō* and *Hokekyō* bibliographically in his *Shōtoku Taishi gyosei hokke gisho no kenkyū* and *Shōmangyō gisho no Jōgū o sen ni kansuru kenkyū*.[42] Based on his observations that the annotations on the three sutras have, since the Nara period, been attributed to *Jōgū ōin*; that other explanatory notes, such as *Hongi*, were written in the Ryō period, prior to Prince Shōtoku's time; and that the written style of the annotations seems to be uniquely Japanese, Hanayama concluded that the annotations were authored by the prince himself.

## SHŌTOKU AS CHAMPION OF BUDDHISM

In Shōtoku's time, Japan began to emerge as a nation under imperial rule. Aristocratic families, such as the powerful Soga, embraced and promoted Buddhism to validate and secure the rule of the imperial family, while the pro-Shintō Mononobe clan was violently opposed to the adoption of a foreign and harmful religion. As prince regent, Shōtoku played an important role in articulating the rhetoric of the imperial family's claim to dominance over Japan. The imperial family wielded the religious power that was believed to reside in Buddhist texts, images, and rituals as a way of justifying their ruling authority.

A clear example of the connection between Buddhism and ruling power can be seen in the political struggle between the Soga and Mononobe. According to the account in the *Nihon shoki*, Moriya no Mononobe, an anti-Buddhist, attempted to kill Shōtoku, but the prince made an alliance with the pro-Buddhist Soga no Umako to protect himself. The Mononobe clan was associated with the worship of the indigenous *kami*, while the Soga family supported Buddhism. After rallying his troops and making a vow to the *Four Guardian Deities* for victory, Prince Shōtoku successfully defeated Moriya and constructed Shitennōji in Naniwa, now in the city Ōsaka, in gratitude to the *Four Guardian Deities*.[43] After the war, according to the text, the Shitennōji was built in Settsu (modern Ōsaka), and half of Moriya no Mononobe's slaves, together with his house, were donated to the institution:

Soga no Umako counseled the Imperial princes and government officials in devising a plan to destroy Moriya no Mononobe. Leading an
army, Umako and the others advanced to attack Moriya. . . . Moriya
also led an army of family and servants. They built a fortress from
bundles of rice and engaged in battle. . . . Moriya's army fought furi-
ously. . . . The army of the Imperial princes and government officials
was seized with fear, and they retreated three times. At this time,
Prince Shōtoku . . . reflected on the development of the battle: "Will
we not be defeated? Unless we make a vow, it will be difficult to
achieve victory." After saying this, he cut down a sacred nuride tree
and quickly fashioned images of the Four [Buddhist] Guardian
Deities. He placed the images on his forehead and made a vow: "If we
are allowed to achieve victory against our enemies, I will build a temple and stupa to honor the Four Guardian Deities who protect the
world." Soga no Umako also made a vow: "If we obtain the benefit of
being saved and protected by the Four Guardian Deities and the protector *kami* Daijinnō, I vow to build a temple and stupa to them, and
to propagate Buddhism." Having made these vows, they prepared
their army and urged them into battle. From a tree, an archer named
Tomi no Obito Ichii shot at Moriya no Mononobe, killing him and
his children. Consequently, Moriya's army was quickly routed. . . .
After the battle, Shitennōji was constructed at Tsunokuni. Half of
Moriya no Mononobe's servants were made servants for the temple,
and Moriya's estate was made into the private rice fields of the temple.
Also, 490 acres of rice field were presented to Tomi no Obito Ichii.
Soga no Umako, in keeping with his vow, constructed the Hōkō Tem-
ple in Asuka.[44]

According to the *Zenkōji engi*, after his triumphant victory over Moriya, Prince
Shōtoku went to the Naniwa Canal to rescue the submerged Amida triad[45] so
that he could enshrine it in the palace.[46]

Once Buddhism gained official government support, a natural movement
emerged that sought to unite the new religion with the indigenous *kamis*; this
is known in its early stages as *shinbutsu shūgō* (unification of *kamis* and buddhas).[47] From ancient times, the center of village life had been constructed
around devotions to the village guardian deities *(ujigami)*. Since Buddhism
was a foreign religion still lacking popular acceptance, it became necessary for
temple masters to seek a means of harmonizing existing beliefs with Buddhist
thought in order to sustain temple *shōen* (tax-free landed estate). According to
Alicia Matsunaga, Shintō priests viewed the development of *shinbutsu shūgō* as
a means of sharing the lucrative government benefits bestowed on Buddhism;

idealistic Buddhists recognized it as a way to approach the masses, and the common people accepted it as a natural phenomenon.[48] The government encouraged such a process by supporting the construction of *jingūji* (shrine-temples). With the construction of *jingūji* and the practice of sutra chanting for the indigenous *kamis*, it was commonly accepted that the native deities had embraced Buddhism and decided to protect the dharma.[49] Matsunaga explains that it is natural to imagine that at this time the great and powerful *kami* could become the guardians of the local temples, while the lesser *kami*, as they grew more humanized, could be treated as unenlightened *kamis* and instructed in the teachings. The assimilation of the indigenous *kami* into Japanese Buddhism was an important and essential development in the evolution of Japanese Buddhism.

## SHŌTOKU AS IMPERIAL ANCESTOR

During the Heian period (794–1185), a gradual shift in the power structure began as the aristocratic landowners, great temples, and shrines managed to evade taxation and acquire huge *shōen*.[50] The centralized bureaucratic system or *ritsuryō* that was modeled after the Chinese brand of government disintegrated and eventually gave rise to the control of local warlords *(daimyōs)*. Plots, intrigues, and corruption abounded, and even the Buddhist temples developed *sōhei* or priest-warriors to protect their interests and make frequent demands at the capital. However, with the decline of the *ritsuryō* government, many of the state-sponsored temples suffered a loss of revenue. Temples found a new financial basis through imperial patronage and support from the aristocracy.[51] The aristocrats had a great deal to gain by supporting Buddhism, since the legal justification for their role diminished along with the disintegration of the *ritsuryō* government. During this time, the Fujiwara house took an active role in promoting Shōtoku worship to maintain a powerful regency.

However, although aristocratic support was a financial blessing, it also became a source of dissension within the orders and temples. Obliged to support the causes of their patrons, by the end of the Heian period many temples were forced into rivalries and hostilities that were totally unrelated to religion. In particular, as Fujiwara control began to waver during the latter part of the eleventh century, temples found themselves entangled in quarrels between their patrons and the retired emperors who sought to assert their authority behind the scenes under the *insei* (cloistered-government) system. An example of such a case was the Shingon Ninnaji temple. Established under the patronage of its abbot, the retired emperor Uda, who had tried to break Fujiwara control at the end of the ninth century, the Ninnaji became a rallying place for pro-imperial, anti-Fujiwara groups. Such political involvement drew many temples into the endless succession disputes at the end of the Heian period. Consequently, besides the political handicaps resulting from aristocratic patronage, temples also had to endure aristocrats as abbots. Just as the retired emperor Uda became the abbot of the Ninnaji, other emperors, princes, and sons of nobles, possessing virtually no religious training or experience, were installed as abbots in the prestigious temples.[52] To legitimize their installations, retired emperors displayed their veneration of Prince Shōtoku, whom they considered their imperial ancestor and ideal Buddhist king.

As a Buddhist holding a position of power in such a crucial period of Japanese history, Prince Shōtoku could have chosen to eradicate the indigenous Shintō *kamis* and set Buddhism in their place. He also had a good motive, considering that major proponents of the native Shintō were the enemies that his clan had to defeat prior to its rise to power.[53] Despite these facts, Shōtoku gave support to the indigenous beliefs. There was no need for conflict. The native Shintō cult was not yet an institution except at court. It lacked a systematic philosophical foundation, and was not completely unified throughout the country. Shōtoku envisioned the union of native Shintō beliefs and Buddhism, and he sought to encourage the development of both in harmony. In 607, he issued the following edict in the name of Empress Suiko: "Now in our reign how can one give up the respect and prayers to the *kamis* in the Pure Land and on the earth? Hence, all of my attendants should make up their minds to rightly worship the *kamis* in Pure Land and the *kamis* on the earth."[54] In this way, the imperial family maintained native Shintō beliefs, while charismatic spiritual leaders of the nation also propagated Buddhism. The imperial family claimed the basis for their authority over the Japanese nation by reason of their divine descent from the sun goddess, Amaterasu. As a result, at the political level, the imperial family was able to become close to the other powerful clans, who also claimed descent from various Pure Land or earthly deities. Consequently, the power of the imperial family was dependent on support from these other clans, which were still virtually autonomous at this time, despite the recent Soga victory.

Promoting the native Shintō cult and solidifying it into a state religion was one method of extending the hegemony of the imperial family and making their power more secure. For instance, when Minamoto no Yoritomo raised an army to conquer Japan and in 1177 claimed his rule to be a shogunate, a government by military rule, this was the first time in Japanese history that a military warlord came into power in Japan. Before the Kamakura government, the Japanese emperor held both political and spiritual power. However, as a result of Yoritomo's successful usurpation of the throne, the Japanese emperor no longer held political power, but did continue to hold symbolic power. Although

Yoritomo's own nobility justified his claim to the throne, he tried to secure his legitimacy by venerating Shōtoku Taishi. He identified with Shōtoku, who also punished those who were considered enemies of Buddhism.[55] It is common knowledge that Yoritomo often sought Shōtoku's divine favor in the healing of his sickly daughter, often visiting the famous Shitennōji to worship Shōtoku Taishi. Just as Shōtoku had been hailed as the victor and protector of Buddhism during the defeat of the Mononobe clan in previous years, Yoritomo attributed his successful defeat of Taira no Kiyomori, who was considered an enemy of the king and Buddhist law, to Shōtoku's guidance and protection. In fact, Yoritomo even considered himself to be an incarnation of Shōtoku Taishi because he, too, was instrumental in protecting and promoting Buddhism in Japan.[56] Following the manner in which Shōtoku Taishi executed Moriya no Mononobe after the civil war, Yoritomo also executed Taira no Munemori. In other words, Yoritomo attempted to establish his government by military rule based on the model of government created by Shōtoku Taishi and Emperor Temmu.

To validate his military rule through veneration of Shōtoku Taishi, it was also important for Yoritomo to be on good terms with temple establishments. To gain a deeper understanding of Shōtoku Taishi, Yoritomo studied the *Goshuin engi*.[57] The *Goshuin engi* described those who robbed temples as the incarnation of Moriya and stated that Buddhist law had to be protected from corruption caused by bureaucrats stealing temple lands. He explained to the leaders of temple establishments that the Buddha had punished the Taira family because they were enemies of Buddhism. Yoritomo gained the support of Enjo-ji, who considered him a guardian and protector of Buddhism, as Shōtoku had been during the Soga–Mononobe conflict. To further strengthen the perception of himself as guardian and protector of Buddhism, Yoritomo showed special favor to those temples that were associated with Shōtoku, and even donated his own taxes to these temples.

As the legend of Shōtoku continued to evolve during the medieval period, some emperors, seeking to more firmly establish their authority, boldly claimed even closer ties to Shōtoku Taishi. In a commemoration of Shōtoku's founding of Hōjō-ji, Eiga Monogatari and Ō-kagami describe Fujiwara no Michinaga as an incarnation of Shōtoku Taishi, since Shōtoku once said that a person who preaches Buddhism was an incarnation of himself. This saying was recorded in an *engi* that supposedly emerged from the Hōtō (treasure tower) of Shitennōji Kondō (Golden Hall) in 1007, and was allegedly written by Shōtoku himself.[58] Consequently, it was not an uncommon practice for an emperor to claim that he was the incarnation of bodhisattva Kannon and guardian of Buddhism. Emperor Shōmu, for example, who was responsible for building the Great Buddha or *Daibutsu* at Tōdaiji in the late Nara period, claimed that he was the incarnation of Shōtoku Taishi.[59] And, according to the *Tōdaiji yōraku*, the Tōdaiji and the Daibutsu in Kamakura were built by the will of bodhisattva Kannon, Shōtoku Taishi, and Emperor Shōmu.

Michinaga's descendants, Yorinaga, Kanezane, and Michiie, also worshiped Shōtoku Taishi. Yorinaga often visited Shitennōji to pray.[60] His prayers during the month of October in 1143 seem to have had particular significance for him as he meditated on Shōtoku's picture and prayed in front of Shōtoku's statue, vowing to follow Shōtoku's Seventeen-Article Constitution. Subsequently, Yorinaga claimed that the emperor's power was endorsed by his respect of both the Buddhist law and the secular law, described in the Seventeen-Article Constitution.[61] Furthermore, in order to strengthen his ties to the imperial court, Yorinaga sent his daughter-in-law to the palace to become the second wife of Emperor Konoe and had her pray regularly at Rokkakudō.

The Seventeen-Article Constitution served as an important source for the aristocracy who used it to criticize the unfair policies of the government as well as to promote their own influence through their connection to Shōtoku. After the downfall of Taira no Kiyomori in 1185, the Minamoto family ascended to power and Go-Toba assumed the emperorship. As a way of reform, Fujiwara Kanezane appealed to the Kamakura shōgun, Minamoto no Yoritomo, to conduct good politics based on sound moral grounds as in the ancient state, found in the Seventeen-Article Constitution. Although Fujiwara Kanezane's attempt to promote ideal politics through the Seventeen-Article Constitution was initially successful, anti-Kanezane powers arose and ousted him.

After the downfall of Kanezane, Michiie of the Kujō family assumed the regency. To reinforce his claim to authority, Michiie arranged a grand ritual to worship Shōtoku Taishi, asking Shōtoku to favor and guide his regency. From this point on, the aristocratic family began to show an avid worship of Shōtoku Taishi, just as Michinaga, who was considered to be an incarnation of Prince Shōtoku, had done. Temples related to Shōtoku, especially the Shitennōji, became like media centers where the aristocratic families could display their deep devotion to their patron saint, Shōtoku Taishi. They constantly reminded the people that Shōtoku was the ideal regent, and that their regency would be modeled after Shōtoku's administration and Buddhist faith.

## SHŌTOKU AS FATHER OF JAPANESE BUDDHISM

Minamoto Tamenori's tenth-century composition of the *Sanbōe*[62] cleverly incorporated all previous legends about Shōtoku Taishi, essentially portraying Prince Shōtoku as the father of Japanese Buddhism.[63] Having been a *monjosho*, a student of literary studies in the Imperial University, and having studied

Chinese histories and Confucian classics under Minamoto Shitago (911–983), Tamenori was able to write the *Sanbōe* with allusions to secular Chinese and Japanese works as well as to a vast number of Buddhist texts. Careful reading of Tamenori's *Sanbōe* reveals that Tamenori skillfully combined various biographical and mythical allusions to Shōtoku Taishi recorded earlier in the *Nihon shoki*, *Jōgū Taishi gyoki*, *Shōtoku Taishi denryaku*, and the *Gangōji engi*. In fact, he even used *jātaka* (Jpn. *honjō-wa*),[64] the corpus of stories about the Buddha's previous lives, to not only emphasize the law of karma, but also to invent his own *jātakas*, in effect portraying Shōtoku Taishi as the father of Japanese Buddhism and the incarnation of bodhisattva Kannon.

The focus of the second volume of Tamenori's *Sanbōe* begins with an account of the establishment of Buddhism in Japan by Prince Shōtoku, who is hailed by Nichira[65] as *guze bosatsu*,[66] "bringer of light, king of this wild little eastern country."[67] Just as it is recorded in the *Nihon shoki*, the text goes on to describe Prince Shōtoku's participation in the battle between the Soga and Mononobe clan and his invocation of the *Four Guardian Deities* who promised to protect Buddhism from its enemies. After the defeat of the Mononobe clan, Tamenori records that Prince Shōtoku kept his promise to build the temple of the *Four Guardian Deities* or *Shitennōji*, the great temple in Osaka, and "Buddhism flourished ever afterward." Three years later, at the age of nineteen, Prince Shōtoku was made regent under his aunt, Empress Suiko, and was given all responsibility for governing the nation. Then, Tamenori adds, Prince Shōtoku was hailed once again, by a prince named Asa from Paekche: "Hail the World-saving Bodhisattva Kannon who has brought the wondrous teaching to the eastern nation of Japan, who will illuminate and expound the teachings for forty-nine years."[68] Tamenori writes, "At that moment, a white light shone from Prince Shōtoku's brow; the beam of light was three yards long. After a while, it shortened and then disappeared." The rest of the biography describes Shōtoku's role in the construction of many temples and his death at the age of forty-nine. In these descriptions, Tamenori portrays Prince Shōtoku in the various images of an ideal general, ideal regent, guardian of Buddhism, and bodhisattva Kannon, all incarnations promoted by ruling authorities attempting to legitimize their claims to authority in medieval Japan.

In the final section on Shōtoku's biography, Tamenori's explanation of Shōtoku's three names helps us to better understand how Shōtoku was worshiped during Tamenori's day:

> The prince is known by three names. First, he is called Umayado Toyotomimi no miko. This is because he was born by the side of the royal stable and could hear about the sufferings of ten people all at one time without missing a word. Second, he is called Shōtoku Taishi.

This is because he behaved like a monk from the time of his birth and later wrote commentaries on the Śrīmālā Sutra and the Lotus Sutra, spread Buddhism, and saved many people. Third, he is called Jōgū Taishi. This is because he lived in the southern wing of the palace during the reign of Empress Suiko and conducted all the affairs of the State himself.[69]

According to Tamenori's explication, Shōtoku's three names correspond to the three traditional ways in which Shōtoku was worshiped during his time: "Umayado Toyotomimi no miko" as a manifestation of Bodhisattva Kannon (karmic lineage); "Shōtoku Taishi" as a reincarnation of the Chinese Buddhist monk, Hui-ssu (the spiritual lineage); and "Jōgū Taishi" as imperial ancestor (imperial lineage).

First, the name "Umayado Toyotomimi no miko" is used several times in *Nihon shoki*. *Umayado*, meaning, "stable," refers to the legend of the prince's miraculous birth in a stable and his speaking with great skill by the age of four months. *Toyotomimi* describes his ears as having supernatural capabilities, and suggests that he possessed the universal hearing possessed by bodhisattvas— namely, Kannon. Interestingly, the element *mimi* (ear) appears in the names of many Shintō deities and may have some other ritualistic or honorific meanings of non-Buddhist origin, which accounts for the *honji suijaku* application.

Second, "Shōtoku Taishi," his posthumous name, suggests the name's general Buddhist character, which explains the espousal by Tendai patriarchs to worship Shōtoku Taishi as a reincarnation of the T'ien T'ai patriarch, Hui-ssu, as a way to validate their authority. The two commentaries mentioned here in connection with this name—the *Shōmangyō gisho* (on the *Śrīmālā sutra*) and the *Hokekyō gisho* (on the *Lotus sutra*)—and a third commentary, the *Yuimagyō gisho* (on the *Vimalakīrti sutra*), are attributed to the prince. Shirai Shigenobu points out that these commentaries rely considerably on Chinese commentaries that may not have been known in Japan during the prince's lifetime.[70]

Third, "Jōgū Taishi" appears in the *Nihon shoki* in sections covering the reigns of Yōmei and Suiko. *Jōgū*, literally "upper palace," means that his quarters were on higher ground than the sovereign's, implying an honorific expression of his governance as regent, or an indication that he was heir apparent. As expected, this name corresponds to the imperial claims to authority through imperial lineage to Prince Shōtoku. Furthermore, we must keep in mind that the two surviving official sources regarding the biography of Shōtoku, the *Nihon shoki* and *Jōgū Shōtoku Taishi hōō teisetsu*, were compiled by imperial command.

Through Tamenori's *Sanbōe*, we learn how Shōtoku was worshiped in three different ways: as a reincarnation of the Chinese T'ien-t'ai patriarch,

Hui-ssu (Jpn. Eshi); as an incarnation of bodhisattva Kannon; and as an imperial ancestor. In an episode of Tamenori's *Sanbōe*, Prince Shōtoku is described as a reincarnation of Hui-ssu who died in 577, three years after Shōtoku's birth:

> The prince sent Ono no Imoko to look for a sutra that, he said, had belonged to him in a former life, when he had lived on Mount Heng in China. "In the southern part of China," said the prince, "there is a mountain called Mount Heng, and on the mountain is the Pan-jo temple. All of my comrades of those by-gone days must be dead by now, but three of them may still be alive. Tell them that you are my messenger and that I had a copy of the Lotus Sutra in one fascicle when I lived there. Ask them for it, and bring it back." Following these instructions, Imoko went to China and made his way to the temple. A monk was standing at the gate, and when he saw Imoko he went in and said, "A messenger has come from Meditation Master Nien."[71]

"Meditation Master Nien" *(Nen zenshi)* is understood here as Prince Shōtoku's name in his previous life. Because of the association of Mount Heng with Hui-ssu, the theory that the prince was a reincarnation of Hui-ssu himself became popular; both Saichō and Kukai adopted it.

Tamenori's *Sanbōe* is especially insightful because we are able to learn how the legend of Shōtoku evolved in different ways according to the needs of various ruling authorities to build their legitimacy. Tamenori's *Sanbōe* did not fully integrate the idea of worshiping Prince Shōtoku as both *kami* and incarnation of bodhisattva Kannon, in accordance with the development of the *honji suijaku* thought in the Heian period. Rather, Tamenori's *Sanbōe* represents a "transitional work" that promoted the worship of Shōtoku as a superhuman being, in accordance with the traditional accounts of Prince Shōtoku found in ancient sources, and as a reincarnation of Hui-ssu and bodhisattva Kannon, in accordance with the continual evolution of Shōtoku worship during the medieval period. A thorough integration of the veneration of Prince Shōtoku as both *kami* and incarnation of bodhisattva Kannon would be achieved through the proliferation of Shōtoku legends in association with popular Shintō images in the medieval period.

These sources indicate that the earliest legends about Shōtoku Taishi were initiated not only by temple establishments, particularly by those temples that were founded by Shōtoku, but also by imperial authorities who promoted the worship of Shōtoku to legitimize their rule. According to tradition, Japanese people continued to regard the emperor as the direct descendant of the sun goddess, Amaterasu, in accordance with Japanese mythology. This notion of the emperor's divine right to reign had been cultivated from ancient times through the observance of rituals and ceremonies centered on rice festivals, and had been passed down, theoretically, from the goddess Amaterasu. Throughout the ages, the emperor continued to foster the perception of his direct imperial lineage to the goddess Amaterasu by performing various rituals resembling shamanistic practices while wearing regal garments symbolizing his divine status. Joan Piggott explains that the concept of emperorship, which is based on the emperors' claim to unbroken succession from the sun goddess Amaterasu and the assumption of absolute powers, was derived from the Chinese concept of the Mandate of Heaven. She notes that Prince Shōtoku's Seventeen-Article Constitution, the Taika Reforms, and the adoption of Chinese legal and bureaucratic institutions were all intended to strengthen the claims of the emperor to be a true "Son of Heaven."

# Chapter 4

## Images of Shōtoku in Medieval Japan

During the medieval period, Prince Shōtoku was portrayed and venerated as a Buddhist saint. Kamakura Buddhists believed that Shōtoku was the first Japanese to fully experience the essence of Buddhism in Japan, so they tended to associate him with the glories of earlier Indian and Chinese Buddhism. Many legends typically identified Shōtoku as a Japanese manifestation of the bodhisattva Kannon, a reincarnation of the Buddhist queen Śrīmālā of India, and Tendai Eshi (Ch. Nanyüeh Hui-ssu, 515–577) of China. With the movement of the capital from Nara to Heian and the newly established, imperially sponsored Buddhist centers at Mount Hiei and Mount Kōya, the sangha developed an effective way to solidify their presence and continue their influence on Japanese society. Through the figure of Shōtoku Taishi and the promotion of Prince Shōtoku as a Buddhist divinity, the sangha found the ideal patron and perfect means for legitimizing their claims of authority at the newly established Buddhist centers at Heiankyō during medieval Japan. Just as earlier sources were compiled on Prince Shōtoku—the *Nihon shoki* and *Kojiki*—to promote Prince Shōtoku as imperial ancestor and *kami* in order for the imperial court to legitimize its rule through their claim of divine ancestry and authority of the emperor, the sangha also compiled Buddhist-originated sources that promoted Prince Shōtoku's Buddhist accomplishments, which also could be used as sources of legitimization to establish their authority at Heiankyō. Thus, during the Heian and Kamakura period, we notice a proliferation of Shōtoku legends through various mediums—*engis*, iconographic representations, and Shōtoku-centered rituals, and ceremonies conducted at temples[1]—whose underlying purpose was to promote Prince Shōtoku as a Buddhist saint and divinity.

71

## LEGITIMACY AND AUTHORITY: *HONJI SUIJAKU* THEORY

In his article "Hagiography and History: The Image of Prince Shōtoku" in the *Religions of Japan in Practice,* William Deal explains that the *Nihon shoki* (Chronicles of Japan), an imperially sanctioned account, portray Shōtoku Taishi in order to validate the claims of the imperial family's right to rule. Deal argues that the *Nihon shoki* places Shōtoku within the larger context of the political and religious struggles occurring in early Japanese history, and that there is strong evidence that it is a compendium of historical, literary, legendary, religious, and other materials placed within the historical chronological framework. Deal cites another source, *Jōgū Shōtoku hōō teisetsu* (the Imperial Record of Shōtoku, Dharma King of the Upper Palace), which shares similar features that portray Shōtoku in both legendary and historical terms for the sake of legitimacy. Composed in the eighth century, the *Jōgū Shōtoku hōō teisetsu* also reveals the importance of Shōtoku as both ruler and Buddhist. Unlike the account in the *Nihon shoki,* the *Jōgū Shōtoku hōō teisetsu* is primarily a Buddhist biography because it emphasizes Shōtoku's Buddhist activities, such as temple building and sutra study. Deal notes that since both texts were written about a hundred years after Shōtoku's death, one has to be careful to not confuse claims about historical fact with the valorization of the prince's political and religious accomplishments. Nevertheless, a closer examination of these sources will help us learn what his image has meant in different historical periods, and how this image was utilized to promote religious practices and political agendas. In the *Nihon shoki* and the *Jōgū Shōtoku hōō teisetsu* biographies, Shōtoku the statesman and Shōtoku the Buddhist are interrelated images, since Buddhism and the state had become inextricably linked in early Japan. During Shōtoku's lifetime and after, aristocratic families like the powerful Soga family utilized Buddhism, at least in part, to legitimate and secure the power and authority of the imperial family. Deal explains that the rising popularity of Buddhism among some of the aristocracy necessitated imperial control over this powerful ideology, which was itself becoming a central part of the imperial family's claim to the throne.

In his work *The Theory of Social and Economic Organization,* the German sociologist Max Weber discussed the three types of legitimate authority, in which the validity of claims to legitimacy is based on rational grounds, traditional grounds, or charismatic grounds.[2] Rational grounds rest on a belief in the "legality" of patterns of normative rules and the right of those elevated to authority under such rules to issue commands. Traditional grounds rest on an established belief in the sanctity of immemorial traditions and the legitimacy of the status of those exercising authority under them. In the case of legal authority, obedience is owed to the legally established impersonal order. It extends to the persons exercising the authority of office under it only by virtue of the formal legality of their commands, and only within the scope of authority of the office. The fundamental source of authority in this type is the authority of the impersonal order itself. Finally, legitimacy on charismatic grounds rests on devotion to the specific and exceptional sanctity, heroism, or exemplary character of an individual person, and of the normative patterns or order revealed or ordained by him. The "charismatic" claim to authority is one that is specifically in conflict with the bases of legitimacy of an established, fully institutionalized order. The charismatic leader is always in some sense a revolutionary, setting himself in conscious opposition to established aspects of the society in which he works.

Weber's description of legitimacy on charismatic grounds is particularly applicable to our study. The founders of the new Buddhist orders during the Kamakura period can be viewed as revolutionary figures, since each one of them—Nichiren, Dōgen, Eisai, Hōnen, and Shinran—left the established institutionalized order at Mount Hiei and propagated their own interpretations regarding the method of realizing enlightment during the time of *mappo*, though some founders were accused of deviating from the orthodox teachings of the established order. For instance, in order to refute the heretical teachings *(itan)* of Pure Land Buddhism, the political and religious authorities issued a ban in 1207 on the *senju nenbutsu* teaching and exiled its "revolutionary" leaders, Hōnen and Shinran. Although both Hōnen and Shinran displayed charismatic qualities, followers of Shinran's *Jōdo Shinshū* especially elevated their master to the status of sainthood. For instance, some of Shinran's followers venerated him as the reincarnation of Kannon and even Amida Buddha. The veneration of Shinran as charismatic individual seems to fit well with Weber's definition of the term "charisma"—a certain quality of an individual personality by virtue of which he is set apart from ordinary men and treated as endowed with supernatural, superhuman, or at least exceptional powers or qualities. These qualities are not accessible to the ordinary person, but are regarded as of divine origin or as exemplary, and on their basis the individual is regarded as a leader. How the quality in question would ultimately be judged from any ethical or aesthetic point of view is entirely irrelevant for purposes of definition. What alone is important is how the individual is actually regarded by those subject to the charismatic authority, by his "followers" or "disciples."[3]

In Weber's treatment, perhaps two points stand out regarding charisma, besides the fact that it is a source legitimate authority. First, charisma is a revolutionary force, tending to upset the stability of institutionalized orders; second, charisma cannot itself become the basis of a stabilized order without undergoing profound structural changes.[4] The initial source of its revolutionary character lies in setting up the authority of an individual against the established order—the *kenmitsu taisei*[5]—the office or traditionalized status of those originally in authority. The Soga imperial court was the first to set a precedent when they successfully established legitimacy for their claims of rule through the figure of Prince Shōtoku in the sixth century, when Japan was in a state of dis-array as a result of the disparate *uji* clans vying for power during Yamato Japan. Through their promotion of Shōtoku worship, the Soga family sought to achieve the following three objectives: (1) to claim their victory over the com-peting pro-Shintō Mononobe clan; (2) to unify the disparate factions in Japan by promoting Shōtoku as their imperial ancestor and *kami*, and subordinating the patron *kamis* from other *uji* clan; and, (3) to establish legitimacy for their claim to rule. To begin with, the Soga family supported and championed their imperial representative Prince Shōtoku, who waved the flag of Buddhism against the flag of Shintō. Reminiscent of the battle cries of the crusaders from the eleventh century, the pro-Buddhist Soga family likewise emerged victori-ous over the pro-Shintō Mononobe clan, as recorded in the *Nihon shoki*. To fur-ther strengthen their position and demonstrate their newly acquired political power, the Soga family instituted national reform measures through the Seven-teen-Article Constitution, which was based on the Chinese model of govern-ment and society.

Moreover, the Soga family's effective promotion of Prince Shōtoku as their champion and imperial ancestor for legitimacy purposes served as a precedent for later political and religious groups or individuals to use the same method, which, as Weber decribes, established a *tradition* of Shōtoku legitimacy.[6] For instance, during the medieval period, retired emperors continued the tradi-tional practice of paying their respects to Prince Shōtoku at the various temples that Shōtoku founded; Go-Sanjō, Shirakawa, Toba, Go-Shirakawa, and Go-Toba all regularly visited Shitennōji for prayer and meditation. Their religious activities at Shitennōji were used to portray the retired emperors as dignified secular and sacred rulers similar to Prince Shōtoku, whom they venerated as an ideal regent and ideal Buddhist king. In some cases, a retired emperor also made bold claims about his ties to Shōtoku Taishi. For example, just as Michi-naga established temples after hearing Shōtoku's words that anyone who preaches Buddhism was an incarnation of himself, Shirakawa also claimed that he was an incarnation of Shōtoku Taishi.[7]

According to Satō Hiroo, a major development during the medieval period was the association of *kamis* with buddhas under *honji suijaku*.[8] With the break-down of the *ritsuryō* government, many shrines, formerly under state control, formed associations with Buddhist temples. Satō explains how *kami* in the an-cient period progressed from *kamis* unrelated to one another, to a more orga-nized group with a genealogy recorded in the *Nihon shoki* and *Kojiki*. Under the doctrine of *honji suijaku*, the mythological structure of *kami* was reorganized as *kami* were incorporated into Buddhist cosmology. *Kamis* and buddhas were no longer seen as separate entities, as they had been during the ancient period. In view of the *honji suijaku* theory as well as the general *mappō* consciousness of the medieval period, people generally believed that Shōtoku was one of the powerful *kami* who appeared in this degenerate world as a manifestation of the bodhisattva Kannon and Amida Buddha.[9]

The close association of shrines and temples invariably began an integration of *kamis* and buddhas under *honji suijaku*, whereby native Shintō *kamis* were gradually assimilated into the Buddhist cosmology.[10] Satō explains that the *honji suijaku* theory was necessary to avoid total warfare between *kamis*. In his *Shinbutsu ōken no chūsei*,[11] Satō outlines the medieval cosmology of *kamis* and buddhas. He explains that there were ten levels of existence in Buddhist cosmology and notes that the upper four realms, which included buddhas, bodhisattvas, pratyeka-buddhas, and śrāvakas,[12] were considered the realms of enlightened existence, while the lower six realms *(rokudō)* from Pure Land downward were the worlds of confusion. Within this order, the Japanese *kami* were below those of Pure Land. Precisely because the Japanese *kami* and the Pure Land figures, like Taishaku, existed within *rokudō*, they had the ability to administer punishment and reward; beings that lived in the enlightened realm only had the ability to rescue people, and thus their functions were cosmologically supported. However, buddhas that existed in this realm of disorder as material manifestations were considered to have different functions than when they existed purely in the enlightened realms. Therefore, Satō asserts that this cosmology is marked by an absence of absolute figures.

According to *honji suijaku*, indigenous Shintō gods *(kamis)* actually represented manifestations *(suijaku)* of various buddhas and bodhisattvas *(honji)*.[13] This required the selection of popular Buddhist divinities, such as the bodhisattva Kannon, and matching them with Shintō *kami*, then endowing the latter with the attributes of the former.[14] The attempt to form a correlation between Shintō and Buddhism resulted in the native *kami* being elevated to a metaphysical status, and acculturated Buddhism to the existing Japanese religious framework. As Satō explains, many shrines, formerly under state control, formed associations with Buddhist temples following the breakdown of the *ritsuryō* government in the ancient period. Having gradually lost the patronage and financial support of the Imperial court before the breakdown of the *ritsuryō* government, shrines found a new source of support in alliances with Buddhist temples.

Satō also notes that during the medieval period specific places, such as the grounds of shrines and temples, came to be seen as Pure Land space within the defiled world. This view was supported by the *honji suijaku* theory and asserted that certain *kami*, such as Hachiman,[15] were the *honji* of important buddhas in otherworldly Pure Lands—in this case, Shōtoku Taishi. He also points out that shrines and temples used stories of miracles in their *engi* to establish lineages, and asserted that they were locations of the Pure Land in order to draw visitors and pilgrims and thus raise revenue. According to Satō, the concept developed in such a way that visitations to these temples or shrines that housed the *honji* of *higan no butsu* (compassionate vow of Buddha) became the "close path" for rebirth into these otherworldly Pure Lands.

The development of the *honji suijaku* thought also played an important role in the promotion of Shōtoku worship among various ruling authorities that attempted to legitimize their authority during the medieval period. Each ruling authority tried to elaborate on the notion of Shōtoku worship by promoting new images of Shōtoku to serve his political interest. For instance, embracing the *honji suijaku* and portrayal of Shōtoku as the reincarnation of Tendai Eshi (Ch. Hui-ssu), Michinaga considered himself the reincarnation of Shōtoku, according to the account in the *Azuma kagami* and *Jōgū Shōtoku Taishi den hoketsuki*.[16] Temple establishments also promoted the worship of Shōtoku by conducting rituals that venerated Shōtoku as a manifestation of the bodhisattva Kannon. By incorporating certains aspects of Shintō into Buddhism, the *honji suijaku* made it easier to portray Shōtoku in legendary terms, thus increasing Shōtoku worship. While ancient sources such as the *Nihon shoki* contain dramatizations of Prince Shōtoku's achievements in their efforts to create Shōtoku legends, medieval sources incorporate a more integrated worship of Shōtoku Taishi as a *kami* and Buddhist divinity as a result of *honji suijaku* thought.[17] One of the sources in which we can see this transformation in Shōtoku worship is the *Jōgū Shōtoku Taishi den hoketsuki*, an addendum that incorporated and elaborated on Shōtoku legends found in ancient sources. Ancient sources on Shōtoku Taishi, such as the *Nihon shoki* and *Jōgū Shōtoku Taishi hōō teisetsu*, portray the prince as a superhuman being and like a *kami*, but not as a manifestation of a Buddhist divinity. Because Shōtoku was a capable and powerful regent who was able to unite Japan, these ancient sources painted him in legendary terms. He was described as having the power to foresee the future. For instance, according to *Jōgū Taishi bosatsu den*, Shōtoku predicted the moving of the capital from Nara to Heian.[18]

The attempts to dramatize Shōtoku intensify with the incorporation of *honji suijaku* in medieval sources. Such sources, like *Shōtoku Taishi denryaku* and *Jōgū Shōtoku Taishi den hoketsuki*, continued to expand on the legendary qualities of Shōtoku's achievements to further promote Shōtoku as a Buddhist divinity. In the beginning of *Jōgū Shōtoku Taishi den hoketsuki*, Shōtoku is presented as a shamanistic, supernatural being, but later is elevated to the status of a Buddhist saint, with attributes of a native *kami*, such as a guardian *kami* of Buddhism. By the beginning of the Heian period, Shōtoku had become a *kami* and at the same time was understood to be the manifestation of a Buddhist divinity, the bodhisattva Kannon. In the religious circle, Shōtoku was considered the father of Japanese Buddhism and elevated to the status of a Buddhist saint; he was described as the reincarnation of Hui-ssu.

## Shōtoku in Chinese, Japanese, and Buddhist Forms: Hui-ssu, *kami*, and Kannon

Although the *honji suijaku* theory represented the final step in the elevation of the native *kamis* and their complete assimilation into Buddhism, an intermediate step to its final evolution consisted in the elevation of the Japanese indigenous *kamis* and historical personages. As a cultural icon, Prince Shōtoku was the first of the historical figures to be elevated to the level of a Buddhist divinity figure through the *honji suijaku* formation. Although he was not granted the title of bodhisattva initially, by the end of the Nara period Shōtoku was considered to be the after-body *(goshin)* or reincarnation of Hui-ssu.[19] The earliest account of Shōtoku as the manifestation of a bodhisattva can be found in Ssu-to's (Jpn. Shitaku) *Tōdaiwajō toseiden* (754), which relates the following story that supposedly took place in China:

> The Buddhist monk Ei-ei went to the Daimyōji Temple and saluted the Great Elder [Ganjin], telling him the reason for his visit. He said "Buddhism came from the West to arrive in Japan and although there was Buddhism, there was no person to teach it. Formerly in Japan, Shotoku Taishi lived and said: 'After two hundred years the Buddhist doctrine will arise in Japan.' Now may you [Ganjin] follow this tradition and go to the East to instruct the people." So the Great Elder answered, "I have heard before that after Nagaku Zenji died he would be born as a prince of Japan to make Buddhism flourish and enlighten sentient beings."[20]

This is one of the earliest correlations between Shōtoku Taishi and Nangaku Zenji (Ch. Hui-ssu; Jpn. Eshi). In Ninchu's biography of Saichō, the *Eizandaishiden*, a similar story is related: "In the Sui Dynasty there lived Shi (Szu) Zenji on Mount Nangaku. This monk always hoped and said 'after my death I will certainly be born in the East—Japan, to introduce Buddhism.' Later Prince Shōtoku was born in Japan. . . . All the contemporary people say that Prince Shōtoku is the *goshin* of Shi Zenji."[21] Here Prince Shōtoku appears as the "after-body" *(goshin)* of Nangaku. Saichō set forth this theory, and supported the belief that Shōtoku was an after-body of Hui-ssu, which made Shōtoku into one of the Tendai saints during the Heian period.[22]

In the medieval period, people worshiped Shōtoku in the image of a child in Buddhist temples as well as in shrines, in accordance with a popular belief that a child, having unlimited potential, had some closer affinity with the sacred. *Shōtoku Taishi denreki* records an account of Shōtoku at ten years old, playing a vital role in warding off an attack by the barbarous people of

Chishima (Kuril Islands), who were camped at Kidō peak north of Miwa-yama in Nara. It describes how the young Prince Shōtoku miraculously transformed himself into a *kami* before the enemy's eyes in order to force them to surrender and submit to his authority. Significantly, this account became a record of war in the Daigo edition of *Shōtoku Taishiden*:

> As Taishi was on his way towards the enemy's camp, he dismounted from his horse in front of the big *torii* (gate of shrine) of Miwa-yama temple, a well known spiritual site of Wakarisho, to pray to the *ujigami* (tutelary *kami*) Miwa Daimyōjin. Then, when Taishi transformed his figure into a *kami* in order to make the barbarians surrender, they became tremendously frightened, thinking that the *kamis* blessed Japan and protected Shōtoku. Thus, they feared that the *kamis* would punish them if they opposed Shōtoku since he was in favor with the *kamis*. Upon learning that young Shōtoku already knew the name of the general and the number of his troops, the barbarous people payed their respects to Shōtoku saying, "Look! Shōtoku really leads the people with the blessing from the *kamis*." Then Taishi persuaded the enemy, who conspired to launch a surprise attack on Japan by saying, "You look like devils and are actually strong as they are because of your great number. Now, it may seem that you will not be defeated by anybody, especially by a country that is as small as ours, I remind you that we have emerged victoriously against other bigger countries because our country was created and protected by *kamis*, we are all *ujiko* (children of *ujigami*). I am just ten years old and it is impossible to defeat your army of thousands by myself, but I remind you that I am a leader of numerous *ujiko*s, empowered by *kami*, so you should not conspire to attack our country!" Thereupon, the barbarians turned back and swore by Miwa *Daimyōjin*, which is Taishi's *ujigami* that they would not hold any grudges towards the future generation— this is the reason why there has not been an invasion of Japan by the Chishima people for seven hundred years since their return.[23]

*Taishiden* points out that Shōtoku's promotion of Buddhism and concern to save people placed a priority on politics. He protected Japan from its neighboring foreign barbarians from the east and west, and brought world peace around Japan. Thereupon, Shōtoku spread Buddhism through the construction of temples and Buddhist statues, compilation of commentaries on classical Buddhist sutras, and promotion of Kannon worship.

*Taishiden* explains that Shōtoku's respect for *kami* and reference to the relationship of *ujigami* and *ujiko* as guardian *kami* and children were widely accepted in *Shingi-shinkō* (idea of respecting *ujigami*). For instance, in the *engi* at Kashima and Suwa Shrine that are recorded in *Shintō shū*, *Chinju sha* (protecting shrine) was called *ujigami*, and *ujiko* were the people who were protected by a Chinju *kami*. The *Kashima Daimyōjin* 9 of the third roll of *Shintō shū* described the *kami*'s protecting people as *Kahima Daimyōjin*'s saving *ujikos*. Among the numerous *kamis* in Japan, Kashima's power to protect people is tremendously strong, and its *ujikos* can live peacefully and go to Pure Land after death. In *Suwa Engi Topics* 50 of the tenth roll, there is a story about Kohga Saburo being protected by the *ujigami* in the Ōmi district.

Furthermore, belief in the *Shingi shinkō*, in which a tutelary *kami* was called *ujigami* who protected *ujiko*, is prevalent in the Bunpō edition of *Taishiden*. According to Imabori, these books were produced during the *Shingi shinkō* era to promote *Taishi shinkō* by establishing a close connection among Taishi, *ujigami*, and *ujiko*.[24] In chapter 35, in the sixth roll of *Shintō shū*, it states, "In Japan the Buddha appears as a human being and experiences pain and ill of society. Then the Buddha becomes a *kami* and saves people living in society." Hence, an aspect of *Taishi shinkō* follows Shintō's idea of *yoshakushigen*, the appearance of Buddha as a human being in the real world where human beings, *kami*, and Buddha are integrated into one entity. Within this context, Shōtoku Taishi is regarded as a *ujigami*, a blessing of *kami*. Thus, if one were to make the connection between Shōtoku, *ujigami*, and *ujiko*, then Shōtoku may be regarded as a Chinju *kami*. In other words, *Shingi shinkō* helped to promote *Taishi shinkō*.

*Taishiden* explains the reasons behind Moriya no Mononobe's conspiracy to exile Shōtoku Taishi. According to *Taishiden*, Moriya had an incorrect idea about respecting the *ujigami*. Moriya said to the Emperor Bintatsu that a recent epidemic was caused by Shōtoku's effort to enshrine *Zenkōji Tathāgata*, which had been floating on the sea of Naniwa at Kohenji, and proposed that Japan should abandon the worship of the Buddha's icon. However, the emperor did not approve. Determined to destroy Buddhism, Moriya prayed to *ujigami* and waited for further guidance. When a devil of the sixth realm heard about Moriya's evil intentions, he decided to send a "devil of disturbance" to Moriya. Then the devil appeared as "Kamiko" (son of *kami*) at Moriya's lodging and said to him, "I am Kamiko. Ujigami can do anything but he never says anything in front of the common people. He always sends a messenger to hear people confess their anxieties. Our country has been infiltrated with the practice of worshiping icons of foreign gods that are abnormal and strange. They ruin *kami* worship and bring epidemic throughout the country. If you want to help people, then you should abandon icons and burn the Buddha's place and books." Encouraged by *ujigami*'s charge through *Kamiko*, Moriya began to destroy Buddhism vigorously and Japan returned to spiritual anarchy. Consequently,

Moriya's actions incited the rage of benevolent *kamis,* and many innocent people suffered from the epidemic.

In contrast, *Taishiden* describes how young Shōtoku, at the age of fourteen, offered incense and prayer to bring about peace. A few years later, Emperor Yōmei, Shōtoku's father, became gravely ill as a result of Moriya's curse. In supplication, Prince Shōtoku wore a *kesa* (Buddhist coat) over his red clothes, held a gold pot of incense, and prayed to both *kami* and the Buddha, along with their manifestations. Meanwhile, Moriya continued to argue that these epidemics were the result of Japan's abandoning respect for *kamis* and turning to the worship of foreign icons of Buddhism. After the death of Emperor Yōmei, Moriya accused Prince Shōtoku as a "great enemy of *kami*" and attempted to exile him. Moriya argued that Shōtoku did not respect *kami,* even though Shōtoku was regarded as an offspring of Amaterasu, born in *kami*'s land, as a son of *kami.* He accused Shōtoku of going against the good custom of the country by embracing Buddhism, constructing temples, and bringing epidemics to the people. Moriya attempted to become a general of *kami*'s army to defeat Shōtoku.

In the last section of "When Taishi Was Eighteen Years Old" in *Taishi denreki,* it is written that Shōtoku was responsible for sponsoring the construction of more than 13,700 shrines, which confirms his deep devotion for native *kamis.* This information, which is based on the *Engishiki shinmei cho,* is often quoted by authors who argue that all *Chinju kamis* (guardian deities) in Japan are incarnations of the Buddha. Imabori explains that the notion of *Jingi shinkō* (respecting *kami* of Pure Land) is based on the understanding that *kami* is an incarnation of the Buddha.[25]

In the "When Taishi Was Twenty-seven Years Old" section of *Taishi denreki,* there is an explanation of *Jingi ron* (logic of Jingi), which is based on *honji suijaku.* An episode of Shōtoku climbing to Mount Fuji while riding on a black horse is translated as follows: "In April, early summer, Taishi sought and found a good horse in the Kai country among hundreds of horses. Pointing to Choshimaru, his horse trainer, he claimed that the horse was a horse of *kami.* In September, Taishi rode the horse and went off into the clouds. Three days later, he returned and said that he rode the horse to Mount Fuji, directly beyond cloud and fog, and saw the country from the sky."[26] This episode is exaggerated to emphasize the close relationship between Shōtoku and *kamis* of famous shrines. In the Daigo account, Shōtoku rides on a black horse that was given to him from the Kai country and says, "I went to pray at all the shrines in Japan and acquired the spirit of dharma," and "I saw the large halls of Buddhism in Japan and paid my respects to them, one after another." Both of these were Shōtoku's long cherished desires. As for Shōtoku's black horse, it was "able to fly freely like a dragon because it had the power and spirit of *kami.*" In accordance with the *Taishi denreki* version, the Daigo account described the black horse as having the spirit of *kami*. Shōtoku also argued that Choshimaru, his horse trainer, who was born in the 'big country,' was better than Kajishimaru, the horse trainer who was born in *kami* country. According to Imabori, Shōtoku said that Kajishimaru was born in a border district and was not able to fly in the sky even if Shōtoku gave him the power of *kami*, whereas Choshimaru was able to fly because he was born in a big country.[27] In other words, the Daigo edition completely denies the *Jingi shinkō*. Also, when Shōtoku went to Kehi Dai Bosatsu, he said that they talked about "*suijaku* and the glory for eternal offsprings" and listened to "glory that was brought by *suijaku*" from Daibenzai Tennyo, Ibuki Daimyōjin, and Mio Daimyōjin of the Omi country. Moreover, Shōtoku argued that he practiced *tsuya* (staying near the spirit overnight) at the spiritual house of Kumano Gongen, and "talked about mercy, gave three sets of clothes to the *kamis*, and vowed to guard the precious dharma." According to the Daigo edition, Shōtoku presented a book recording a talk with the *kamis* in Japan to the emperor. At the conclusion of his book, Shōtoku pointed out that although he recognized the distinction of Daimyōjin, Daibosatsu, and Daigongen in the Shinmei (figure of god), the origin of Shinmei was *Butsu bosatsu* (Buddha).

In the chapter "When Taishi Was Thirty one-Years Old," the author explains the origins of the Itsukushima Daimyōjin and other shrines in Itsukushima. According to the Daigo account, people prayed at the *Itsukushima Daimyōjin* in Aki country for the first time when Shōtoku was thirty-one years old. When Saeki Anshoku, governor of Aki, came across three aristocratic women cruising on a dragonhead ship, one of the women told the governor: "I want to learn about the country's fortune in the island (Itsukushima) and protect the Buddhism that Shōtoku is preaching to a hundred kings. You should construct both big and small shrines with a long corridor of 180 *kens* (1 *ken* is 1.8 meters) above sea level in order to pay your respects to me. Solemnity of the island makes the will of *kami* to stay there. Therefore the name was called Solemn Island (Itsukushima) *Daimyōjin*."[28] She then revealed a sentence that Shōtoku interpreted and gave to the emperor, saying, "Though the real body exists in Jōdo surrounded with celestial light, the same kinds of entity give light into a wave of ocean to be harmonized." The Daigo edition clearly emphasizes that Shōtoku's instructions brought respect to numerous *kamis* and their original *bosatsu* (bodhisattva), such as Dainichi, Amida, Fugen, and Miroku. Furthermore, the relationship between *bosatsu* and Japan's *kamis* concerning its origins and incarnations is explained from a quotation in the *Hokekyō*, which says that every spirit of *bosatsu* definitely appears as a *kami* during *mappō*. *Taishiden* also quotes the words of the saint Teikei, who confirmed the phenomenon of the *honji suijaku* theory, who believed that Buddha came to

Japan to protect people during the harsh and corrupted condition of *mappō*. It also explained, "All *kamis* and buddhas, whether they are in a different form, like in the form of real body or in their incarnation, act with the same sense of charity." Therefore, Shōtoku argued that "in Japan, Daijō and Shōjo's law made *kami's* life longer and saved everything from depletion and floating."

*Taishiden* also describes the relationship between *kami* veneration at shrines and among Buddhist priests. It points out that all *kamis* rely on the Three Treasures (Jpn. *Sanboē*) and are given the mercy of the original spirit:

> Ise Amaterasu ōmi *kami* had venerated Shōtoku Taishi and promised to elevate her law. Usa Hachiman Daibosatsu had venerated Oshō and accumulated merit through the good law of Han-nya. Taishō Daimy-ōjin had venerated Kobo Daishi to guard the law of Tōji temple and increase the happiness of the emperor. Gion Gyuto Tennō (not emperor) believed So-ō Oshō and venerated Ryobu-no Taihō to grant mercy to all people. Kehi daibosatsu in Echizen country and It-sukushima Daimyōjin in Aki country promised Shōtoku Taishi to guard the Buddhist law. Yahiko Daimyōjin in Echigo believed Shodaitoku and given high quality of Buddhist law so that they did not suffer the three kinds of pain.[29]

With regard to the veneration of *Chinju-shin* (guardian deities) in the medieval period, Buddhist monks believed that *kamis* were incarnations of *bosatsu*, like the relationship between *Daimyōjin* and monks that is described in the *Shintō shū*. According to the account in the *Suwa engi-goto* (historical facts) in the *Shintō shū*, Koga Saburō walked around the countries beneath the earth and came to the Ima country, then returned to Mount Asama in Shinshū in Japan. When he returned, *Hyoju Daimyōjin*, Saburō's *ujigami*, revealed that Hakusan Gongen, wearing white clothes, *Fuji Sengen Daibosatsu*, wearing a hat, and Ku-mano Gongen, sitting on a saddle, were all *Daimyōjins* who protected the cas-tles of kings—Hiyoshisannoh, Matsuo, Inari, Umemiya, Hirota, and so on. Considering these two accounts in the *Shintō shū* regarding *kamis* receiving Buddhist law from the monks, we learn that certain *kamis* were considered in-carnations of *Butsu bosatsu*. Moreover, monks supported the notion of *honji-butsu* (origin or real entity in Buddhism like *bosatsu*) to protect people at shrines in every country. Thus, *Taishiden* argues that Chinju *kamis* of many countries received Buddhist law from monks who promoted *Taishi shinkō*.

By the mid-Heian period, the legend of Shōtoku had evolved to the point that he was transformed from merely the "after-body" or manifestation to a *honji*. For instance, Shōtoku's own manifestations became such personages as Emperor Shōmu, Kūkai, and Rigan Daishi.[30] On the other hand, the *honji* of Shōtoku also developed, becoming not only Hui-ssu in China, but also figures such as *Dainichi Tathāgata* (Sk. *Vairocana*) and Kannon. Such beliefs were further popularized with the compilation of the *Taishi-wasan*[31] and *Taishi-koshiki*[32] of later periods. Furthermore, both Nichiren and Ippen also venerated Shōtoku. Nichiren (1222–1282), the founder of the Buddhist tradition that is based on the Lotus Sutra, also wrote more than twenty hymns in praise of Shōtoku Taishi, calling him "the origin of Japanese Buddhism." Ippen (1239–1289), the founder of the Jishū school, received inspiration from Shōtoku while praying at the mausoleum at Taishi-byō for three days. Although most of Ippen's writings were destroyed before his death, a religious writing by Kūkai states that Ippen believed that Shōtoku was a manifestation of Kannon.

The image of Shōtoku Taishi as an incarnation of bodhisattva Kannon was recorded in the *Denryaku*, compiled during the middle of the Heian period. Recorded in 618 (the twenty-sixth year of Suiko Tennō reign), the *Denryaku* describes a miraculous story of Shōtoku Taishi telling his wife about his past lives and wishes for the future:[33]

In October, Shōtoku Taishi summoned his wife and explained to her about his past lives saying, "I was born very poor, and I met a Hokke priest. I cut off my hair to renounce the world and to become a sramanera (a wanderer). After thirty years of training, I left this world at Kōzan (Heng Shan), which was at the end of the Shin Era (around 376 B.C.E.). Later I was reborn as a member of the Kan family (a renowned family in South Korea). Again, I renounced the world and became a monk. I climbed Kōzan (Heng Shan) and trained for another fifty years until I left this world again at the time of the So (Sung) era. Then I was born again as a male and a member of the Ryu-family and renounced the world after thirty years of training. Next I became a member of the Ko-family and trained at Kōzan (Heng Shan) for sixty years before I left this world again at the time of Seiou (King Sei)'s reign. Then during the Ryō-era (502–557) I was born again as a member of the Ryō family and trained at Kōzan for seventy years. In the Chin and Shū (Chou) era, I was born as a member of the Yo family. Then I aspired to be born in the Tōkai province (near the eastern ocean area) to spread Buddhism, which will occur in my seventh reincarnation. Finally I was born as a member of the Japanese royal family. After many years of training and reincarnations and even though the number of priests is increasing now, the goal of Ekayāna has not yet been achieved. Thus, I trained myself and gained merit and virtue as a prince of the royal family. Due to my social status, however, I am not able to knock on each door to spread Buddhism; therefore, I will leave this body and be re-born in a lower-level

family. Then I will renounce the world to save *sattva* (sentient beings).
This is my religious aspiration (or wish), and after 500 reincarnations,
I will then enter Higan (the other shore; i.e., nirvana)."

In the later part of the *Denryaku*, there is an account of Shōtoku Taishi's
prediction of his own death in two years. It recalls how his grieving wife
mourns with tears because her husband was leaving her alone in this world.
Moved by compassion for his wife, Shōtoku Taishi then invites her to come
with him. *Denryaku* explains that soon after he said these words to his wife,
Shōtoku built his own grave and, after taking a bath, they died together, and
were buried together in 621. The *Denryaku* is filled with such dramatic descriptions describing Shōtoku Taishi as a savior-figure on a great mission, as
*guze* Kannon. By the middle of the Heian period, since Shōtoku Taishi was
venerated as a *kami* and incarnation of bodhisattva Kannon, these articulate expressions of Shōtoku's achievements had attained mythological proportions.
They continued to instill in the minds and hearts of the Japanese people a profound sense of devotion for Shōtoku Taishi, whose quest was to usher in a "new
world" and offer hope and salvation to the poor and needy people of Japan.

The compilers of *Denryaku* apparently went to great pains to create and incorporate these miraculous myths surrounding the events of Shōtoku's life. A
close reading of the *Denryaku* reveals the compilers' intention to convey the
idea that Shōtoku Taishi was going to be reborn into the world on a continual
basis. For instance, *Denryaku* explains that: "In August 604, while visiting
Kadono (near Kyoto), Shōtoku Taishi predicted that 250 years after his death
there will come a priest who will build a temple there. This priest is the reincarnation of me and he will spread Buddhism during the time of *mappō*." Here
Shōtoku Taishi predicted the appearance of the founder of the Tendai School
on Mount Hiei, the great master Saichō, as his incarnation during the Heian
period.[34] Moreover, Shōtoku also examined the Heiankyō (Kyoto) more closely
and stated: "This area is dominant. The southern part is sunny and open while
the northern part is dark and closed. A river runs from the west to the east and
there is a dragon that lies in a coil, watching over and protecting this area. In
300 years, I predict that a saint will build a Miyako (capital) here and the Buddhist sutras will prosper." This prediction also reflects the historical transfer of
the capital from Nara to Heian by Kanmu Tennō. Accordingly, when Shōtoku
Taishi visited Nara, he also predicted the rise of Shōmu Tennō and the building of the Tōdaiji. When he visited the Ōmi (Shiga prefecture), Kawachi
(Osaka) area, Shōtoku Taishi again predicted the appearance of Tenji Tennō,
the transfer of the capital to Otsu (Otsu kyō sento), and the appearance of
Gyōgi (668–749).

From these examples, we can conclude that the writers of the *Denryaku* painstakingly correlated these miraculous accounts of predictions made by Shōtoku Taishi, presumably a fictional figure in history, with actual and significant events in Japanese history. Fujii Yukiko contends that the *Denryaku*'s purpose was to incite people's interest in Buddhism through the use of such creative myths surrounding Shōtoku Taishi's miraculous abilities. Interestingly, the mythological and prophetical accounts based on the belief of Shōtoku Taishi's numerous reincarnations sparked the emergence of a genre of prophetical books following the medieval period in Japan. Usually referred to as *Miraiki* (Accounts of Future Events), such as the well-known *Taishi gyōkibun* (Taishi's Documents) and the *Meno seki kibun* (The Agate Stone Records), these prophetical books were often based on the alleged memoirs that Shōtoku Taishi wrote just before his death. Although we strongly doubt the historical truth of such accounts, the fact remains that these prophetical accounts reflect how people in medieval Japan longed for such hope-filled messages, particularly during the time of *mappō* when Japan was undergoing a volatile change in society.

In the chapter "When Taishi Was Forty-five Years Old," in the Daigo edition of *Taishi denreki*, Shōtoku is regarded as an incarnation of *guze* Kannon, and the relationship between Kannon and Shinmei, the figure of *kami* as an incarnation of the Buddha, is also mentioned:

> Japan is connected with Kannon. The *honji* (origin of celestial spirit) of eleven *kamis* is Kannon. This is the mainstay of Japan's Buddhism. The *honji* of Hakusan Gongen in the Kaga country is the *Jūichimen* (eleven-face) Kannon, and the *honji* of Nishi-no gozen, the first of the Kumanon junikasho (twelve-place) Gongen is Senju (thousand-hand) Kannon, and so on. Therefore, all the spiritual *kamis* in Japan are incarnation of Kannon. Thus, Shōtoku Taishi said, "The *honji* of every *kami* is Kannon. Why don't people from both upper and lower classes venerate Kannon?[35]

Shōtoku asserted that all manifestations of *kamis* were incarnations of Kannon, and that one should venerate them rather than venerating certain famous shrines that were believed to be incarnations of Kannon. For instance, Imabori points out that according to the *Kitano Tenjin engi*, people believed that the Kitano shrine was an incarnation of Kannon. In the *Ko-rui Kitano Tenjin engi*, Kitano Tenjin is described as a *kami* protecting kings' castles. The degree to which the shrine is highly respected by all people depends on the level of merit or power of the *chinju-shin* (guardian *kami*) associated with a particular shrine.

For instance, in the Kenkyū edition, the merit of the Kitano shrine is assessed through *Jūichimen* (eleven-face) Kannon's appearing as Tenman Tenjin, in order to help people in the two worlds *(gento nisei)*: the worlds before and after death. In the Daigo edition, Buddhist monks protected people over the two worlds through *kamis* that were incarnations of the spirit of *honji*, like Kannon. In the *Tenjin engi* and *emaki* (painting scrolls), the merits of the Tenjin and Kitano shrine are accumulated through the spirit of *honji* Kannon. The *Tenjin ko* (meeting) was also a religious meeting held at the Tenjin shrine, where people went to pray for birth in the Pure Land after death through the compassion of Kannon.

In *Tenjin shinkō* (veneration of Tenjin), *Jōdo ōjō* (birth in the Pure Land after death) was explained through the relationship of the *honji* (true nature) and *suijaku* (manifestations) between Tenjin and Kannon, *kamis* and Buddha. In *Taishi shinkō*, however, it was explained through Shōtoku and Kannon, a person and Buddha. This explanation supported the phrase written in "When Taishi Was Seven Years Old" of *Taishiden* that says, "All people, both *zaike* (one who stayed home to practice Buddhism) and *shūkke* (one who left his home), rich and poor, men and women, born in this country equally receives Shōtoku's mercy. Every one receives Shōtoku's mercy and attains birth in the Pure Land." According to the *Taishiden*, it is said that the "Living Kannon, who appeared through her compassion, left Jōdo and came down to this marginal Japan." In the "Birth Time" chapter, *Taishiden* records Shōtoku's statement, "I am the incarnation of *guze daihi* (great compassion; i.e., Kannon). I used to live in *an'yo* (peaceful) world but came to this dirty world in order to save people." In the section "When Taishi Was Forty-seven Years Old," the relationship between Shōtoku and Kannon is reemphasized.

Finally, in the last chapter of the Daigo edition of *Taishiden*, "When Taishi Was Fifty-one Years Old," there is an account of Choshimaru's prayer of *nenbutsu* just before his death: "My master (Shōtoku) is Kannon *bosatsu* with great mercy. Before his birth, he received religious training and our relationship as master and attendant lasted forty years." Through their close relationship, Choshimaru hoped that he, too, would flee from the restraint of this world and be born in the Pure Land, as he prayed *nenbutsu* with all of his heart for seven days and nights. After the seventh day, purple clouds appeared on the mountain, music played in the air, and Choshimaru sat facing west, pressing his hands together in prayer as he attained *gokuraku ōjō* (dying peacefully to be born in the Pure Land). Here we learn that *Taishi shinkō* involves worshiping Shōtoku as Kannon and praying *nenbutsu* intently.

It is safe to say that the purpose of the *Taishiden* is to advocate *nenbutsu ōjō* (birth in the Pure Land via nembutsu) by tying it closely to Shōtoku, who is regarded as an incarnation of *guze* Kannon. The author seems to suggest that association with Chinju *kamis* of many countries who are incarnations of *bosatsu* and association with Shōtoku were the same. Thus, during the medieval period, the meaning of *Taishi shinkō* was broadened throughout the country through the notion of *Jingi shinkō*, in which Shintō *kamis* are the incarnation of bosatsu.[36] In this context, the contents of *Taishi shinkō* and *chinju-shin shinkō* are considered the same. Therefore, *chinji-shin* became unnecessary for people who venerated Shōtoku, which also meant that they could leave the *ujigami shinkō*. Thus, in the medieval period, *Taishi-dō* (hall) seems to have played a role similar to Chinju shrines.

The idea of *jingi shisō* is found in *Shōtoku Taishi denki* of the Daigo Temple. According to Gorai Shigeru, in the medieval period, *Taishi shinkō* of common people was related to *jōdo shinkō* and *shisha-tsuifuku shinkō* (praying for the happiness of the dead). Prayers for the dead were done before a Shōtoku Taishi icon, which was used as the object of *jōdo shinkō*. Hayashi Mikiya also explains that *Taishi shinkō* was equal to Kannon worship. Shōtoku Taishi served as the object of *gokuraku ōjō* (going to the Pure Land after death) and *sokushin jōbutsu* (becoming Buddha or good spirit after death). Shōtoku supposedly led the people to the Pure Land after their death since he was regarded as the first one to be born in the Pure Land. The relationship between Shōtoku and *jingi shinkō* is repeatedly mentioned because *Taishi shinkō* was an integral part of *jingi shinkō*. For instance, Hayashi argued that Risso of the Risshū faction, Zenso of the Zenshū faction, and *Sanmai-shū* (people who prayed with all their heart) all went to the Pure Land because they prayed to the Shōtoku Taishi icon and gave him respect in the *Taishi-dō*. Hayashi asserted that *Taishi shinkō* was the belief of special people called Risso and Zenso in Old Buddhism. Also, *Taishi shinkō* was especially important for *hinin* who are *bessho* and *sanmai-shū*; these people were able to attain birth in the Pure Land through the power of "*honji* of *butsu bosatsu*."

In the *Nomori kagami*, the relationship between Zenshū and *kami* is stated as: "Friends of Zenshū lose the promise of rebirth, the power of *kami* declines, and punishment remains. It is the law of *kenmitsu* that *shinmei* protects." It goes on to say that Shōtoku Taishi was born in this country in order to preach the dharma, recommended by Daruma Oshō, but the gods in this country did not love the dharma and the country itself was weak and small. As a result, Daruma Oshō appeared on *kataoka-yama* to show his spirit. Then Shōtoku made a song to confess the reason for his failure, saying, "People in the poor and peripheral country are not only suffering from famine but are also like orphan travelers falling down on the road"—that is, it was difficult to spread the religious law unless the people accepted the idea that the *kami* protected their spirit. It also stated that both Risso and Zenso were not loved by the gods in this country and were unable to attain *jōdo ōjō* (birth in the Pure Land) through the *kamis*.

In the Old Buddhism faction, people who were called *hinin* did not have any connection to Shintō, in which *bosatsu* appeared as other *kamis*. It can be argued that *Taishi shinkō* were composed of *jōdo shinkō* from the lower class of monks who were rejected by *jōdo ōjō*.[37]

## THE CULT OF SHŌTOKU: PORTRAITS, RELICS, AND WOMEN

Idealized portraits in sculpture and painting for Shōtoku worship were first made soon after his death, but the production of images dramatically increased from the late Heian and Kamakura periods. Portraits of Shōtoku depict a variety of significant episodes and legends about his life, which fall into one of four categories: (1) "Mantra Chanting," or Namubutsu Taishizō; (2) "Offering Filial Piety,"or Kōyō Taishizō; (3) "Lecturing on the Sutra," or Kōsan Taishizō; and (4) "Regent Taishi statues," or Sesshō Taishizō.[38]

Namubutsu Taishizō depict the prince at the age of two when, on the fifteenth day of the second month, he reputedly faced east, placed his palms together, and recited the Namubutsu, a prayer honoring the Buddha's name and calling up his grace. This precocious act is recounted in the early legendary histories such as the *Shōtoku Taishi denryaku*. The earliest record of the image is found in an entry from 1210 of the *Azuma kagami*, which mentions the image installed in the private chapel of Shogun Minamoto no Sanetomo (r. 1203–1219). Among the oldest extant Namubutsu Taishizō are the wooden images in the Fogg Art Museum (ca. 1292) and Hōryūji (1307).

Kōyō Taishizō, often called "Shōtoku Taishi at the Age of 16," is generally thought to represent Shōtoku praying for the recovery of his ill father, Emperor Yōmei (r. 585–587). The prince is said to have prayed by his father's side day and night, dressed in court attire, and holding a long-handled incense burner. Yōmei recovered thanks to his son's faith, and converted to Buddhism. Images of a youthful Shōtoku in prayer, however, may represent another incident from Shōtoku's sixteenth year, in which he is said to have stopped to pray during a battle between his clan, the Soga, and the Mononobe faction. The earliest known Kōyō Taishizō was sponsored by the Tendai sect. The oldest known Kōyō Taishizō is a painting from the set of portraits of esteemed Tendai monks (Ichijōji, Hyōgo prefecture, late eleventh century). Shōtoku is shown seated cross-legged on a low dais wearing a monastic surplice, kesa, and holding a long-handled incense burner. Inscriptions on the Ichijōji set suggest that the paintings were patterned after wall paintings of Enryakuji on Mt. Hiei produced before 946. The inclusion of Shōtoku in the set is based on the acceptance of the prince as an incarnation of the second Chinese T'ien-t'ai patriarch

Hui-ssu (Jp. Eshi, 515–577). Another early image of Kōyō Taishizō is included in a painting of thirty-six venerated monks, from Ninnaji, Kyoto (1163). In other early Kōyō Taishizō, references are made to Shōtoku as the reincarnation of Kannon. These images were apparently worshiped by those seeking salvation and protection from disease and disaster, just as Kannon images were worshiped. From the late thirteenth century on, the majority of Kōyō Taishizō in painting and sculpture assume a standing posture. The fourteenth-century Kōyō images depict him holding a scepter, along with the censer. The scepter, representative of secular authority, contrasts with the censer, which is indicative of spiritual pursuits.

Kōsan Taishizō represents an episode from Shōtoku's thirty-fifth year, when he was ordered by Empress Suiko to discourse on the *Shōmangyō* sutra. According to the *Shōtoku Taishi denryaku*, Shōtoku sat on a lion's throne, holding a yak's tail fly whisk, and lectured on the sutra. When finished, huge lotus petals fell miraculously from the heavens. Suiko erected a temple, Tachibanadera, on the site. Painted and sculpted Kōsan Taishizō show the prince crowned and seated, usually holding a fan. The oldest record of a Kōsan Taishi image is found among inventory documents of the Tōin at Hōryūji, dated 761.

Sesshō Taishizō shows Shōtoku as regent, between the ages of thirty-two and forty-nine. He is usually depicted seated, wearing courtly attire, and holding a scepter. The oldest known Sesshō Taishizō image is a painting from the early Nara period in the Imperial Household Collection, which is traditionally called the "Chinese Style Portrait of a Nobleman" (Karahon no Miei). Shōtoku stands with scepter in hand, flanked on each side by the smaller princes Yamashiro and Eguri. The earliest extant sculpture of Sesshō Taishizō is from the Shōryō'in at Hōryūji (1121). In this work, the prince is seated, flanked by four figures.

Shōtoku Taishizō became prevalent from the twelfth and thirteenth centuries. It has been suggested that the Namubutsu, Kōyō, Kōsan, and Sesshō Taishizō images represent the principal stages in the prince's life: infancy, youth, and manhood, based on the widely disseminated *Shōtoku Taishi denryaku*. The popularity of these particular scenes from Shōtoku's life is more likely due to their use by the new, popular sects of Buddhism such as Jōdo, Shinshū, Ritsu, and Hokke, which venerated Shōtoku Taishi as founder and promoter of Buddhism in Japan, as well as an incarnation of such important Buddhist figures as Śākyamuni (Shaka) and Kannon. One factor in the appeal of Namubutsu Taishizō seems to have been the parallel between the story of the two-year-old Shōtoku reciting the Namubutsu and the pictorialized story of Śākyamuni as an infant, pointing one hand to heaven and the other to earth, roaring like a lion, "I am the Lord of the World." Similarly, Kōsan Taishizō images seem to parallel the account and depictions of the enlightened Śākyamuni's lecture at the Deer Park, also delivered at age thirty-five. During a time of political and social upheaval such as that of the late Heian and early Kamakura periods, when the faithful feared that the period of *mappō* was at hand, the direct connection between Taishi and Śākyamuni provided reassuring evidence of the authenticity of Japanese Buddhism and the benefits and salvation promised specifically in the teachings of these sects.

Shōtoku worship was also connected with the worship of Buddha's relics, which was called *Shari-shinkō*. For instance, in the section entitled "When Shōtoku Taishi Was Two Years Old" in the *Shōtoku Taishi denreki*, a belief was recorded that Shōtoku's left hand remained closed for the first two years. When he finally opened his left palm after two years, he was holding something crystal clear, which turned out to be Śākyamuni Buddha's left eye. In 1220, a chapel called Yumedono or "dream pavilion" at Hōryūji was dedicated to worship Shōtoku and Buddha's crystal eye. Ever since, worship of Shōtoku and Buddha's relic has been popular. Takada also points out that *Shari-shinkō* is connected to the reason why Kaidatsu Shōnin began the practice of *kanjin* (urging people to do meritorious acts) in 1211, through the collection of alms and chanting of the Shaka *nenbutsu*. Furthermore, the practice of *gyakushū* (the performance of a Buddhist service for a person before he dies) was also influenced by *Shari-shinkō*.[39]

As a result of this legend, *Taishi shinkō* flourished. The relic was enshrined in Yumedono. As *Shari-shinkō* became popular, the *Shariden*, a special hall for keeping the Buddha's bones as a relic, was constructed in 1220. Subsequently, monks gathered at the *Shariden* for "Shari-ko" and *Taishi shinkō* became very popular. When *Shariden* was being renovated in 1943, there was a big basket that contained a small, wooden statue of the Buddha, a "Sasa-sotoba" (grave posts made of bamboo), a bowl for bones of five rings, a bowl for bones made of bamboo, and a certificate of thirty-three sacred sites. From the very few writings on the graveposts and bone bowls, these artifacts seem to have been created sometime between the end of Kamakura and the Muromachi period. Although Hōryūji, which is located near three of the thirty-three temples, is not included among the thirty-three sacred sites, many people visited *Shariden* to worship the bones from Shōtoku's palm.

*Shari shinkō* is also related to the practice of *Shaka nenbutsu* inside *Shariden* that was recommended by Gedatsu-Shōnin in 1221. A ceremony related to *Shari-shinkō* is described in the ten volumes of *Koshiki* (a manual book on rituals). Many of Shōtoku's belongings were kept inside the *Shariden*, which further promoted *Taishi shinkō*. Furthermore, in the effort to further spread *Shari-shinkō*, a Namubutsu Taishizō (statue of a two-year-old Shōtoku), signed in 1307, was constructed and placed in Hōryūji for Shōtoku worship.

*Taishi shinkō* also continued to prosper during the Muromachi period (1338–1573) through the worship of *Jizō bosatsu-zō*,[40] which replaced the *Seiko mandara* that served as an object of worship, and was located inside the east room of the *Shorei-in*. Originally brought by Hyakusai (Korea), the *Jizō bosatsu-zō* was moved from Tachibana-dera to the *kondō*, the Golden Hall, at Hōryūji in 1080. According to the *Seiko mandara-ki* (record), this statue was given to Shōtoku Taishi by Seimei-ō (king) of Hyakusai, who was also regarded to be an incarnation of *guze* Kannon.[41] This legend is also found in *Shōtoku Taishi denshiki*, which means that the legend has existed since the medieval period. Based on this legend, the Jizō statue was installed in *Shorei-in*, the original place of *Taishi shinkō*, and *Jizō shinkō* was also included in *Taishi shinkō* at Hōryūji. The fact that many *Jizō bosatsu-zō* were installed at *Jibutsu-dō* of *Sannaishi-in* between the end of Kamakura period and the Muromachi period indicates the popularity of such worship of Jizō. Also, in the *Jizō-ko-shiki* that is kept at Hōryūji, Shūnsei Daihoshi explains that *Jizō shinkō* and *Taishi shinkō* were inseparable.

Women played an important role in promoting Shōtoku worship in medieval Japan. Perhaps the most influential promoters of Shōtoku worship within the Fujiwara family were Komyo (701–760); the wife of Emperor Shōmu (724–749); and Tachibana Michiyo, the wife of Fujiwara Fuhito. According to the *Hōryūji tōin engi shizaichō*, the official record of treasures kept in *tōin*, the east pagoda hall of Hōryūji, Tachibana collected Buddha's ashes, bones, and bow and-arrow to be used as sacred objects of worship at Horyūji, a state-sponsored temple that was originally founded by Shōtoku. Apparently Tachibana was quite instrumental in collecting sacred objects of the Buddha to be used for worship both at Hōryūji and Shitennōji because her connection to the imperial family gave her free and convenient access to the state-sponsored temples.[42] As a cousin of Tachibana, Komyo also joined Tachibana's cause in collecting Buddha's relics *(shari-shinkō)* to promote Shōtoku worship at Hōryūji and Shitennōji. According to *Jōgū Taishi bosatsuden*, Tachibana and Komyo both believed in Saichō's claim that Shōtoku was a reincarnation of Hui-ssu.[43]

Soon after Prince Shōtoku's death, Empress Anahobe no Hashihito, Shōtoku's mother, with Lady Tachibana, one of the prince's consorts, and Komyo Kogo, wife of Emperor Shōmu, meticulously prepared a proper burial mound at Hōryūji, which became an important site for the development of Shōtoku cults during the medieval period. According to the *Nihon shoki*, Shōtoku is buried in a funerary mound, which is the *Shinaga misasagi* (imperial tomb).[44] The tomb is mentioned in a tenth-century document, *Engishiki*, in the section corresponding to *Shōryō-e* (Office of Imperial Tombs). In the document, "the tomb of Shinaga" is identified as belonging to the son of the Emperor Tachibana no Toyohi (Yōmei), named Shōtoku, located in the village of Ishikawa in the county of Kawachi, and occupying a space of three *cho* (327 meters) from east to west and two cho (218 meters) from north to south.[45] According to the inscription of the *Tenjukoku shūcho mandara*, Empress Ana- hobe no Hashihito died on the twelfth month of Suiko 29 (621), and Prince Shōtoku on the second month of Suiko 30 (622). The same information is recorded in the controversial inscription of the Hōryūji Amida triad, which also indicates that Princess Kashiwade hikikimi no iratsume, one of the prince's consorts, died a day before the prince. According to Umehara Sueji, who en- tered the burial chamber in 1921, the tomb was constructed to be the burial place of Empress Anahobe, but since the prince and his consort Kashiwade died within a few months, the three of them were buried together. He also re- ports that the empress is buried at the back in a stone coffin, and the prince and his consort are in lacquered coffins that sit on stone pedestals, on the right and left, respectively. The tomb type is a corridor tomb *(yokoanashiki)*, which con- sists of a horizōntal hallway leading from the slope of a mound to a stone-lined burial chamber.[46]

The funerary mound is now a part of the Buddhist temple complex of Ei- fukuji. The temple legend claims that its history began after the death of the prince, when Empress Suiko ordered the performance of memorial services at the site to protect the tomb, and on that occasion a small building was con- structed. The legend also states that a temple complex was built in the first year of Jingi (724), under the patronage of Emperor Shōmu (724–749). Various sources mention the popularity of the site, and a number of stories associated with the site further developed the cult of Prince Shōtoku. Temple records show that emperors made donations, and that important religious figures, such as the Tendai priest Jien (1155–1225), Shinran (1173–1262), the priest Eizōn (1201–1290) from Saidaiji, and Ippen (1239–1289) visited the site. Most of the early records refer to the site as the "tomb of the prince" *(Taishi no haka or Taishi no byō)*; only the sixteenth-century documents call it Eifukuji.[47] The late Heian text *Fusō ryakki* indicates that there was a procession in which people carried flowers, recited laments, and chanted Buddhist sutras for the funeral of Prince Shōtoku.[48] Abe Yasurō explains that during the ancient period, Shintō did not have a strong funerary ritual, but Buddhism's funerary practices enabled a pu- rification process.[49]

Further evidence regarding the role of women in promoting Buddhism through Shōtoku worship is found in the *Tenjukoku shūcho mandara*. The *Ten- jukoku shūcho mandara* are fragments of an embroidered curtain that depict *Ten- jukoku (ten*, heaven; *ju*, span of life; and *koku*, land), which was made some time after the death of Prince Shōtoku and his mother, Empress Anahobe no Hashihito. On the center of the *mandara* is an Amida triad-like representation that consists of Prince Shōtoku, sitting in Amida Buddha's usual place, flanked by his mother Empress Anahobe no Hashihito and his consort Lady Tachibana,[50] who replaced bodhisattva Kannon and Seishi. According to the inscription recorded in the *Jōgū Shōtoku hōō teisetsu*, the curtain was commissioned after Prince Shōtoku's death by his mother to represent him in *Tenjukoku*, the paradise where he was reborn after his death. This legend confirms that of Shōtoku described in *Shōtoku Taishi den*, where Shōtoku Taishi was portrayed as the first person who attained birth in the "Land of Pure Landly Longevity."

According to Maria del Rosario Pradel's study of the *Tenjukoku shūcho mandara*, the original embroidered curtains were most likely used as a part of funerary paraphernalia during the performance of rituals to honor Prince Shōtoku's death. Pradel concludes that the curtains were considered relics of the patron of Chuguji, Empress Anahobe no Hashihito. Pradel observes that the art motif in the *Tenjukoku shūcho mandara* is an example of the pictorial art of the Asuka period (552–645). During the ascension of female power in the Asuka period, the promotion association with Prince Shōtoku through the *Tenjukoku shūcho mandara* gave women an important justification of power.[51]

Although the curtains were not associated with Buddhist ideas during the Asuka period, the artifact was replicated for a Buddhist temple by the Kamakura period in 1274. Ōhashi Katsuaki's study of the fragments of *Tenjukoku shūcho mandara* in his book *Tenjukoku shūcho no kenkyū*[52] focused on the turtles with four characters on the shells. The inscriptions on the turtles, which are recorded in the *Jōgū Shōtoku hōō teisetsu*, show the genealogy of Prince Shōtoku and Lady Tachibana.[53] They then describe how the empress-consort Anahobe no Hashihito, Shōtoku's mother, passed away in the twelfth month of Suiko 29 (621) and how the prince died on the second month of the following year, Suiko 30 (622). It states that Lady Tachibana talked to her grandmother, Empress Suiko, and expressed her grief at the loss of her husband and her mother-in-law. She said that, because the prince respected the Buddhist law, she knew that he was in *Tenjukoku*. However, she could not visualize this world, and expressed her wish to have a pictorial representation of the prince in that world, to cherish his memory. Consequently, Empress Suiko ordered the ladies of the court to make a pair of embroidered curtains with the inscription "the Buddhist paradise where the prince was reborn."

However, the underlying reason why women were especially active in promoting Shōtoku worship may be due to the Pure Land teaching that enabled women to attain enlightenment, a topic of debate within Buddhism. One of the earliest sources of the *ōjōden* (biographies of those born into the Pure Land) was the *Nihon ōjō gokuraku ki* (A Record of Japanese Born into the Pure Land), which was compiled by the scholar Yoshishige no Yasutane (934?–997) in 985. This book is composed of the spiritual biographies of pious women, often from aristocratic or bureaucratic families, who had gained rebirth in the western paradise. Moreover, the Lotus Sutra clearly stated that women were capable of gaining salvation. The "Devadatta" chapter (chapter 12) of the Lotus Sutra tells the story of the eight-year-old daughter of the Dragon King, who is said to have attained enlightenment on hearing the Lotus Sutra preached despite the disbelief by some bodhisattvas. The dragon girl appears before the assembled bodhisattvas, one of whom questions her, saying:

> You say that in no long time you shall attain the unexcelled Way. This is hard to believe. What is the reason? A woman's body is filthy; it is not a Dharma-receptacle. How can you attain unexcelled bodhi [wisdom]? The Path of the Buddha is remote and cavernous. Throughout incalculable kaplas [ages], by tormenting oneself and accumulating good conduct, also by thoroughly cultivating perfections, only by these means can one then be successful. Also, a woman's body even then has five obstacles. It cannot become first a Brahmā god king, second Śakra, third King Māra, fourth a sage-king turning the Wheel, fifth a Buddha-body. How can the body of a woman speedily achieve Buddhahood?[54]

The dragon girl, in response to these doubts expressed about her ability to gain enlightenment, instantaneously turns into a man and achieves Buddhahood.

Further support for women's salvation is provided in chapter 23 of the Lotus Sutra, "Former Affairs of the Bodhisattva Medicine King," which makes explicit the possibility of birth in the Pure Land for women who uphold the Lotus Sutra.

> If a woman, hearing this chapter of the Former Affairs of the Bodhisattva Medicine King, can accept and keep it, she shall put an end to her female body, and shall never again receive one. If after the extinction of the Thus Come One [Tathāgata], within the last five hundred years, there is then a woman who, hearing this scriptural canon, practices it as preached, at the end of this life she shall straightway go the world-sphere Comfortable (Sukhāvati) [the Pure Land], to the dwelling place of the Buddha Amitāyus [Amida], where he is surrounded by a multitude of great bodhisattvas, there to be reborn on a jewelled throne among lotus blossoms, never again to be tormented by greed, never again to be tormented by anger or folly, never again to be tormented by pride, envy, or other defilements.[55]

It is notable that in tales of birth in the Pure Land, men are often depicted as engaging in a combination of Lotus Sutra rituals and nembutsu practice. Women, however, are usually portrayed only as reciting the nembutsu. Thus, the religious lives of Heian men and women, though directed toward the same goal, were distinguished by conceptions of spiritual differences based on gender. Men apparently held the attitude that women were only capable of the "easy" practice of the nembutsu, whereas men, able to read and understand the profundity of the Lotus Sutra, could engage in both kinds of rituals. Further gender distinctions are evident in the fact that women are not often identified by name, but rather in terms of their relationship to men, such as to their husbands, fathers, and brothers.

## SHŌTOKU WORSHIP AT MOUNT HIEI, HŌRYŪJI, AND SHITENNŌJI

The Shōtoku Taishi cult reached its peak at temples and Kannondō associated with Shōtoku Taishi, particularly at the Tendai center at Mount Hiei where many Buddhist monks regularly practiced *sanrō* (worship involving a set period of days and nights dedicated to a specific veneration and often a distinct vow). Akamatsu explains that in the middle of the Heian period it became popular for people to shut themselves for days in a chamber, where a statue of a Buddhist figure was enshrined for the purpose of praying for guidance and inspiration.[56] Shin scholars Takemitsu and Hayashi point out that, by the Kamakura period, Shōtoku Taishi was worshiped with the same amount of veneration as Kannon.[57]

As the center of Tendai Buddhism, Mount Hiei actively promoted the Hui-ssu legend and developed institutional ties to the Shitennōji, which was one of the centers of Shōtoku worship. The medieval Japanese scholar Fujii Yukiko explains that the tale of Prince Shōtoku's reincarnation as Kannon was actually based on the story of Hui-ssu's reincarnation recorded in the *Hui-ssu kōshin denshō*, which was compiled at the end of the Nara period and became popular in the Heian period. Fujii explains that the *Shōtoku Taishi shinkō* (Shōtoku cult) was started by those who mourned his death. Since the Hui-ssu reincarnation tale was compiled before the *Denryaku*, which first described Prince Shōtoku as the reincarnation of Kannon, Fujii points out that there is a high probability that the compilers of *Denryaku* were heavily influenced by *Hui-ssu kōshin denshō*.

Closer examination of the *Hui-ssu kōshin denshō* and the *Denryaku* reveal a chronological discrepancy, which suggests that the tale of Prince Shōtoku reincarnation as Kannon was not accurately constructed in accordance with historical sources. According to *Hui-ssu kōshin denshō*, it is recorded that the Tendai-sect priest Nangagu Hui-ssu (517–577) was trained in Mount Nangaku and wished to be born in the Eastern sea (Japan) to spread the Buddhist teaching to the people. In contrast, the *Denryaku* claims that Hui-ssu was reborn as Prince Shōtoku, which corresponds to Prince Shōtoku's birth in 573. However, Prince Shōtoku would have been four years old at the time of Hui-ssu's death in 577. There is a four-year overlap that is unaccounted for, which subsequently weakens the claim of Prince Shōtoku's reincarnation as Kannon in the *Denryaku*.[58]

In fact, Ganjin (688–763), the Chinese monk who founded the Japanese Ritsu sect, apparently came to Japan in 754 and studied at Tōdaiji because he believed that Hui-ssu would be reincarnated as Prince Shōtoku there. Ganjin's disciple, Shitaku (730–800), who came to Japan with Ganjin records this account in his book, *Enryaku so roku* (Record of Enryaku Temple Priests). During the Nara period, the Hui-ssu reincarnation tale was promoted enthusiastically, primarily by Shitaku in support of the Ganjin group, while Kōjō, one of Saichō's disciples, promoted the Hui-ssu reincarnation tale during the Heian period.[59]

In Shitaku's *Enryaku so roku*, there exists a well-organized biography of Shōtoku Taishi in a chapter titled "Jōgū Kōtaishi bosatsu den." The beginning of the chapter describes Hui-ssu's training at Kōzan and his desire to be reborn in the Eastern world (Japan) where there was no Buddhist teaching. Toward the end of the book, it explicitly records that "Hui-ssu was reborn in Japan as Tachibana no Toyohi no Sumera-mikoto no miya (Prince of the royal family)" and presents Prince Shōtoku's miraculous accomplishments as evidence of Hui-ssu's reincarnation in Japan, confirming earlier predictions. Two other historical books, Shitaku's *Ganjin den*, presumably written around 763–777, and Mahito Genkai's *Tōsei den*, which is an abridged version of the *Ganjin den*, confirm the notion that Ganjin's primary reason for coming to Japan was based on his belief that Hui-ssu was reincarnated as Prince Shōtoku. Furthermore, in Kōjō's book, the *Denjutsu isshin kaibun*, the Hui-ssu reincarnation tale is referenced in a poem that was composed by Mahito Genkai when he accompanied the Tennō to Shitennōji in 767. Along with the Hui-ssu reincarnation tale, Mahito Genkai's poem also contained the *Nangaku shūkyō denshō*, a story that explains how Shōtoku Taishi sent the Japanese envoy, Ōno no Imoko, to a stone cave of Nangaku Hannyadai to retrieve the *Hokekyō* (Lotus Sutra), which Hui-ssu kept in a treasure box. Although the trip to the Nangaku is fiction, the fact that Imoko was sent to the Sui dynasty as a Japanese envoy has been confirmed as a historical fact.[60] These accounts substantiate that the Hui-ssu reincarnation tale held a special meaning for Ganji and his disciples during the Nara and Heian period.

In his *Shōtoku Taishi Hui-ssu zenshi kōshin setsu ni kanrensure gi* (A Doubt about Hui-ssu-Reincarnation Story), Tsujī Zennosuke suggests that the followers of Ganjin invented the Hui-ssu reincarnation tale by altering some aspects. The earlier version of the Hui-ssu reincarnation tale regarding

Shōtoku's rebirth as a member of the royal family was widely regarded as a traditional story in mainland China. According to historical documents, people readily accepted the new version without much objection since there was a prevalent belief that Hui-ssu would continue to live eternally and reappear in the world in various reincarnations. For instance, in Kyōto Shigemitsu's *Shōtoku Taishi no Hui-ssu zenshi kōshin setsu ni tsuite*, it is written that "the great priest (Hui-ssu) would keep Lotus Sutra for two decades and later after his death, he will be born again as a prince of overseas and govern the country using the sutra." This document confirms that the Hui-ssu reincarnation tale was already widespread before 760 at the Choan center during T'ang dynasty in China. Another book titled *Myōitsu den* (~767), which contains the "Hui-ssu shichidai ki," states that when Hui-ssu was training at Kōzan, Daruma, the founder of Zen Buddhism, visited him and encouraged Hui-ssu to be reborn in the Eastern ocean area and spread the Buddhist teaching to the desperate Japanese people who were living in corruption. Additionally, Kōjō's book, the *Denjutsu isshin kaimon* also contained the "Hui-ssu shichidai ki," which gives evidence to the fact that the Hui-ssu reincarnation tale must have directly influenced the compilation of *Denryaku*.

The reason the Hui-ssu reincarnation tale was so popular in China can be traced back to the notion of "kuon jitsujō" (the true attainment of enlightenment in the remotest past) in the Lotus Sutra, which Hui-ssu always kept with him. The concept of "kuon jitsujō," which is repeatedly mentioned in the Lotus Sutra, deals with the idea of the release of Śakyamuni's absolute existence. "Kuon jitsujō" is the idea of the eternal presence and continuous returning of Śakyamuni, who teaches the Buddhist dharma to people not only in this human world but also in the world beyond all worlds. In other words, through the concept of "kuon jitsujō," Śakyamuni goes beyond the actual historical person who attained enlightenment in India, but is regarded as an eternal god. Thus, the Tendai sect, which is founded on the fundamental principles from the Lotus Sutra, promoted the Hui-ssu reincarnation tale, which was similarly based on the idea of the eternal presence and reincarnation of Hui-ssu.[61]

Ganjin, who introduced the Ritsu to Japan in 753 and established the Tendai sect on Mount Hiei, and his followers incorporated the popular Chinese version of the Hui-ssu reincarnation tale and connected Hui-ssu with Prince Shōtoku, using the concept of "kuon jitsujō" in the Lotus Sutra. Ganjin and his followers employed this clever way of promoting Buddhism in Japan for the purpose of gaining legitimation of their own authority, which was based on the successful method of establishing a viable theory that connected Hui-ssu with Prince Shōtoku. This theory finds support in chapter two, "Ju Ko So Sha Mon Shaku Shitaku Den" of Shitaku's book *Enryaku so roku*, where he mentions that his master Ganjin was slandered by Japanese people when he moved to Tōshō daiji (Tōshō temple) in Nara. Shitaku explained that even though Ganjin received a sincere invitation from Yōei and Fūsho, the two Japanese monks in Nara, and though Ganjin suffered through numerous shipwrecks and even lost his eyesight to visit Japan, he did not receive a heartfelt welcome from the Japanese monks in Nara. Therefore, in order to strengthen Ganjin's position among the opposing monks in Nara, Shitaku decided to write the *Ganjin den*, cleverly incorporating the Hui-ssu reincarnation tale, applying the concept of "kuon jitsujō" in the Lotus Sutra, and establishing legitimization through the important figure of Shōtoku Taishi.

During the Heian period, the Hui-ssu story was advocated by Saichō and his disciples. In his book *Wakaki hi no Saichō to sono jidai*, Saeki Yūsei explains that the Saichō originally became interested in the Hui-ssu reincarnation tale through Ganjin's followers. In chapter 7 of his book *Ken kai ron* (816), Saichō states that "Nangaku Daishi (Hui-ssu) became an enlightened one in Tang dynasty in China and out of his compassion for our country, he was reborn as a prince in Japan and started Buddhism." This *Ken kai ron* was submitted to the imperial court to refute Sogo—a government official who controlled monks—in Nara, who criticized *Shijō shiki*, which is a part of the *Sange gakushō shiki*, a document that supported the independence of the Tendai sect. Just as with Ganjin, the Hui-ssu reincarnation tale was used to silence the criticism from the Sogo. However, Saichō did not use the Hui-ssu reincarnation tale for political purposes. Before he wrote the *Ken kai ron*, Saichō composed a poem worshiping Prince Shōtoku in front of Taishi-byō (mausoleum) at Shintennōji. This event is recorded in Kōjō's *Denjutsu isshin kaibun*:

In 816, the great priest Saichō visited Taishi's mausoleum at Shitennōji and said the following before he composed a poem: "Our Shōtoku Taishi is the reincarnation of Nangaku Hui-ssu Daishi. He was born in a stable and sent an envoy to T'ang China to search for his Lotus Sutra. The Tendai sect preserved the profound teachings of Buddhism. I, Saichō, a śramana (mendicant monk) of Kofuku-ji, am still young and immature, but I sincerely desire my master's teaching and will never stop worshiping you. Out of respect and reverence, I have composed the following poem: 'My heart came to this place as I searched the power of destiny in the ocean. I now devote myself to spread the Myōhō (Myōhō renge kyō; 'I take refuge in the Lotus Sutra') as your teaching is endless . . . I ask you to protect this country and help me to make this country a great nation.' It has been surmised that Saichō wrote the poem just before or after the vernal equinox day on February 22, which is Shōtoku Taishi's Memoral Day. Also in the year of 816, Saichō decided to separate himself from Kūkai's Shingon esoteric Buddhist principles in order to devote himself wholeheartedly to the Tendai teachings. To commemorate this decision, Saichō visited the Shitennōji to give homage to Prince Shōtoku."[62]

After the death of Saichō, his disciples Kōji,[63] Ennin,[64] and Chishō further propagated the belief. The belief that Shōtoku was the reincarnation of Hui-ssu was not confined to the Tendai sect, but was also believed by Kūkai.[65]

Kōjō's *Denjutsu isshin kaibun* contains many references to the Hui-ssu reincarnation tales, particularly when the Tendai establishment became vulnerable to attack soon after Saichō's death. For instance, in 824 when Kōjō made a request to the imperial court to appoint a Tendai priest to Shitennōji's *ango kōji* position (a lecturer during the training period), his request was denied because one of the chief priests at Enraykuji, Tomono Kunimichi (768–828), vehemently opposed it. Kōjō wrote the *Denjutsu isshin kaimon* to provide a defense against Tomono's opposition by asserting that the Tendai sect strictly adhered to the Lotus Sutra, and claimed that the Lotus Sutra was a legitimate successor of the Buddhism that was promulgated by Shotoku Taishi. Kōjō also cited Saichō's poem, which contained the account of the Hui-ssu reincarnation tale in order to emphasize the legitimacy of the Tendai sect. Kōjō's petition was approved by the government and on February 8 of the following year (825), the government issued a permit to appoint Tendai priests to Shitennōji and Horyūji's *ango kōji* and *chōjū* (attends court hearings) positions. Since then, the Tendai sect consistently used the Hui-ssu reincarnation story to support its legitimacy and achieve their goals.[66]

The Hui-ssu's reincarnation tale is also found in the work of another disciple of Saichō, Ennin (794~864), who wrote the book *Nyuto guhō junrei koki* (The Account of the Pilgrimage of Searching the Teaching, Which Entered T'ang). In particular, chapter 3 in the May 16 Article in the year of 840 recounts a conversation that Ennin had with Shien, the master of the Godaisan Daikegonji (a temple in China): "When Shien asked about Ennin about the prosperity of the Japanese Tendai sect, he replied that Nangaku Daishi (Hui-ssu) was reborn in Japan to spread the Buddhist teaching. When the people heard this, they became overjoyed. Shien also was very delighted that Hui-ssu was born in Japan to spread the Buddhist teaching." Moreover, when Ennin returned from China he brought back Honji Myoku's *Shōmangyō gisho shisō*, which also contained the Hui-ssu's reincarnation story and the *Nangaku shūkyū denshō*. When the Kaimyo and Tokūjō went to China in 772, they presented Shōtoku Taishi's *Hokke gisho* and the *Shōmangyō gisho* to Ganjin's leading disciple, Reiyu. When Myoku read these books, he was impressed to the point that he decided to write an annotated edition of the *Shōmangyō gisho*, which was called *Shōmangyō gisho shisō*. One can see both the Hui-ssu's reincarnation tale and the Shōtoku Taishi's in this work. Thus, Hui-ssu's reincarnation story originated in China from Lotus Sutra; when it came to Japan, compilers successfully created a new version that incorporated the tale of Hui-ssu's reincarnation as Shōtoku Taishi.[67]

How did Hui-ssu's reincarnation story develop into Kannon's incarnation story? Again in Kōjō's *Denjutsu isshin kaimon*, there is a Poem titled "A Poem about the Summer Visit to Jōgū's Mausoleum in Shitennōji and Hokke." The poem begins by saying that "Nangaku Hui-ssu Daishi and Tendai Chisha Daishi (Chigi) are priests of the holy mountain. They started training at Kōzan and Hui-ssu was born again in Japan." Later in the same chapter, it reads, "Our Shōtoku Taishi is the reincarnation of Nangaku Hui-ssu Daishi. He became a prince as one of Kannon's thirty-three transformations, taught the three ways to attain enlightenment, and showed the people how to realize Buddhahood with the Buddha's teaching." As the title of the poem indicates, Kōjō read the *Fumonbon* (Kannon Sutra) section of the Lotus Sutra—regarding Kannon's thirty-three transformations—in front of Shōtoku Taishi's mausoleum. In essence, Kōjō was claiming that Kannon became Shōtoku Taishi in one of his transformations; this statement also confirms that the Tendai sect was so determined to legitimize the Tendai sect as an expression of Mahāyāna Buddhism. Shōtoku Taishi thus began to be considered as a reincarnation of Kannon.[68]

From the *Nihon shoki*, we learn that Shōtoku worship was already widespread from the Nara period. People worshiped Shōtoku as an incarnation of Kannon, especially at the three temples that were associated with Shōtoku—Hōryūji, Shitennōji, and Shinaga, the site of his tomb in the Kawachi district. Devotees of Shōtoku constructed statues in his image to pray for Shōtoku's healing during his illness just before his death. Following Shōtoku's death, the government and temple establishments constructed temples and Buddhist statues in dedication to Shōtoku, Kannon, and the Buddha.[69] Hōryūji became one of the centers of Shōtoku worship. Other temples, such as Horinji and Hokkiji, were newly constructed to honor Shōtoku along with statues of the Amida triad.

According to Hōryūji history, the ailing Emperor Yōmei ordered the construction of a Buddhist temple in 587 C.E. in hopes of recovering from his illness. When Yōmei died shortly after this commission, the heir Empress Suiko and her regent, Prince Shōtoku, completed the project in 607. The Hōryūji that they built, however, is not the one that is located 12 kilometers outside central Nara. The construction of the temple was halted just before completion because Soga-no-Iruka attacked the Ikaruga shrine in 643 and killed Jōgū (aristocratic) families, such as Yamase Oeno-ōji's. Hōryūji was burned in 670 and other temples related to Shōtoku also suffered severe damage. Historians continue to debate the precise year of reconstruction, but most agree that it preceded 710, the dawn of the Nara period (710–784), which preceded the court's move to Kyoto. The four surviving structures from the Asuka era, considered one of the oldest in history, include the five-story pagoda in the central grounds, which is the centerpiece of the temple complex; the Golden Hall *(kondō)*; the inner gate south of the ancient pavilions; and most of the corridor that wraps around the central precinct.

Two principal images of Shōtoku are placed on top of the altar platform inside Hōryūji. On the back of the images, the history of the formation of the icons is inscribed: "In 586, the Emperor Yōmei, who was gravely ill, requested that Empress Suiko and Prince Shōtoku build the Hōryūji and to enshrine an image of Yakushi in the hope of his recovery. However, Emperor Yōmei's abrupt death postponed the construction of the temple until it was later completed by the Empress Suikō and her nephew, Prince Shōtoku, in 607." The inscription also records the death of the Dowager Empress, Shōtoku's mother, "in the thirty-first year of Hōkō (i.e., after the founding of Hōkōji, 621?)." The inscription then notes that "the Priestly-Prince of the Upper Palace" (Shōtoku) also fell gravely ill in the beginning of 622 and recounts how one of Shōtoku's consorts died from "the fatigue of nursing him." Filled with great anxiety and concern, all the people in the court gathered together to pray for the prince's recovery and made an image of Shaka with the same measurements as Shōtoku's figure.

Facing south on the platform altar of the *kondō* at Hōryūji, three statues with references to Pure Land Buddhism are depicted: the Shaka Trinity at the center, a single Yakushi (the healing Buddha) to the east, and a single Amida to the west. Although it has been warranted that the Kondō possessed no large Amida icon on its altar until the thirteenth century, the inscriptions on the back of the Amida statue, which record the biography of Shōtoku, reveal the true intention of its placement: the desire to include the prince, identifying him as a manifestation of Kannon, to be worshiped among the great Buddhist icons in the Golden Hall he had founded. Moreover, the fact that Shōtoku's biography is inscribed on the back of Amida serves as another piece of evidence, confirming that there was a considerable effort to promote the belief of Shōtoku as a manifestation of Kannon.

However, closer examination of the statues reveals a discrepancy with the dates of the two inscriptions, 607 in Yakushi's and 623 in Shaka's, and gives further evidence to the strong possibility that the Amida statue was actually placed at a later time. Soper postulates that the wording of the dedication record "of 607" may contain evidence for the actual lateness of its origin. He explains that both *kondō* inscriptions seem to reveal a special, local veneration for Shōtoku by the lofty impersonality of their references to him. For instance, although he is claimed to be the cofounder in the *Gangōji engi*, Shōtoku is referenced simply under the nickname that describes his miraculous ability to hear ten people at once, Prince Toyotomimi, or under the quasinickname that describes the manner of his birth, Prince Umayado. Even the inscription on the *Tenjukoku Shūcho mandara*, the embroidered scene of the Pure Land paradise that was supposedly commissioned by his surviving consort as a memorial to Shōtoku immediately following his death, refers to him simply as Taishi, the Crown Prince.[70] In contrast, the Kondō inscriptions use the term "the Priestly-Prince of the Upper Palace." In the Yakushi inscription, these descriptions reach their climax by an inclusion of the adjective *shō*, or "saintly," the first syllable of his posthumous title Shōtoku.[71]

However, on a mid-eighth-century version found in Hōryūji, a Yakushi inscription describes Shōtoku with an even more elevated title: *Tōgū Jōgū Shōtoku hōō*, "the Priestly-Prince of saintly virtue, heir-apparent of the Upper Palace." Between this text and the time of Shōtoku's death there is no datable evidence bearing on the problem beyond that given in the *Nihon shoki*. In the account given of the prince's life, he is designated by simple titles. The character *shō* is first applied to him immediately after his death, in the course of an anecdote that (whether literally true of not) has a general plausibility.[72]

There are also many works of art expressing Pure Land motifs at Hōryūji. The reason may be due to the influence of *Tenjukoku shūcho mandara*, which was created to pictorialize the Pure Land where Shōtoku had gone after his death. Besides the painting of the *Miroku jōdo* on the south wall inside the *gojū-nō-tō* (five-storied tower), there are four large paintings inside the *kondō*, filled with images of Shōtoku, Kannon, Amida Buddha, and Pure Land. Though Pure Land was not understood as a special place at that time, through the influence of Kannon worship from the end of the Nara period, there was a tendency to combine faith in Amida Buddha's Pure Land and Shōtoku worship; they were fully integrated by 1072.[73] In that year, some monks at Hōryūji requested that the political section move to the west manor of the temple in a newly constructed hall, *zanmaidō*. Meanwhile, a new chapel, called *kongo-in* West Annex of Hōryūji, became a place where monks could go to recite nembutsu for Shōtoku Taishi for as long as they desired. The recitation of nembutsu, an essential meditation practice of Pure Land Buddhism, may have been one of the significant developments that further promoted Shōtoku worship toward the end of the Heian period. For instance, the belief in *Seiho ganjō* (westward prayer), mentioned in a verse in "Ryōjinhishō," was recited during a ceremony of *Taishi-kō* (speech) of *Shōryō-e*.

From 670 to the Tenpyo era (729–749), Takada explains that *Taishi shinkō* was beginning to form among Shōtoku devotees who hoped for Shōtoku's return, as evidenced by the construction of new temples in memory of Shōtoku, such as Hokkiji, Shūguji, Horinji, and the reconstruction of Hōryūji.[74] For instance, on statues at the *Gōjū-nō-tō* (five-story tower), which was built in 711, there are inscriptions that describe Buddha's works and identify Shōtoku as an incarnation of the Buddha. Also, in the *Tōinbukkyō shizaichō*, edited in 761, there is a description of a life-size statue of Kannon as Shōtoku, who is described as the incarnation of Kannon.[75]

According to the *Hōryūji garan engi*, Tenpyo 19, the annual ceremony to honor Shōtoku was conducted on February 22, the presumed date of his death. It is recorded in the *engi* that on the anniversary of Shōtoku's death, February 22, 734, Komyo Kogo, the wife of the emperor, gave a gift to Hōryūji. On the same date two years later, it is recorded that the Empress Murō and other people gave gifts to Hōryūji. Moreover, some gifts were given to the tower where the Ima statue was located, which tells us that the ceremony most likely took place at the *kondō* in front of the tower, by the statues that commemorate the life and times of Śākyamuni Buddha and Shōtoku Taishi. Based on this evidence, we may deduce that the reconstruction of Hōryūji commenced in 670, and memorial services for Shōtoku most likely started in the Tenpyo era when Horyūji was completely rebuilt.

The *Hōryūji tōin engi* (747) tells how Shōtoku Taishi spread Buddhism at *Jōgū-ōin*, how it was destroyed, and how it was rebuilt by Gyōshin in 739. There is also a section that explains that the *guze* Kannon statue, later called *Yumedono Honzōn*, was made when Shōtoku Taishi was alive. Another book, the *Hōryūji engi narabini shizaichō* (761), reports that the *guze* Kannon statue was made to match the size of Shōtoku Taishi; this indicates that during the Nara period the Kannon statue was commensurate with the Shōtoku Taishi statue. Moreover, one can see the obvious effort by the orginators to construct a long and historical account of Shōtoku Taishi's connection to the founding of the Hōryūji.

An article from the *Kokin ichiyo shū* explains the history behind the Hōryūji continuous renovations by Gyōshin and Dōsen, until it became ruined again. Then, in 1023, the Fujiwara no Michinaga, who was supposedly regarded as an reincarnation of Shōtoku Taishi, visited the Hōryūji for the first time. Surprised by the destruction of the temple, he ordered its reconstruction. By the time of the Heian period when Hōryūji was ruined, and following the compilation of the *Denryaku*, *Taishi shinkō* was quite popular. The extent of the devastation of Hōryūji is recorded in the latter part of the *Hōryūji tōin engi*, which says, "Minamoto no Yoshitsune was wanted by the government, so the government officials came to Hōryūji with the suspicion that Yoshitsune was hiding there. The priests of Hōryūji exclaimed, 'Hōryūji is Kannon's holy and historical site, which was built by Shōtoku Taishi. This was where the first *samgharama* (where priests are trained) and origin of the Buddhist *dōjō* (training place). However, after 600 years, *samgharama* is completely destroyed. Only Shōtoku Taishi's *sharira* (remains) and the Lotus Sutra that Ōno no

Imoko brought from China are left and enshrined in the hall located there.'"[76] Here we can deduce that the priests were proud of the Hōryūji history, even though records indicated how it was destroyed. After the Emperor Kammu transferred the capital from Nara to Heian, Hōryūji's status began to wane. In an effort to reestablish Buddhism, the priests of Hōryūji attempted to create a link between the *Yumedono honzōn* with the growing popularity of *guze* Kannon worship, as in the case of *Denryaku*. However, this scheme did not yield any results until the Kamakura period (1192–1333).

According to the account in the *Hōryūji shizaichō*, the main goal for Gyoshin's reconstruction of *Jōgū ōin* was to remember Shōtoku's accomplishments and to further promote Shōtoku worship.[77] After the reconstruction, Hōryūji grew from a private temple into one of the seven great temples during the Nara and Heian period. The traditional anniversary ceremony for Shōtoku, which had previously been celebrated at Hōryūji, was held at *Jōgū ōin* after the reconstruction of Hōryūji. Consequently, the reconstruction of *Jōgū ōin* had a different meaning from the reconstruction of Hōryūji. Hōryūji was reconstructed to promote state Buddhism as well as *Taishi shinkō*. But the reconstruction of *Jōgū ōin* was entirely for the improvement of Shōtoku worship, and was the sacred site where Shōtoku's belongings were kept. This difference is made clear by the fact that their account books are separated. For instance, from the end of Tenpyo to 1116, there are no records of Shōtoku's ceremony for more than 300 years, as *Jōgū ōin* was incorporated into Hōryūji. The *Tōin engi* indicates that the beginning of Shōtoku worship at *Jōgū ōin* was February 22 of Tenpyo 8 (736).

In 1069, the fifth year of Chireki, a statue of Shōtoku Taishi as a child called *Taishi dozi keizō*[78] was built at Hōryūji. One of the mantras of bodhisattva Kannon is found on that statue. This means that, by that year, the belief that Shōtoku was a reincarnation of Kannon was firmly established, and worship of Shōtoku and Kannon was integrated. Also, in the chapel of *Jōgū-ōin*, the oldest chapel dedicated to Shōtoku, Buddhist monks painted *emaki*-like scenes and images of Shōtoku's life *(Taishi eden)* along with a seated image of Shōtoku as a child. This was likely in preparation for the upcoming celebration in 1071, the third year of Enkyū, of the 450th anniversary of Shōtoku Taishi's death. These images further promoted Shōtoku worship and influenced the formation of the annual ritual of Shōtoku worship, the *Shōryō-e*, sometime between 1074 and 1096.[79] Following the typical ritual format of Nara temples, the *Shōryō-e* ritual included singing hymns, reciting sutras, giving offerings, recognizing donors, and saying prayers. Since its incorporation into Hōryūji, *Shōryō-e* has continued to the present time to be the most important event at *Jōgū ōin* and *Se-in*. The practice of praising Shōtoku was also performed when *Shōrei-in* was newly built in honor of Shōtoku.

In 1121, in the second year of Ho-An, a chapel called *Shōrei-in* was built, in which the principle divinity image was that of Shōtoku Taishi giving a lecture from the Queen Śrīmālā Sutra *(Shōmangyō Kosan-zō)*.[80] Within the image are smaller images, of Kannon as *guze*, produced during the Nara period, along with the Lotus Sutra, Queen Śrīmālā Sutra, and Vimalakīrti Sutra. A *guze* Kannon statue standing upright on Horai-san, and three scriptures of *Hokekyō*, *Shōmangyō*,[81] and *Yuimagyō* are placed beside the statue of *Shōmangyō kosan-zō*, which is the main icon for worship at *Shōrei-in*.

Among the earliest surviving examples of Namubutsu is the mid-thirteenth-century statue of the infant Shōtoku Taishi, dressed in a modest robe and standing with his hands joined in childlike piety, now housed in the Seattle Art Museum.[82] The representation of the two-year-old Shōtoku resembles the tanjōbutsu (image of the Buddha) in pose and attire, but is also characterized by significant distinctions. Whereas the *tanjōbutsu* (infant Buddha) is typically depicted with a commanding and royal presence, by contrast, the infant Shōtoku is portrayed as a humble and obedient servant, endowed with wisdom beyond his age. By his reverent gesture of prayer, Shōtoku is clearly summoning a greater outside power rather than relying on his own power, and demonstrating that salvation is achieved through faith, a message that clearly reflected Shinran's notion of *shinjin* (sincere mind entrusting). Moreover, the notion that the powerless in this world might achieve sacred power through childlike piety was a message that was especially fitting for those who were forgotten or rejected by society.

In 1335, in the second year of Kemmu, an image of Nyoirin Kannon,[83] the wish-fulfilling Kannon, was also enshrined in the west *zuishi* (small shrine) of *Shōrei-in*. At the same time, various liturgical texts that dealt with the worshiping of Shōtoku and hymns that were dedicated to Shōtoku were produced. Such veneration of Shōtoku Taishi was discussed in *Taishi kōshiki* and *Taishi wasan*—two of the numerous hymns on Shōtoku Taishi that were composed during the medieval period. Depending on their preferences, Nara temples emphasized different aspects of Shōtoku worship in conjunction with other aspects of their worship and ritual. The fact that a large number of statues in Hōryūji are of Kannon is related to the further development of *Taishi shinkō* in medieval Japan.

In contrast to Hōryūji, the ritualism surrounding Shōtoku worship at Shitennōji was quite effective. Believed to have been written by Shōtoku Taishi, but clearly authored by someone else, the *Shitennōji goshuin engi* was a well-written book produced around 1007 that records the founding of Shitennōji by Shōtoku Taishi. In the opening section, the *engi* begins with the claim that Shitennōji was the place where Śākyamuni spread Buddhism in Japan, along with mythological accounts stating that the temple would always be protected by a blue dragon, and including other stories of miscellaneous miraculous accounts, such as the healing effects that one could receive from the water that springs from the rocks. Soon after the book was written, members of the Tennō family began a custom of visiting the Shitennōji to pay tribute to Shōtoku Taishi. Thus, on the day of Shōtoku Taishi's memorial, it became an important custom for the royal family, aristocrats, and even common people to attend the annual memorial service to honor the sarira, give homage to *guze* Kannon that was located in the *kondō*, and worship the Taishi statue, while the priests gave lectures on the Lotus Sutra in the *Seirei-in* and performed visualizations of the Pure Land by gazing at the setting sun.

In his book *Shōtoku Taishi shinkō no seiritsu*, Tanaka Tsuguhito contends that the similar characteristics found in the activities practiced at Shitennōji and by the *ango kōji* strongly suggest that *Denryaku* must have been written with the context of Shitennōji in mind, especially in *Denryaku*'s use of the expression "*guze* Kannon," which was consistent with the charitable activities being performed at Shitennōji.[84] Although there is no conclusive evidence to show that *Denryaku* was actually invented by the priests at Shitennōji, there are other similar versions of *Denryaku*, such as the *Shitennōji-ki* and the *Shichidai-ki*, which were based on Myōitsu's *Myōitsu den* and shared many similar characteristics with the *Shitennōji shoji den*. Hence, there could be a connection between the *Denryaku* and the Shitennōji, even though both temples did not fully submit themselves under the control of the Tendai sect, which was trying to expand its influence by dispatching the *ango kōji*. Shitennōji reacted with sensitivity to the instability of the Tendai sect, and effectively used the fact that the *ango kōji* was worshiping the Shōtoku Taishi's mausoleum at Shitennōji to gain the people's support for the importance of the temple. Moreover, the fact that Shōtoku Taishi was considered *guze* Kannon also reflects the Bodhisattva path in Mahāyāna Buddhism, which was brought to Japan. Later, from the end of the twelfth century until the beginning of the sixteenth century, the image of Shōtoku was brought back to represent a more human figure because it was more persuasive to use such an image, particularly during the time of *mappō*, to show that all could be equally saved.

Thus, as a result of the development of *honji suijaku* during the medieval period, *Taishi shinkō* continued to be the subject of legend as it became connected with other deities of popular worship. Most important, Kannon worship was always at the center of *Taishi shinkō* and played an important role in mediating other forms of popular worship during the medieval period. In other words, the essential aspect of *Taishi shinkō* was Kannon worship. Moreover, the evidence of Shōtoku worship and the integration of Shōtoku and Kannon worship found at Hōryūji confirm the fact that Shōtoku was worshiped as a bodhisattva Kannon and guardian *kami* figure, within *kenmitsu* Buddhism.

# Chapter 5

## Shōtoku and Shinran's Buddhism

The transition from the Heian to the Kamakura period was a volatile time for Japan, both in the secular and religious realms. During his lifetime, Shinran witnessed the downfall of the glorious Heian period and the rise of the turbulent Kamakura period. This era included one of the bloodiest civil wars in Japanese history, the Gempei War (1180–1185), when two prominent clans, the Taira and Minamoto, fought for control of Japan. When Minamoto no Yoritomo emerged as the victor and subsequently established the *bakufu* or "tent government" in Kamakura, there was an inevitable power shift in the traditional forms of rule. In particular, the Fujiwara emperor who was previously regarded as the central power figure in early Japan was forced to seek alternative means of authority because his political power was significantly undermined by the military rule of the *shōgun* or "supreme general," who essentially ran the country from Kamakura. The sangha proved to be that ideal place where the emperor, and later the retired emperor, could continue to exert symbolic power and control the economic benefits that the religious institutions enjoyed from the tax-free *shōen* (estate) system. By claiming his imperial ties to Prince Shōtoku—the ideal imperial ancestor and Buddhist figure who served as an effective bridge between the imperial court and the sangha—the emperor retired from public duty as emperor and became actively involved in the sangha by assuming the position of head of the sangha and giving himself the title of *hōō* or "dharma-emperor." During this period, known as the *insei* or "cloistered-government" period (1086–1156),[1] the retired emperor used his imperial connection to Shōtoku as a way to legitimize his claim to religious authority, enabling him to enjoy the best of both worlds: he continued to hold imperial

107

authority and, as head of the sangha, also enjoyed religious authority and control of the *shōen* holdings of temple establishments.

During the *insei* period, the retired emperor strengthened his influence and control over temple establishments by setting up essentially an emperor-ship within the sangha. The retired emperor appointed his own ministers to high religious positions within the sangha and enforced the observance of rituals aimed at securing the longevity of the emperor, such as the *Taigen* ritual performed at the imperial palace from the eighth to the fourteenth of the first month. However, the increasing involvement of the retired emperor and other political bureaucrats gradually converted the sangha into a religiopolitical bureaucracy; traditional Buddhist practice was also compromised as a result. Buddhist monks, who were mostly from an aristocratic background, were more interested in securing material benefits and parading in religious garb than in adhering strictly to the *vināya* (rules of discipline). By the Kamakura period, for instance, it was common knowledge that many monks had a wife or wives. Some Buddhist monks, such as Shinran, left the Tendai center at Mount Hiei to seek Buddhism elsewhere because they were dissatisfied and disillusioned with the promotion of state Buddhism by the emperor and political authorities.

Upon leaving Mount Hiei, Shinran spent a hundred days at Rokkakudō, a hexagonal temple dedicated to Shōtoku Taishi, to pray for spiritual inspiration. On the ninety-fifth day, Shōtoku Taishi miraculously appeared in Shinran's dream as a manifestation of bodhisattva Kannon and gave him spiritual guidance. Soon after, Shinran met his master Hōnen and joined his effort to spread the exclusive or *senju nenbutsu* teaching, a practice that was centered on chanting the name of Amida Buddha for one's salvation. The simple message of the *senju nenbutsu* teaching attracted many people from the countryside, eventually causing concern for religious and political authorities who felt threatened by the growing popularity of the *senju nenbutsu* movement. In response, the leaders of mainstream Buddhism made a successful appeal to the retired emperor to ban the *senju nenbutsu* teaching as heresy and to exile the leaders of the movement. However, closer examination of Shinran's teaching reveals that, like all the other ruling authorities and *kenmitsu taisei* during the medieval period, Shinran used *Taishi shinkō* in connection with *honji suijaku* to legitimize his innovative teaching.

## GATES OF POWER IN MEDIEVAL JAPAN

Kuroda's theory of *kenmon taisei* (the gates of power system) may help us to better understand the sociopolitical context of Shinran's time in medieval Japan. According to his theory, during the twelfth and thirteenth centuries, Japanese rulership was shared by three elite groups known as *kenmon* ("gates of power" or "influential families"): the court nobles (*kōke* or *kuge*), the warrior aristocracy *(buke)*, and temples and shrines *(jisha)*. Each member of the *kenmon taisei* played a significant role in the responsibility of government and supported each other's privileges and status. First, the court nobility, consisting of the imperial family and the capital aristocracy, held the administrative and ceremonial responsibilities of the state. Supported by their private organizations and assets, the nobles maintained their privileged access to government offices and remained the formal leaders of the state. The emperor, serving as the outstanding symbol of the state itself, made all important appointments, including the shōgun and monks for important Buddhist ceremonies at the imperial court. Second, the warrior aristocracy's main responsibility was to maintain peace and control the warrior class. Beginning in the mid-twelfth century, these duties were entrusted to prominent warrior leaders from the Minamoto and Taira clans, an assignment that was finally formalized with Minamoto no Yoritomo's (1147–1199) establishment of the shogunate in the east (the Kamakura *bakufu*) in the 1180s. During this time, even though the *bakufu* could have easily outpowered the court in the capital area—which actually happened in the Jōkyū War of 1221—it did not eliminate the court because the *bakufu* needed the administrative and bureaucratic apparatus of the court to extend its rule.

What is particularly interesting for our study is to understand how the third member of the *kenmon taisei*, the religious establishment—an entity that was traditionally separated from political affairs—gained such power and influence during that period. Kuroda explains that in medieval Japan religious institutions were not merely locations of worship and religious rituals but also sociopolitical institutions, integral to the government and its rule. Temples such as Enryakuji, Kōfukuji, and Onjōji had become not only centers of Buddhist studies but also important political allies with considerable wealth and numerous followers. Along with its general role in providing spiritual protection for the state, the religious institutions performed important rituals and ceremonies aimed at legitimizing and securing temporal power of ruling authorities, particularly the emperor or retired emperor.[2] Such rituals were instrumental in creating and maintaining the social stratification that supported the court hierarchy, since the ability to finance and perform such elaborate and expensive ceremonies augmented the status of those involved. For instance, the *Sandai'e*, or "annual lecture-rituals," which were held at Kōfukuji, Yakushiji, and at the imperial palace, were controlled by the Fujiwara chieftain and had been instrumental in the regent's ability to obtain funding, including private estates, for Kōfukuji. Participation in and performance of these ceremonies, especially the *Yuima'e* at Kōfukuji, were also crucial for determining promotion of monks to the Office of Monastic Affairs, which still constituted the main framework for the top-ranking offices in the religious hierarchy. Performing these rituals aimed at legitimizing the rule of those involved was mutually beneficial for the temples, as court officials rewarded ritualistic leaders with funding and promotions. Occasionally, for instance, the retired emperor Shirakawa donated more extensive funding, estates, or taxes for the construction of pagodas, cloisters, or Buddhist images, or the copying of sutras.[3]

One of the main reasons religious institutions were able to gain such political power and influence was their ability to amass much wealth through the tax-free *shōen* system. As Kuroda points out, private estates *(shōen)* became the main source of income for most temples during the late Heian and Kamakura periods. Records indicate that close to three hundred estates were registered in Enryakuji's name in the premodern era.[4] Aristocrats and noble chieftains donated their estates to secure spiritual and political support from influential monks and temples. The wealth that was amassed through *shōen* holdings by religious institutions enticed, for example, the retired emperor, who wanted to privatize *shōen* holdings. Shirakawa, for instance, managed to allocate large portfolios of land under the private control of the imperial family through the establishment of a new set of imperial temples headed by monk-princes, which favored Shingon and Tendai monks.

However, although the *shōen* treasure at religious institutions gave religious leaders some degree of political power and influence, it also created contention and strife among other members of the *kenmon taisei*. Members of the Fujiwara family and retired emperors, for example, competed for control of these temple assets. Consequently, the *bakufu* played more of a peripheral role in such affairs, and he only entered the scene after the "dust settled" to clean up the mess and reestablish societal order. According to Kuroda, the first signs of a *kenmon* system appeared late in the eleventh century, when members of the imperial family reasserted their dominance as retired emperors. Beginning with Shirakawa, who retired from the throne in 1086, the imperial house transformed itself into a private elite, amassing estates and attracting retainers of its own. The period from 1086 to 1185 is therefore known as the era of "rule by retired emperors" *(insei)*. During this period, retired emperors, particularly during the reign of Shirakawa (1086–1129), Go-Shirakawa (1159–1192), and Go-Saga (1246–1272), infiltrated the sangha in order to gain control of the wealth from the large *shōen* holdings of the religious institutions. By appointing himself as the official representative of the sangha, the retired emperor asserted his influence and used various tactics, such as appointing his own ministers to key positions in the sangha, even though they had no formal religious training.

One of the methods that the retired emperor used to wield the power of religious institutions was to appoint an abbot of his own choosing at key Buddhist temples, such as Enryakuji and Shitennōji, despite the protests by leaders of those religious centers who wanted an abbot appointed from their own ranks. Located on Mouth Hiei just northeast of Kyoto, Enryakuji—arguably the most influential temple in premodern Japan—housed some three thousand monks, well known for their various methods of putting pressure on the imperial court in issues that concerned the temple. Court nobles, mainly spearheaded by the retired emperors Go-Shirakawa and Go-Saga, attempted to appoint their own handpicked abbots. This caused the vehement disapproval from monks at Enryakuji, who responded with *gōso*[5] or "forceful protests," and resorted to unconventional violent means, such as taking arms, hijacking palanquins transporting key appointed figures, or even setting fire to their own temple compounds. The *gōso* were apparently effective to the extent that they caused concerns for the imperial court, whose financial interests in the *shōen* holdings were located at these elite temples.[6] In 1264, for instance, frustrated by the lack of acknowledgment of such protests against the retired emperor Go-Shirakawa's appointment of a monk from Onjōji to the abbotship of Shitennōji, monks at Enryakuji burned the ordination platform, grabbing the attention of court officials and ultimately the *bakufu*, who played a "referee" role in such disputes. These incidents and strife reveal that monks at Enryakuji were in the pursuit of spiritual rewards but were also quite involved in political pursuits, and adamant about resisting or relinquishing efforts to be controlled by the court or ambitious individuals, who wanted to tap into the financial base of the *shoen* system via appointment of handpicked abbots. It can be estimated that some three hundred protests were staged by religious institutions in the capital from the late eleventh to the sixteenth centuries, and more than one-fourth of them were staged by Enryakuji.[7] Evidence for the significant frustration that was caused by these *gōso* protests was recorded by the retired emperor Shirakawa (1053–1129), who once said, "The flow of the Kamo river; the roll of the dice, and the mountain monks [of Enryakuji] are things I cannot control."[8]

Religious institutions in premodern Japan were not merely locations of worship and religious rituals, but also home to important members of the ruling elite. While religious institutions may not have had enough power to form an independent government as the warrior aristocracy did, the leading Buddhist temples like Enryakuji and Kōfukuji were legitimate shared rulers of the premodern Japanese realm, according to Kuroda's *kenmon taisei* theory. Enryakuji played a pivotal role in both the spiritual and political well-being of the state and, according to the prevailing doctrine of mutual dependence of the Imperial law and Buddhism *(ōbō-buppō sōi)*,[9] the destruction of Enryakuji would also result in the decline of the court itself.[10] Go-Shirakawa himself once said that the imperial court and government were dependent on the continual presence and influence of the Buddhist institutions. Enryakuji and other main Buddhist centers, Shitennōji and Kōfukuji, were very much sociopolitical centers. This was a time when monks took arms to defend not their beliefs but their wealth from the tax-free *shōen*s. Although the Buddhist institutions enjoyed a shared ruler-ship with the court and *bakufu*, there was continued struggle for control over *shōen* holdings, which were publicized through *gōso* and destruction of temple properties by monks. This politically saturated atmosphere and gradual demise of Buddhist practice at Mount Hiei must have led conscientious monks like Shinran to leave the Tendai center and seek Buddhism elsewhere.

## Mappō

The emergence of an exclusive form of practice in Kamakura Buddhism was closely connected with the development of *mappō* consciousness. Integrated into the Pure Land tradition by Tao-ch'o (562–645), the idea of *mappō* involves a qualitative view of time that is envisioned in relation to the lifetime of Śākya-muni.[11] *Mappō* refers to the degenerating age of Buddhism—lasting 10,000 years—when people are no longer able to realize enlightenment because they are far removed from historical Buddha's teachings and practices. In other words, the spiritual, moral, and physical conditions on earth are seen to pro-gressively deteriorate in direct proportion to the time that has elapsed since the Buddha's parinirvana (death). During the Heian period, 949 B.C.E. came to be accepted as the date of the Buddha's death, and Buddhist circles adopted the explanation that the period of True Dharma and Counterfeit Dharma each lasted for 1,000 years, placing the commencement of *mappō* in 1052 C.E.[12] The *mappō* doctrine provided a way to account for the desperate situation in Japan, and instilled a new fear with its implication of an age when the dharma would be lost. As the foundation of the central government began to collapse, the focus of Buddhism shifted from protection of the state to personal salvation.[13] Hoping to escape from the disastrous world in which they lived, nobles began to devote themselves to building family temples, worshiping Amida Buddha, and seeking rebirth in his Pure Land. LaFleur cites the court diaries, which blamed the collapse of the social structure on the advent of *mappō* and voiced their authors' despair at having been born in this evil era.[14] In the *Shōzōmatsu wasan* (Hymns of the Dharma-Ages), Shinran recalls the monks of his day:

> As evidence of (how common are) the five perversities, the monks and masters of today are like low-grade servants, and the term "monks" and "masters" is synonymous with vulgarity. A mark of the evil of the five defilements is that the titles "monk" and "teacher of dharma" are used for serfs and servants and have become derogatory terms. Al-though monks are so in name only and keep no precepts, now in this

defiled world of the last dharma-age they are the equals of Śāriputra (Jpn. Sharihotsu) and Maudgalyāyana (Jpn. Mokuren), and we are urged to pay homage to and revere them.[15]

In line with Shinran's account of Mount Hiei, Norihiko Kikumura describes Mount Hiei during Shinran's day:

> Enryaku Temple on Mount Hiei was founded to "pacify and preserve" Japan, yet incantations were sold there in the belief that magical rites could affect a desired outcome. Many monks completely disregarded their vows and spent all their time and energies performing rites which would bring them popularity and financial gain. Their incantations were not always effective, however. Efforts to bring about recovery from illness often resulted in death. Efforts to bring about good fortune often had just the opposite effect. But in offering to perform magical rites, these monks strengthened the superstitious beliefs of the people. It is no exaggeration to say that in the superstition they spread, these monks were incarnations of the devil, rather than seekers of spiritual understanding.[16]

Apparently many monks disregarded their vows and spent all of their time and effort performing rites that would bring them popularity and financial gain. In offering to perform magical rites, these monks strengthened the superstitious beliefs of the people. Shinran must have found it very difficult to accept this corruption in the place where he sought enlightenment. In fact, it must have been difficult for any conscientious monk to practice spiritual discipline in an increasingly religiopolitical atmosphere of hypocrisy among aristocratic monks.

The *mappō* doctrine influenced Shinran, who believed that Shōtoku Taishi was the incarnation of Kannon who compassionately appeared in Japan during *mappo*. This is the main reason Shinran referred to Shōtoku Taishi as *guze* Kannon in one of his hymns. Shinran's concern with the problem of *mappō* can be seen in his *Ken jōdo shinjitsu kyōgyōshō monrui* (Collection of Passages Elucidating the True Pure Land Teaching, Practice, and Proof). In the final chapter, "On the Transformed Buddha Land," Shinran reaffirms Hōnen's conclusion that only the nembutsu of the Original Vow can lead ignorant people to salvation in the age of *mappō*. Far more than Hōnen, Shinran identified the degeneracy of the age with his own sense of sinfulness and further explicated the distinction between self-power and Other-power. He concluded that people in the degenerate age of *mappō* could not perform even the slightest good deed, for one's virtuous acts are invariably tainted by self-calculation and will remain essentially egotistical. Although he did not deny that attaining enlightenment through difficult disciplines by traditional methods was effective, Shinran was convinced that such methods were inevitably useless during the age of *mappō*. He believed that relying on meritorious acts for one's rebirth implied reliance on one's own power, and thus fell short of perfect trust in Amida's power. The *mappō* consciousness of Shinran focused on human depravity and powerlessness to achieve salvation through personal effort, and opened the way to attain immediate rebirth in the Pure Land by renouncing all self-reliance and placing total faith in Amida Buddha's vows. Hence, among the forty-eight vows of Dharmākara, Shinran emphasized only the Eighteenth Vow, which stressed faith and absolute reliance on Amida Buddha.

## SHINRAN ON MOUNT HIEI

In his *Takada kaisan Shinran shōnin shōtōden*, Goten Ryōku says that Shinran became a monk at the age of eight and proved to be an outstanding student; he studied rigorously the entire body of Buddhist sacred literature until the age of twenty-three. In the second month of his twenty-fourth year, Jien summoned him and "engaged in conversation about *Shōshikan* (Method of Contemplation) and *Ōjōyōshū*," asking many difficult questions about these works. Shinran answered all questions with ease. On the second day of the sixth month, Jien thereby "conferred the rank of *Shōsōzō* and appointed him head of Shōkō Temple, which was associated with the Imperial Court." This tradition was widely accepted during the Tokugawa period (1600–1868) primarily because there was no evidence to show that it was not true.[17] From Eshinni's account, we learn that Shinran was a *dōsō*: "The lord [Shinran] sought enlightenment by descending [Mount Hiei], where he was a *dōsō*, and secluded himself in Rokkaku Temple for 100 days."

Based on the information from court diaries in Shinran's day, we learn that there were three basic classes of monks on Mount Hiei: student monks *(gakushō)*, attendant monks *(dōshu)*, and ordinary temple monks *(dōsō)*.[18] The *gakushō* position was filled by those of aristocratic blood, whereas *dōshu* were the former retainers of court nobility who served their former-masters-turned-student-monks, and also performed the menial labor required to maintain the temples.[19] *Dōsō* was the lowest of these three classes of monks, and their primary duty consisted of a devotional practice known as the *jōgyōzanmai* (constant practice of meditation on Amida), which prescribed ninety days of continuous chanting of the sacred name of the Buddha Amida, "Namu Amida Butsu," while circling around the statue of Amida Buddha in an attempt to attain enlightenment.[20] A training hall for that purpose, the *jōgyōzanmai-dō*, exists even to this day at Yokawa on Mount Hiei.

A *dōsō* was expected to strictly and rigorously uphold monastic precepts and disciplines. As a typical *dōsō*, Shinran's daily activities would follow the standard monastic career on Mount Hiei in those times. One began by entering the Buddhist path at about the age of ten, becoming partially ordained after five years, and receiving full ordination of Buddhist precepts after another five years of study. Then, for the next twenty years, he would progress along a course of study and meditation that dealt with the Tendai school's two major practices—cessation and realization *(shikangyō)*, and meditation on the Buddha Mahāvairocana *(shanagō)*.[21]

In regard to his personal religious practice at Mount Hiei as a *dōsō*, Shinran may have felt the futility of trying to attain enlightenment through the continuous chanting of nembutsu (i.e., self-power) at the *jōgyōzanmai-dō* (constant practice of meditation on Amida). It is likely that Shinran's conscience also tormented him because he harbored some impure thoughts and desires, such as the desire to be with a woman, later revealed by his decision to marry and have children. Furthermore, since it was considered common knowledge that many monks had secret affairs with women, it is not unimaginable that Shinran might have witnessed the *gakushō* or *dōshu* having relations with women behind closed doors as he made his rounds cleaning the temple. Shinran did not follow the hypocrisy of such monks. Rather, he decided to marry openly and live an ordinary life, starting a family and associating with common people. Hence, Shinran described himself as being "neither monk nor layman" *(so ni arazu zoku ni arazu)*, which implies that he did not consider himself a monk because of his marriage and lay lifestyle. On the other hand, he did not see himself as a layman either since he was truly a Buddhist in heart and mind. The phrase "neither monk nor layman" may sound like a paradox, but not if we understand Shinran's self-description with the notion of Other-power *(tariki)* teaching that he learned from Hōnen. Shinran once explained that "even the most evil practitioner could attain birth in the Pure Land" by calling the name of Amida Buddha with *shinjin* (sincere mind entrusting) since the practitioner attains birth not by self-power but through the Other-power of Amida Buddha's compassionate Primal Vow to save all sentient beings. In the same line of reasoning, his master Hōnen repeatedly taught that marriage was no hindrance to birth in the Pure Land.

After twenty years of spiritual discipline and training at the Tendai Buddhism center, Shinran left Mount Hiei and headed toward Rokkakudō for a hundred-day retreat to seek spiritual guidance and inspiration. No one really knows exactly why Shinran left Mount Hiei. Traditional explanation argues that Shinran departed because he had fallen into despair after practicing nembutsu in self-power for many years without seeing any improvement in his spiritual life, particularly in regard to controlling his sexual impulses. We only have speculations and various theories regarding Shinran's decision to leave his home

and spiritual training ground.[22] Japanese scholarship is generally divided into
two approaches. One approach, represented by such scholars as Iyenaga
Saburō, Tamura Enchō, Shigematsu Akihisa, and Akamatsu Toshihide, adheres to the view that the corruption of the religious practice occurred as a result of the political downfall of the Heian government with the rise of the
warrior class at the onset of the Kamakura period. Hence, these scholars deduce
that Shinran's abandonment of the Tendai practice at Mount Hiei was due to
the overall decay he found in the religious atmosphere of the Tendai order.[23]
They feel that the influx of unqualified monks into this socioreligious establishment, the corrupted and violent behavior of monks *(sōhei)*[24] who were concerned primarily with securing material benefits, the constant dissension
between the student monks and priests, and the routine performance of rituals
dedicated to worldly benefits must have deeply disturbed a sensitive religious
mind that was searching for a way to salvation.[25] However, before we can accept
this interpretation, we must confirm that Buddhist practice was indeed decadent, as in reflecting the mood of *mappō*, to the point that a conscientious and
dedicated monk would feel propelled to "leave his nest."

The dissenting approach, represented by such scholars as Kuroda Toshio,
Satō Hiroo, Taira Masayuki, and Imai Masaharu, rejects the "corruption theory" in favor of a "positive" interpretation of the religious atmosphere within
the sangha during the political instability of the late Heian period. After further investigation into certain internal factors in the sangha, these scholars contend that religious practice did not wane, but actually remained strong and even
intensified as a result of *mappō* consciousness. Hence, Kuroda Toshio, for instance, argues that Shinran left Mount Hiei because he rejected the orthodoxy
of *kenmitsu* Buddhism "after carefully studying the scriptures of the orthodoxy."
Taira Masayuki supports Kuroda's explanation by claiming that the founders of
the Kamakura Pure Land schools were leaders who rebelled against the religious orthodoxy at its center.[26]

Kuroda's study of Kamakura Buddhism from an economic perspective
sparked a movement toward a closer examination of the internal context of the
sangha during the Kamakura period.[27] Basing his conclusions on a closer investigation of the *shōen* system, Kuroda shows that the sangha was able to
maintain a strong continual religious practice and presence by way of *kenmitsu
taisei*, the system of Buddhist doctrine and esoteric ritual that infused the
Tendai, Shingon, and Nara schools, without being affected by the political instability of the government during the late Heian and early Kamakura periods.
Kuroda's theory thus refutes the explanation that Shinran left Mount Hiei because of the growing corruption of Buddhist practice. In any case, Kuroda made
a significant contribution by encouraging scholars to further investigate internal factors that may help us to better understand the situation within the

sangha during Shinran's time. In my opinion, the issue is not to judge whether one approach is right or wrong, but rather to use valuable information from both approaches that helps us, as sociologist Clifford Geertz would say, to gather a "thick description" of the sangha during the late Heian and early Kamakura periods.

After conducting a deeper study into Shinran's teachings, I have to disagree with Kuroda's interpretation that Shinran's teaching reflected a rebellion against the scriptures of the orthodoxy. Shinran's concept of *shinjin*, for instance, is consistent with the Mahāyāna notion of emptiness and nonduality. It may appear that Shinran's teaching, which emphasizes the worship of Amida Buddha, suggests a heretical tendency, that is, the dualistic nature of the worship of a savior-like figure in Amida Buddha. To dispel such misinterpretation, Shinran explains that the fundamental nature of Amida as transcendent reality and the worship of Amida Buddha are only provisional. While Amida Buddha is said to emerge from true reality or dharma-body as suchness, he manifests into form and time in the samsaric world because of his compassion for all unenlightened beings. According to the *Larger Sutra*, the Amida Buddha is described as the "Buddha of Boundless Light," which Shinran explains: "With the light of the sun or moon, when something has come between, the light does not reach us. Amida's light, however, being unobstructed by things, shines on all sentient beings; hence, he is named Buddha of Boundless Light."[28] Amida's light is unhindered because it does not stand in dualistic opposition to samsaric existence, but illuminates blind passions and evil karma. Moreover, Shinran's teaching of *shinjin* and "immediate birth" in the Pure Land with nonretrogression affirms that the worship of Amida Buddha is only provisional. Throughout most of the Pure Land tradition, it was taught that one attains birth in the Pure Land at the moment of death and thereafter continues to practice until one realizes enlightenment. In other words, it had been usual to understand reaching the Pure Land and later realizing enlightenment as lying in a temporal line along which the practitioner progresses from samsaric existence to Buddhahood.[29] Shinran's teaching of "immediate attainment of birth" shifts the perspective in accordance with basic Mahāyāna teaching regarding the nonduality of samsara and nirvana. Hence, I do not believe that it was a doctrinal issue that led Shinran to leave Mount Hiei, as both Kuroda and Taira suggest. Rather, I believe that one of the main reasons behind Shinran's departure of Mount Hiei was the fact that he witnessed the corruption of Buddhist practice due to the religiopolitical atmosphere being fostered there, and not the fact that he "rejected the scriptures of the orthodoxy."[30] In particular, Shinran rejected the corrupt practices that were instituted by imperial and political authorities who sought to reinforce the symbolic authority of the emperor and promote state Buddhism.

The theory that Shinran left Mount Hiei because he rejected the scriptures of the orthodoxy is also not supported by Shinran's writings. I agree with Kuroda's assertion that the *kenmitsu* Buddhist establishment remained strong during Shinran's days and was the place where Shinran spent many years as a *dōsō*, practicing *jōgyōzanmai*, which would provide the context of his spiritual upbringing and development. The dissension is more of a private matter. Shinran was not against the teachings of the *kenmitsu* Buddhist establishment, but was not in support of the growing political atmosphere within the sangha. Hence, I believe that his decision to leave Mount Hiei stemmed from his desire to practice Buddhism elsewhere.

Hirota Fukushima supports the view that Shinran left Mount Hiei because he rejected the regulation of state Buddhism by secular authorities using secular law. Saichō, the founder of the Tendai center at Mount Hiei, had originally established his school to criticize state Buddhism in the Nara period and make Buddhism independent of secular power. Many monks at Mount Hiei, however, became involved in criticizing the Shingon school at Mount Kōya because of their favoritism toward the aristocracy and service to the emperor.[31] These priests employed soldiers and even armed themselves like secular rulers. Shinran must have also been troubled by the fact that warrior monks *(sōhei)* were recruited to defend temple properties. For instance, in 1108, the monks from Enryakuji and Onjōji protested against Shirakawa's appointment of a monk from a Shingon sect to perform an important ritual. Fujiwara no Munetada, a courtier in Shirakawa's service, fearfully noted in his diary: "Previously, the clergy were clad in protective armor when they came to the Imperial palace, but this time, they are already armed, carrying bows and arrows. It is possible that the mob now reaches several thousand."[32] In time, these warrior monks exercised considerable power and it was inevitable that corruption would invade the sacred grounds of Mount Hiei. Shinran did not choose to be a part of the growing corruption and the increasing involvement of Buddhist temples with secular affairs, so he left Mount Hiei to seek Buddhism elsewhere.[33]

Shinran's disdain for political influences within the sangha can be seen from his explicit comments toward the emperor and his ministers in the postscript of the *Kyōgyōshinshō*, a section that was later censored by governing authorities. In this postscript, Shinran accuses "the emperor and his ministers" of "acting against the dharma and abandoning all integrity" when the emperor issued the imperial edict to ban the *senju nenbutsu* teaching and exile its prominent leaders. There is no disagreement among scholars that Shinran felt profoundly wronged by the political and religious establishments, which, according to his account in the *Kyōgyōshinshō*, were blind to the true teachings of Buddhism:

Thinking to myself, I have come to understand that the various teachings of the Path of the Sages, practice and proof no longer exist anymore, and that the very essence of the Pure Land teaching is now the important and popular path toward realization of enlightenment. However, monks during Śākyamuni's time in various temples did not have a clear understanding of the teaching and were ignorant of the distinction between ultimate and provisional; at the capital, scholars of the Chinese classics were confused about practices and also unable to make a distinction between right and wrong paths. Thus, educated monks of Kōfukuji temple drafted a petition to the retired-emperor in the first part of the second month in 1207. The emperor and his ministers, acting against the dharma and abandoning all integrity, became enraged. Subsequently, Master Genkū—the recognized founder and vigorous messenger, who actively spread the essence of Pure Land teaching [in Japan]—and several of his followers, without receiving any fair trial for their alleged crimes, were executed or exiled to distant provinces; I was among the latter.[34]

Shinran's attitude against the emperor and political authorities, as expressed in this passage, shows the degree to which he regarded their actions as detrimental to Buddhism. It is apparent that he perceived the secular authorities in Kantō as obstructers of the *senju nenbutsu* teaching, and that he considered them karmically destined to punishment in the next life. In fact, Shinran even disowned his son, Zenran, for appealing to political authorities and not religious leaders to resolve religious disputes.[35]

There is no simple answer to the question of why Shinran left Mount Hiei since Shinran never recorded his thoughts on this in writing. As illustrated in the previous arguments, this question remains a rather complicated one; however, I think the answer lies in a combination of various but relevant inner thoughts that stem from Shinran's dissatisfaction with the religiopolitical atmosphere on Mount Hiei, disillusionment from having witnessed hypocrisy among aristocratic monks who secretly had affairs with women, a desire to live an open, honest, and free life as an ordinary person, including having a wife and children, a need to seek a lifestyle different from the one he lived as a *dōsō*, and to see more of the world beyond Mount Hiei, as well as the desire to spread Buddhism among the masses in the countryside.

My explanation of Shinran's descent from Mount Hiei draws from both the corruption theory and Kuroda's positive interpretation of the religious atmosphere within the sangha. My study also includes Satō Hiroo's insightful study of the *honji suijaku* culture during the medieval period. I believe that one of the important and highly relevant events in Shinran's life that helps us to understand why he left Mount Hiei is his one hundred-day retreat at Rokkakudō, where, after ninety-five days, according to Eshinni's letter to her daughter Kakushinni, Shinran had a dream that would change his life. His dream involved the two important Buddhist figures, Prince Shōtoku and the bodhisattva Kannon, mystically becoming one and conveniently transforming into a woman.

## THE *SENJU NENBUTSU* MOVEMENT

Disillusioned by the ritualistic and aristocratic Buddhism of the Nara and Heian periods, the protagonists of the new sects of Buddhism during the Kamakura period propagated an exclusive teaching that emphasized just one kind of nembutsu practice as a way to attain enlightenment.[36] The idea that a single form of practice could benefit all people equally was relatively new in Buddhist history. According to Stone, the period in which the Pure Land message of salvation was propagated was remarkably different from the height of the Heian period in which the sangha, supported by the state and the nobles, offered a selective and comprehensive system of practices designed to harmonize various doctrines and appeal to people of diverse backgrounds and capacities.[37] Pure Land Buddhism was closely associated with the Tendai sect centered on Mount Hiei. The roots of the exclusive practice of vocal nembutsu actually began at Mount Hiei, where Buddhist monks fervently engaged in scriptural studies and other forms of nembutsu practices and meditations. By chanting the nembutsu, the monk could assure his rebirth in the Pure Land where he could practice the necessary disciplines under Amida's compassionate instruction to attain enlightenment.[38]

Another important aspect of Kamakura Buddhism was the shortening of the length of time required to attain enlightenment by traditional Buddhism. Many Mahāyāna sutras describe at the six *parāmitās* (perfections, Jpn. *haramitsu*) or bodhisattva practices of almsgiving, upholding precepts, forbearance, assiduity, meditation, and wisdom are to be perfected one by one. Mastering each *parāmitā* required a hundred *kalpas*; one *kalpa* (Jpn. *kō*) was generally estimated as 15,998,000 years. Hōnen taught that anyone who chants the *nenbutsu* is assured of attaining rebirth in the Pure Land upon his death. Subsequently, one also attains "the stage of nonretrogression" when one has advanced so far in his spiritual development that he cannot regress and is certain to attain the goal. Hōnen taught that by chanting the nembutsu, one could attain the stage of nonretrogression in one's very next existence, which was a drastic shortening of the time traditionally thought to be required. Shinran decreased this time even further. His doctrine of instantaneous rebirth held that one attains the stage of nonretrogression not after death, but in the very moment that *shinjin* (sincere mind entrusting) first arises in his heart, that is, in this present life.[39]

After his conversion experience at Rokkakudō, Shinran met and received religious training under Hōnen, who was actively spreading the *senju nenbutsu* teaching[40] to the masses in the countryside. After a long period of spiritual quest, Hōnen came to believe that the Buddhist practice of nembutsu, the simple calling of Amida Buddha's name, was an effective way to attain eventual enlightenment. According to this belief, a practitioner attains birth in the Pure Land through a wholehearted reliance on the mercy of Amida and the recitation of nembutsu. Hōnen insisted that in the *mappō* era common people were too weak and depraved to achieve spiritual advances through their own efforts. Shinran further conceptualized the exclusive teaching of vocal nembutsu and attracted many followers to the Pure Land faith. Since the nembutsu practice of invoking Amida Buddha's name was easy and did not require any special education, many common people embraced this message of salvation by faith, especially farmers, local *bushi*, and villagers in central provinces. The laypeople who did not have access to the traditional practices of monks and nuns also accepted his message of salvation by faith in Amida Buddha. He explained that it is through the power of Amida Buddha rather than through one's efforts that one is purified of evil karma. Therefore, one need not be a monk or nun, or learned, or even virtuous; liberation is due to Amida Buddha's gracious act, which is available to anyone who simply invokes Amida Buddha's name.[41] Accordingly, Shinran regarded the nembutsu as an expression of gratitude to Amida rather than a practice leading to birth in the Pure Land. As practitioners hear the name, they awaken *shinjin* that is within them; they entrust themselves to the Primal Vow of Amida Buddha to save all sentient beings.[42]

The *senju nenbutsu* teaching offered an easy path toward individual salvation as opposed to the difficult path that required years of religious discipline and training at Buddhist institutions. However, as the number of followers to the *senju nenbutsu* teaching gradually increased, leaders of the mainstream Buddhism at Nara and on Mount Hiei became jealous and began a campaign to stop the *senju nenbutsu* movement from spreading any further. In 1205, the leaders of mainstream Buddhism, led by Jōkei of Kasagi, drafted a carefully worded petition that accused Hōnen, Shinran, and their disciples of spreading heretical teaching.[43] One of the central points of criticism was the claim that their teaching had antinomian tendencies that encouraged lawlessness and immoral conduct, since the observance of precepts and performance of good deeds were not regarded as necessary for attaining birth in the Pure Land. They also pointed out that some aspects of the *senju nenbutsu* teaching challenged the emperor's symbolic authority and threatened to upset the harmonious relationship that mainstream Buddhism had with imperial and political authorities.

Because mainstream Buddhism enjoyed the patronage of the court, the emperor and political authorities approved the petition to ban the *senju nenbutsu* teaching and subsequently exiled its leaders to remote locations.

Akamatsu Toshihide, a post-Marxist scholar of Jōdo Shinshū, has attempted to explain the reason for the approval of the petition by the emperor and political authorities. Akamatsu observes that Kōfukuji monks should have attempted to discuss the problems with the leaders of the *senju nenbutsu* movement. Instead, because many Kōfukuji aristocratic priests had close ties to the emperor, they appealed to him, asking him to issue an Imperial edict banning the *senju nenbutsu* teaching.[44] Akamatsu explains that the Enryakuji monks' problem stemmed from the fact that they appealed to political authorities to resolve religious debates. Initially, the retired emperor Go-Toba (1180–1239) was against neither Enryakuji nor the Jōdo Shinshū, but when he found out that two of Hōnen's disciples, Gyōku and Junsai,[45] were associating closely with his concubines[46] he was furious and immediately took action to force a court decision in the Kōfukuji suit. Seven days later, on January 24, 1207, he proclaimed the ban on the *senju nenbutsu* movement.[47] Subsequently, both Gyōku and Junsai were put to death; during the same month, Hōnen, Shinran, and several other important disciples were exiled. Thus, Akamatsu and Takamichi seem to suggest that secular authorities suppressed the *senju nenbutsu* movement on the basis of the immoral conduct of two troublesome disciples of Hōnen.

The Gyōku and Junsai incident was not timely for Hōnen and Shinran, but Akamatsu and Takamichi are shortsighted in suggesting that that incident alone provoked Go-Toba to approve the ban and punish the leaders of the *senju nenbutsu* movement. A more plausible explanation for the ban is related to the underlying political reasons that caused the retired emperor to stop the spread of the *senju nenbutsu* teaching. First, if Gyōku and Junsai's reckless conduct was not reason enough to justify the retired emperor's approval of the ban, there is a more profound basis for his strong disapproval. In particular, the Pure Land faith that was centered on the worship of Amida Buddha posed a challenge to the retired emperor's symbolic religious authority. Having been stripped of his political power with the rise of the shogunate, the retired emperor's only remaining source of symbolic power and authority was his religious role as the official head of the sangha, which he legitimized through his imperial connection to Shōtoku Taishi. But when Shinran taught that only faith in the Amida Buddha was necessary for salvation, the retired emperor approved the ban because the *senju nenbutsu* teaching undermined his religious authority. Consequently, the validity of the accusations of heresy made by the leaders of mainstream Buddhism remains in question because the retired emperor did not have the capacity to judge whether or not the *senju nenbutsu* teaching was heresy. Although the retired emperor was, by title, the arbiter of such doctrinal debates because of his role as the official head of the sangha, his discernment was based solely on protecting his political interests, not on judging doctrinal issues. For this reason, it is important that we closely examine the grounds for the petition prepared by the leaders of mainstream Buddhism accusing the leaders of the *senju nenbutsu* movement of teaching heresy.

One of the significant things that occurred after the ban of the *senju nenbutsu* teaching and exile of its leaders was that Shinran's teaching continued to be embraced by both the aristocracy and common people, even though it was officially banned as heretical teaching *(itan)*. Shinran's Buddhism continued to be embraced by the masses because his teaching not only offered an easy path toward individual salvation, but also because the *honji suijaku*, in connection with *Taishi shinkō*, legitimized his innovative teaching. Moreover, taking into consideration the particular religious context in which it arose, *senju nenbutsu* teaching was indeed consistent with the orthodoxy of traditional Buddhist teaching; the underlying objective of the ban was to suppress a "bottom-up" reform movement against state Buddhism.

Other aspects of Hōnen and Shinran's teaching of *senju nenbutsu* raised concerns for the *kenmitsu* leaders as well as the emperor. As followers of the Easy Path grew in number, there were fewer visitations to temples and shrines to pay homage to the various *kamis*. It was customary for people to visit the various temples and shrines to pay their respects to the emperor and give donations as a way of gaining merit for the pursuit of enlightenment. There was an economic triangular relationship of exchanging merits between the emperor, the monks, and the people. People came to the temples and shrines to pray for their welfare and offer donations to obtain merit. Then the monks would pray for the welfare of the people, which was a way of gaining merit for themselves. Finally, the emperor would assume control of the funds, take a percentage for himself, and also keep the temples and shrines in business. When Shinran reinterpreted the concept of *ekō* or gaining merit to be the merit that Amida Buddha graciously gives to his believers out of compassion,[48] it upset the economic relationship that had been enjoyed by the political and religious establishment.

Shinran's more personal, faith-oriented Buddhism did not require the believer's effort to accumulate merit for the sake of salvation, leading many people in the countryside to eagerly embrace his innovative teaching.[49] Since birth in the Pure Land was already assured by their complete reliance on the Other-power *(tariki)* of Amida Buddha, nembutsu followers felt it was pointless to go to temples and shrines for prayer since they could pray just as well at home. When the numbers of temple-goers decreased, it caused serious concerns for the leaders of mainstream Buddhism since their livelihood and growth depended on the revenues they amassed from donations. The decrease in income also affected the emperor, who took a percentage of the sangha's revenue.[50]

Shinran's worship of Prince Shōtoku as *guze* Kannon undermined the imperial and political authorities' efforts to legitimize their rule through their imperial connection to Prince Shōtoku. In his *Sanbōe* (The Three Jewels), Tamenori explains that there are three traditional ways of worshiping Prince Shōtoku: as imperial ancestor, as a reincarnation of the Chinese Buddhist monk (the karmic lineage), and as Kannon (the spiritual lineage). When Shinran connected his reverence for Prince Shōtoku with the worship of Kannon in his visions, he emphasized the spiritual lineage over the other two traditional aspects of worship. In the *Nihon shoki*, the name "Shōtoku Taishi" refers to the general Buddhist character of the prince's name. Significantly, Shinran does not mention any kind of worship that involves Prince Shōtoku as the imperial ancestor, thus implying that the imperial lineage is less important than the karmic lineage or worshiping Prince Shōtoku in the spiritual sense. Shinran's emphasis on the karmic and spiritual lineage undermined the authority of the emperor, who gained his symbolic power through his imperial lineage to Prince Shōtoku. By promoting Shōtoku as a manifestation of bodhisattva Kannon during *mappō*, Shinran appears to have been attempting to keep Buddhism free from any involvement with various ruling authorities, such as the emperor, who were using Shōtoku to promote their political interests.

## SHINRAN'S ATTITUDE TOWARD EMPERORSHIP

According to Futaba Kenkō, there are two streams of Buddhism in Japan: one that began from Shōtoku Taishi and state Buddhism, which was created for the emperor. Before the end of World War II, Buddhist scholars had stated that orthodox Buddhism was one that protected the state, contributed to giving more power to the emperor, and had its connection with the state. Futaba argues that Shōtoku Taishi Buddhism was based on *muga,* or the absence of selfishness.[51] In the Seventeen-Article Constitution, Shōtoku Taishi stated that all people can be led astray by secular things, but through the study of Buddhist teachings they could live unselfishly. In contrast, state Buddhism regarded the emperor as the judge, which was not part of the traditional teachings of Buddhism.

Shinran alleged that the most authentic Buddhism was that started by Shōtoku Taishi, revived by his master Hōnen, and based on the *muga* and the notion of equality, that all people are able to become Buddha after death. In contrast, Futaba says, state Buddhism, which he calls "surface Buddhism," was set up for the purpose of strengthening the state and increasing the emperor's prosperity, based on the *yuiga,* to satisfy one's own desire.[52] Futaba also points out that, in Japan, religious authorities and political authorities are one and the same. However, after the Kamakura period, when the *bakufu* stripped the emperor of his political power, the emperor continued to exert great symbolic power by legitimizing the government of new political leaders through his god-like influence over the general masses.[53]

Although his strong reaction against the emperor in the postscript of the *Kyōgyōshinshō* might lead some to believe that Shinran was opposed to the emperorship, his *wasans* praising Prince Shōtoku contradict that idea. One of the reasons Shinran wrote so many *wasans* praising Prince Shōtoku was to restore the nature of ideal emperorship that was lacking among the emperors of his day. For Shinran, Shōtoku Taishi was the ideal emperor who embodied the virtues of a worthy *cakravartin*.[54]

Without making any direct attacks against the emperor or secular authorities, Shinran was able to cleverly use Shōtoku Taishi through subtle rhetoric to criticize and subordinate imperial authority to the superior authority of the Buddha. In our previous examination of the origins of imperial rule in Japan, we learned that the emperor acquired his political authority by convincing his subjects that his imperial authority had been inherited through his imperial connection to the goddess Amaterasu. The emperor was considered the off-spring of the goddess Amaterasu and the earthly representative of Amaterasu's will. Elaborate rituals and ceremonies fostered the notion that the emperor possessed a divine right to rule the nation. When the emperor was on the verge of death, he passed on this mystical power to his sons or brothers. In other words, the emperor's mystical power was passed through his bloodline. Even though Prince Shōtoku was not an emperor, the imperial authorities claimed religious authority through their lineage to him and used that connection to justify entering the sangha and promoting state Buddhism for their own polit-ical interests. Since Shōtoku Taishi was widely venerated both as a great polit-ical and religious figure, imperial and political authorities were successful in claiming that religious authority. Shinran wanted to drive out the imperial and political authorities from the sangha by deemphasizing Prince Shōtoku's polit-ical role and instead emphasizing his religious role as a manifestation of bod-hisattva Kannon. In particular, Shinran stressed the karmic lineage rather than the imperial lineage to Prince Shōtoku. To Shinran, Shōtoku Taishi was pri-marily the father of Japanese Buddhism and a manifestation of bodhisattva Kannon, who compassionately brought the Buddha-dharma to Japan during the age of *mappō*. Unlike other new forms of Buddhism during the Kamakura period, Shinran's Buddhism included Shōtoku worship; though Amida worship remained its primary focus, Shōtoku worship served to legitimize Shinran's innovative teaching.

James Dobbins explains Shinran's attitude toward political authorities as one of ambivalence.[55] Shinran accepted the actions of the authorities against those individuals who freely committed wrongdoing in the name of licensed evil.[56] But he felt it a grave injustice that they did not distinguish between the faithful followers of the *senju nenbutsu* and the adherents of licensed evil. It was probably difficult for the authorities to differentiate Shinran's faithful followers from the adherents of licensed evil since both rejected the traditional forms of religion in favor of undivided devotion to the *senju nenbutsu* teaching. Perhaps the only *senju nenbutsu* advocates exempted from suppressive measures were those who preached the necessity of good deeds *(kenzen shōjin)*, which, from Shinran's point of view, was no truer a path to Pure Land than licensed evil was. Hence, Shinran referred to the local lords, constables, and overseers who could not understand the difference as persons without sight and without hearing. Dobbins examines Shinran's antagonism toward the emperor and political authorities, which he dared to write in the postscript of the *Kyōgyōshinshō*: "The emperor and his ministers, acting against the dharma and violating human rectitude, became enraged and embittered. As a result, Master Genkū—the eminent founder who had enabled the true essence of the Pure Land way to spread vigorously [in Japan]—and a number of followers, without receiving any deliberation of their [alleged] crimes, were summarily sentenced to death or were dispossessed of their monkhood, given [secular] names, and consigned to distant banishment. I was among the latter."[57] Although he refrained from directly and publicly attacking the emperor and political authorities regarding their abuse of political power, Shinran's life and writings following his exile reveal a strong reaction against their oppressive policies and the promotion of the emperorship through the sangha.

## SHINRAN'S ATTITUDE TOWARD SHINTŌ *KAMIS*

Shinran was a Buddhist who did not compromise his beliefs. He strove to keep Buddhism free of the influence of the state and the mixing of traditional Buddhist rituals and practices with aspects of Shintō. In the chapter *Keshindō* of the *Kyōgyōshinshō*, following his counsel against "believing in the deva gods," Shinran condemns certain astrological practices. The historical Buddha was the first to point out that the reliance on *kamis*, astrological signs, and so forth presented an improper escape from one's own personal responsibilities and ethical practices. Shinran also considered such beliefs in *kamis* as hindrances to individual moral and ethical conduct. He believed that they represented a furtherance of the interests of the ego, since man appeals to the *kamis* to order the world to his own liking. And in time, the *kamis* he appeals to become the products of his own illusions, whereby he transforms favorable experiences into the actions of beneficent deities and unhappy experiences into the machinations of evil spirits. Ultimately he loses all control over his own destiny and is swayed by chance events, taking no hand in ordering his own life to avoid the results of improper *karma* (actions). Thus, as a product of self-effort, faith in other buddhas, bodhisattvas, or *kamis* cannot continue after *tariki* (Other-power, i.e., Amida's) faith has been established.[58]

Shinran's attitude toward Shintō was apparently not favorable. In one of his hymns he lamented: "How deplorable it is that both priests and lay people observe auspicious times and lucky days. They worship the *kami*s of heaven and earth, and perform divination and Shintō ceremonies *(saishi)*." Shinran considered the worship of Shintō *kamis* to be one of a vast array of beliefs and practices aimed at securing worldly benefits and avoiding calamity. Others included propitiation of ghosts and evil spirits; divination of good and evil; belief in auspicious days, times, and directions; and observance of taboos *(monoimi)*, in the form of seclusion or abstinence to avoid misfortune. These elements, Shintō and otherwise, had long been integrated into the established forms of religious behavior that *kenmitsu* Buddhism affirmed. Worldly concerns were well mixed with the transcendent goals of Buddhism that, in the popular consciousness, all merged into a seamless tissue of religious behavior. Shinran, however, did not agree with this worldview. Rather, he singled out certain elements of Shintō for acceptance and others for rejection. Reverence for the Shintō *kamis* fell into the latter group, which he classified as "falsehoods, teachings lying outside the pale of Buddhism" *(gekyō jagi)*. The harshness of his language suggests that he regarded such practices as blatant heresy.

It is important also to understand that Shinran himself did not encourage followers to denigrate other buddhas, bodhisattvas, or *kamis*.[59] On the contrary, he saw such denigration as offensive and certainly not the product of faith. The philosophy of assimilation was not to be wholly abandoned. In his writing, Shinran indicated that reciting the nembutsu was in effect honoring the *kamis* and obtaining their protection. In a letter addressed to all followers in the Kantō, dated by scholars at 1254 or 1255,[60] Shinran admonished:

> To scorn buddhas and bodhisattvas and to denigrate Shintō *kami* and spirits is something that should never be. Over countless rebirths and lifetimes, by means of the aid of innumerable and unlimited buddhas and bodhisattvas, people have undertaken all types of beneficial religious practices. Nonetheless, these people have not escaped this world of samsara through any efforts of their own, and so buddhas and bodhisattvas have urged them forward over many *kalpas* of lifetimes. Because of their urging, these people have not encountered Amida's vow, which is extremely difficult to encounter. But, not realizing their indebtedness for this, they speak ill of buddhas and bodhisattvas. Surely it is that they do not realize their profound indebtedness to them.

The *kami* of heaven and earth watch over people who have a profound faith in the Buddhist teachings, accompanying them as if they
took the form of their shadow. Therefore, if people have faith in the
nembutsu, they should never entertain thoughts of disclaiming the
*kami* of heaven and earth. If the *kami* are not to be discarded, then
how much less should they speak ill of or look down on buddhas and
bodhisattvas. If people speak ill of buddhas and bodhisattvas, then
they are individuals who utter Amida's name without having faith in
the nembutsu.

In short, it is only to be expected that lords, constables, and overseers in the area, speaking falsehoods and inclined toward error,
should now take measures to suppress the nembutsu aimed at nembutsu followers. Among the sayings of the Śākyamuni Tathāgata, it is
said that someone who reviles those practicing the nembutsu is a person without sight or a person without hearing. Master Shan-tao (Jpn.
Zendō) accurately interpreted these words, saying: "In this age when
the five corruptions abound, doubt and revilement are widespread.
Priests and lay people alike are filled with abhorrence, and have lost
their ability to hear. When they see people adhering to religious practices, they are filled with poisonous hatred. On some pretext they
work havoc upon them, and endeavor to vent their hostilities." This is
a common occurrence in our world. Local lords, constables, and overseers of the area seem to be those who would obstruct the nembutsu.
Nonetheless, you should not say things against them. Rather, people
who practice the nembutsu should have compassion and feel pity for
those who would pose obstructions, and they should say the nembutsu
fervently, hoping that Amida will save even those posing these obstructions. Our (illustrious) predecessors have taught this to us. You
should reflect on it well.[61]

This passage is particularly revealing, for it shows Shinran's attitude not only
toward followers denigrating *kamis* and buddhas but also toward the authorities
who sought to suppress the nembutsu. It is clear that Shinran does not de-
nounce the observance of *kamis* because he sees them as working together to
help believers of nembutsu. However, Shinran clearly states that those who
suppress the nembutsu are deaf and blind. They are ignorant of the "indebtedness" they have toward Amida Buddha. Shinran encourages other believers to
have compassion on such people and pray that Amida will save even them.
Shinran seems to be accepting the fact that people were living in times of *mappō*
and that it was meaningless to fight against the ignorant authorities who
refused to acknowledge the validity of the *senju nembutsu* teaching.

Instead of denigrating *kamis* and buddhas, Shinran urged his followers to integrate the vast pantheon of Shintō and Buddhist deities into their spiritual practices. Shinran acknowledged the existence of these deities and even ascribed a minor role to them in Amida's grand scheme to deliver all living beings into the Pure Land. Since they helped and protected people during the countless lifetimes of their journey toward Amida's teachings, the believer's natural response to them should be a sense of indebtedness. But ultimately Shinran viewed these deities as subordinate to Amida and overshadowed by his promise of salvation to all sentient beings. Shinran lamented that people often became fixated on these *kamis* and buddhas without comprehending the message of Amida's vows. Moreover, Shinran urged people to turn to Amida single-mindedly. Faith in Amida is the ultimate religious state; it frees a person from any need to worship or supplicate other *kamis* or buddhas, but by no means should it inspire a person to denigrate them.

In Shinran's judgment, gratitude, not only to Amida but also to other buddhas, bodhisattvas, and *kamis*, and even to one's religious teacher and fellow believers, is a way that faith can manifest itself in a person. Shinran thus implies that devotion to other buddhas, bodhisattvas, or *kamis* may be included within *tariki* faith.[62] In the verses of the *Genzeriyaku wasan*, Shinran himself pays respects to other *kamis* within nembutsu:

> When one chants "Namu Amida Butsu," Brahma and Indra pay homage and all the good deva *kamis* protect him day and night. When one chants "Namu Amida Butsu," the Four Guardian Deities together protect him day and night, keeping evil spirits away. When one chants "Namu Amida Butsu," the *kamis* of earth pay homage. And just as the shadow pursues the object, they protect him day and night. When one chants "Namu Amida Butsu," the Dragon King and multiple dragon *kamis* pay homage to the devotee and protect him day and night. When one chants "Namu Amida Butsu," King Yama pays homage and together with the Judges of the Five Existences, protects him day and night. When one chants "Namu Amida Butsu," the king of the *Parānirmita vasavartin* heaven appears before Śākyamuni and makes his pledge to protect. All the *kamis* of heaven and earth should be called good spirit *kamis*. Together these good *kamis* all protect the man of the nembutsu. The faith of incomprehensible vow-power is the great mind of enlightenment. The evil spirit *kamis* who fill Pure Land and earth all fear that faith.[63]

Here the practitioner receives the mind of Amida, and within that mind everything in harmony with enlightenment is reflected. The difference is that the nembutsu follower goes through Amida to show respect or veneration for other buddhas, bodhisattvas, and *kamis*. Shinran writes in one of his letters that "those who profoundly believe in the dharma are protected by the *kamis* of Pure Land and earth." He particularly stresses that it has been through the guidance of the buddhas, bodhisattvas, and *kamis* that *tariki* faith has been established; therefore the follower is bound to be grateful and express thanksgiving. In short, Shinran believes that all the buddhas, bodhisattvas, and *kamis* are manifestations of enlightenment.

# Conclusion

The objective of this study is to demonstrate the importance of Shōtoku worship in Shinran's Buddhism. From his 190 *wasans* that were dedicated specifically to Shōtoku Taishi, there is no question that Shinran profoundly worshiped Shōtoku as a manifestation of the bodhisattva Kannon, who compassionately appeared in Japan to guide beings to the Pure Land path just as the world was entering *mappō*. In one of his hymns, Shinran referred to Shōtoku Taishi as *guze* Kannon. The timing of Shōtoku Taishi's birth also coincided with the timing of *mappō*, which furthered strengthened Shinran's belief in Prince Shōtoku as a manifestation of the bodhisattva Kannon. Traditional Shin scholars have overlooked Shōtoku worship in Shinran's Pure Land Buddhism because of their concern for maintaining a pure doctrine free from the addition of indigenous elements, and perhaps due to the subjective nature of Eshinni's account of Shinran's dream. However, as evidenced from his *wasans* in praise of Shōtoku, the fact remains that Shinran's conversion experience at Rokkakudō did play an important role in the subsequent development of his innovative teaching, which was propagated to the masses during the Kamakura period and after. This study investigates the relationship between Shinran and Shōtoku in order to better understand the unique and complex nature of Shinran's Buddhism and the context in which it arose.

To understand the evolution of Shōtoku worship in Japanese history, I traced the provenance and development of Shōtoku legends from the ancient period. In an effort to portray the image of Prince Shōtoku as the great imperial ancestor who legitimized their claim to the throne, imperial and political authorities in the early period sponsored the compilation of two official historical records, the *Nihon shoki* and *Kojiki*. However, when we examine ancient sources that were sanctioned by imperial authorities, the various discrepancies and lack of historical information about the figure of Shōtoku Taishi raise serious doubts about whether he truly existed.

My investigation into the historical and legendary status of Shōtoku Taishi has led me to agree with some scholars, such as William Deal and Ōyama

Seichi, that Shōtoku may have been a fictional character who was invented and promoted for religious and political agendas. In examining the various sources that describe Shōtoku Taishi, one cannot help seeing that, for the most part, the compilers of the ancient and medieval sources on Shōtoku painstakingly and effectively constructed Shōtoku legends that became very real in the minds of the Japanese people. For that reason, the central question should not be whether the existence of Shōtoku is true or fictitious, but rather the more significant question of why Shōtoku was invented and promoted, and by which individuals or groups. To answer this question, I used a synchronic study model[1] in the spirit of Kuroda and Satō to take a closer look at the religious and political culture of the three periods, Nara, Heian, and Kamakura, to better understand the context in which the Shōtoku legends were developed. I also traced the evolution of Shōtoku legends from the ancient to the medieval period through a close examination of all forms of relevant material from those periods—*engis*, rituals, practices, paintings, sculptures, embroideries, hymns, Shinran's writings—that dealt with Shōtoku themes.

In medieval sources, the attempts to dramatize Shōtoku intensified with the development of *honji suijaku*—the synthesis of the Shintō and Buddhist pantheons. Medieval sources, like *Shōtoku Taishi denryaku* and *Jōgū Shōtoku Taishi den hoketsuki*, continued to expand on the legendary qualities of Shōtoku's achievements to further promote Shōtoku as a Buddhist divinity. In the *Jōgū Shōtoku Taishi den hoketsuki*, for instance, Shōtoku is presented as a kind of shamanistic, supernatural being, and then elevated to the status of a Buddhist saint, combined with the attributes of a native guardian *kami*. A thorough integration of the worship of Shōtoku as both *kami* and incarnation of bodhisattva Kannon is achieved through the proliferation of Shōtoku legends in association with Shintō images. The meaning of *Taishi shinkō* (Shōtoku cult) was broadened through the notion of *Jingi shinkō*, where Shintō *kamis* are viewed as the incarnation of *bosatsu*. People worshiped Shōtoku in the image of a child in Buddhist temples and shrines, in accordance with the belief that a child, having unlimited potential, had some closer affinity with the sacred. For instance, *Shōtoku Taishi denreki* records an account of how the young Prince Shōtoku miraculously transformed himself into a *kami* before the enemy's eyes in order to bring them to surrender and submit to his authority. *Taishiden* also explains that Shōtoku's respect for *kami* and reference to the relationship of *ujigami* and *ujiko* as guardian *kami* and children were widely accepted in *Shingi-shinkō* (idea of respecting *ujigami*). In other words, *Shingi-shinkō* helped to promote *Taishi shinkō*.

The unique phenomenon of *honji suijaku* teaches us that the compilers and visionaries of the *Taishi shinkō* cult cleverly integrated their indigenous Shintō beliefs of *kami* with a Chinese version of Buddhism in the early Nara period, which evolved into a more "Japanese version" in the Heian and Kamakura periods. In this regard, modern Shin Buddhists owe a debt of gratitude toward the compilers of the *Taishi shinkō* cult because they successfully created an effective means of promoting Chinese Buddhism by formulating an intricate mythology and mystique surrounding the charismatic—albeit fictional—personage. In the figure of Shōtoku Taishi, Toyotomi Umayado, Prince Shōtoku, the father of Japanese Buddhism, the originator of the Japanese Constitution, and the reincarnation of the Chinese T'ien-t'ai patriarch Hui-ssu, the manifestation of *guze* Kannon, they have provided a very well-packaged brand of Japanese Buddhism, which has survived the early periods of its provenance and has continued to evolve into rich and diverse forms of expression in the Japanese culture. The old and new schools of Buddhism—Pure Land, Zen, Nichiren, Shingon, and older Nara schools—need not argue about superiority or inferiority, but instead celebrate the rich diversity in the expressions of Japanese Buddhism, which is nestled in the fabric of *honji suijaku* culture and shares the commonality of Shōtoku worship.

Of the several new schools of Buddhism that emerged during the Kamakura period, Shinran's Buddhism was widely embraced by the masses because Shinran incorporated *honji suijaku* in connection with *Taishi shinkō* into his version. By the Kamakura period, *Taishi shinkō* was well ingrained in the minds of Japanese people; Shinran's emphasis on Shōtoku worship thus played a vital role in legitimizing his innovative teaching even though it had been banned as heresy by *kenmitsu* Buddhism. The *honji suijaku* culture was prevalent and remained influential throughout the medieval period because it served as the underlying ideology that legitimized the claims of ruling authorities. Similarly, Shinran legitimized his new teachings through the medieval Shōtoku cult in the same way that the *kenmitsu* establishment (i.e., *kenmon taisei*), consisting of the Fujiwara court, Kamakura shōgunate, and powerful temples, legitimized their power within the fabric of the *honji suijaku* culture.

Whereas imperial families in Japan have traditionally justified their rule by emphasizing their imperial lineage to Prince Shōtoku and passing on the emperorship through blood lineage, Shinran tried to deemphasize the importance of imperial lineage and strongly emphasized the spiritual and karmic lineage of Prince Shōtoku. Hence, Shinran promoted the worship of Shōtoku primarily as the founder of Japanese Buddhism and manifestation of Kannon rather than as an imperial ancestor and great political figure. In other words, Shinran did not support the worship of Shōtoku within the framework of state Buddhism that was promoted by the imperial and political authorities.

By promoting the worship of Shōtoku Taishi, Shinran was calling people of all sectors, both religious and political, to reform. Shinran regarded the era of Shōtoku Taishi as the ideal and model age for Japan, when *ōbō* and *buppō* were in harmony and the nation was ruled by a righteous Buddhist ruler who sought to faithfully govern the country according to the dharma. By using the image of Shōtoku Taishi as an example, Shinran was indirectly criticizing the emperor of his day for not ruling the nation according to the dharma, although Shinran directly criticized "the emperor and his ministers" in the postscript of the *Kyōgyōshinshō*, which was censored by the Japanese government in publications before World War II. Shinran's veneration of Shōtoku Taishi thus reveals his strong nationalistic identity. By promoting the worship of Shōtoku Taishi as the direct incarnation of Kannon, Shinran was essentially cutting off the historical transmission of Buddhism from Korea and China by establishing a direct karmic lineage to Kannon. Japanese Buddhism would no longer be indebted to Korea or China or India, but solely to the ideal Buddhist ruler and *cakravartin* in Japan, Prince Shōtoku Taishi, whom Shinran regarded as the *guze* Kannon during *mappō*.

Closer examination of Shōtoku legends of the ancient and medieval periods reveals that Shōtoku appeared often in the rhetoric of ruling authorities in their attempts to establish legitimacy. Applying Max Weber's works on legitimacy and authority, my bedrock thesis is that Shōtoku was effectively used by both political and religious authorities to establish the legitimacy of their rule and authority. I believe that Shōtoku is the key figure for helping us better understand the political and religious agendas that existed in the minds of the early and later compilers of Shōtoku legends. The interesting aspect of Shōtoku is that he embodied both political and religious interests by his linkage to the imperial family through his royal ties and his designation as the father of Japanese Buddhism. The legend of Prince Shōtoku is based on a very complex and thorough web of creative inventions. The imperial court clearly went to great lengths to substantiate their claim of imperial authority and rule by way of composing a mythology, false but effective, that hypnotized the Japanese for generations. The early works, *Nihon shoki* and *Kojiki*, played an important role in laying down the foundation of the mythical narratives that explained not only the origin of the Japanese people and its land, but also the creation of a figure that became the source of legitimacy for centuries to come. With the timely entry of Buddhism, the newly formed sangha, based on Mount Hiei and Mount Kōya, joined the imperial court in the effort to promote Shōtoku worship because their livelihood was largely dependent on their legitimization through their connection to Shōtoku. In their efforts to promote Shōtoku as the father of Japanese Buddhism, he became the spiritual ancestor who was an incarnation of Hui-ssu, and was then manifested in Japan as Shōtoku, who was actually the incarnation of Kannon.

Shōtoku enabled the imperial court to claim its divine lineage and legitimize the changing political policies of the government, particularly through the Seventeen-Article Constitution, whose true purpose was to centralize authority and promote the power and authority of the emperor, based on the Chinese model. During this time, Japan wanted to follow the Chinese bureaucratic system, but needed someone, more than an ordinary man but one descended from the imperial line, to be the focal point for bringing about change. Shōtoku served many purposes in this regard.

Shōtoku legends began to evolve as Buddhism received the patronage of the government, and they were gradually assimilated into the belief system of indigenous *kamis*, known in its early stages as *shinbutsu shūgō* and fully expressed in the medieval period as *honji suijaku*. By the beginning of the Heian period, Shōtoku became a *kami* and was also regarded as a manifestation of the bodhisattva Kannon. *Taishi shinkō* continued to evolve during the Heian period as Prince Shōtoku was transformed from the "after-body" or manifestation to a *honji*. For instance, Shōtoku's own manifestations became such personages as Emperor Shōmu, Kūkai, and Rigan Daishi. The *honji* of Shōtoku also developed, known not only as Hui-ssu in China, but also as *Dainichi Nyorai* (Sk. *Vairocana*). Meanwhile, temple establishments compiled their own versions of historical records in the form of *engi*, which contained mythical allusions and *Jātaka*-like stories that portrayed Prince Shōtoku as an incarnation of the bodhisattva Kannon. Moreover, the worship of Shōtoku as a reincarnation of the female form of the bodhisattva Kannon became an effective way of legitimizing female claim to the throne and attracted many female devotees to the Pure Land path. All these factors paved the way for the development of an effective and powerful source of political legitimacy through Shōtoku worship in the medieval period.

The key issue here is not whether the existence of Shōtoku Taishi in Japanese history is true or false. For the sake of argument, if we were to simply agree that Shōtoku Taishi was a fictitious character, the focal point of a mass conspiracy that has captured and paralyzed the Japanese people, it does not change the fact that so many people have been influenced by their belief in his actual existence. Their faith in and worship of this figure is meaningful and significant. Our task is to understand how that belief influenced their acts and shaped history. This study leads to a few important points. First, the imperial court played a significant role in formulating the rhetoric, the conspiracy itself, that captured the imagination of the Japanese people. The Japanese seem to have unquestioningly followed the rhetoric of the imperial court, even though it went against logic. That rhetoric revolved around the mystique and wonder of the emperor and the imperial court, with all its pomp and circumstance and pageantry. Second, we learn that people want to know their roots and will be satisfied with lofty tales, even if they are the inventions of creative writers. In addition to the issue of Shōtoku Taishi, it would be useful to study the origin of Shintō. The fact that there is no trace of the origins of Shintō or its founder hints that it also was a story invented by the compilers to fill the imagination of the people, using whatever was possible in their context, such as stories of deities like Amaterasu, Susanoo, Ninigi—all gods whose primary connection is the agricultural society in early Japan. Third, even though Japanese people may borrow ideology from other countries, they still want to make it their own, as in the case of Buddhism and the promotion of Shōtoku as the father of Japanese Buddhism.

An important insight from this work is that the term "Japanese Buddhism" is in itself significant. From the time of the inception of the Chinese culture in Japan during the early seventh century, the Japanese imperial authorities played a groundbreaking task of creating, establishing, and developing the Chinese form of Buddhism that they received through Korean Buddhist envoys to suit their indigenous needs, particularly to unify the nation during a period of political dissension and instability among aristocratic conservatives. This group resisted all foreign influences and moderates, like the Soga family who advocated a new order based on a Chinese makeover to provide a solid foundation for the new emerging Japanese nation and identity. It is no surprise, then, to see that Japanese Buddhism was sponsored by imperial authorities who endeavored to establish and shape their own version of state Buddhism. This form of Buddhism assimilated political and religious aspects of Chinese culture and Buddhism, but still maintained its Japanese identity by simply but painstakingly integrating Buddhism with the native Shintō.

Another significant point is that the very character of Japanese Buddhism includes *kami* worship and is thus syncretic by nature. From the perspective of pure and sectarian Buddhists, *kami* elements, specifically the worship of Shōtoku, may be viewed as a form of heresy *(itan)*, as Kuroda argues. But if one understands that the very character of Japanese Buddhism contains *kami* worship and Buddhist ideals, then, from the perspective of nonsectarian Japanese Buddhists, the element of *kami* worship is actually a reflection of the orthodox character of Japanese Buddhism. This explains the fact that virtually all of the new schools of Buddhism that emerged during the Kamakura period were accused of heresy at some point in their early development.[2] My thesis claims that all the new forms of Kamakura Buddhism, Zen and Nichiren, contain an aspect of Shintō tradition, whether Shōtoku worship in Pure Land Buddhism or the presence of Shintō guardian deities in Zen and Nichiren schools of Buddhism—all stem from the same pool of Shintō and reflect the monistic *kami* worship in Japanese culture. In other words, to fully understand Japanese Buddhism, one must understand not only the Japanese context but also the Japanese culture. Japanese culture and Buddhism are inextricably linked.

While some people have a clear allegiance to one or another sect, there are many features of popular devotion of *kami* worship that cut across sectarian distinctions. Continuing studies on the Shintō aspects in Zen, Nichiren, and Shingon schools may likely confirm that all the new forms of Buddhism in the Kamakura period contained some integrated aspect of *kami* worship. Many Buddhist temples were constructed with Shintō figures, such as the Lokapala or Yaksha guardian deities one finds surrounding Zen temples; Kishimojin who appears in the twenty-sixth chapter of the Lotus Sutra and is venerated in Nichiren circles; Kariteimo in Shingon Buddhism as auspicious protectorate deities of children and mothers; and, the cult of Hachiman,[3] the Japanese Shintō god of war, and divine protector of Japan and the Japanese people. The deity of Hakusan also played an important role in medieval Buddhism, and was one of the key elements in the territorial expansion of the Sōtō sect.[4] The *Genkō shakushō* contains, in the section on "gods and immortals" *(shinsen)*, information about five great Japanese *kami*, who play an important role in esoteric Buddhism: Amaterasu, Hakusan Myōjin, Nyū Myōjin, Shiragi Myōjin, and Tenman Daijizai Tenjin. Its author, Kokan Shiren (1278–1346), was well versed in the Buddhist esoteric tradition, and his work reflects the influence of the *honji suijaku* theory.[5]

Sectarian scholars may attempt to create divisions and dissension among Zen, Nichiren, and Pure Land and even Shingon Buddhists in their effort to preserve some pure teachings of the founder's vision. But following the tradition of the Protestant Reformation advocated by such scholars as Hara Katsurō, the three dominant schools of Japanese Buddhism can now find a reason to celebrate their common heritage and unique expression of Japanese Buddhism without subordinating one expression to another. We can appreciate diversity within the unity of religious belief in Japanese Buddhism. Diverse expression but unified belief, in this case Shintō and Buddhism, provided a new but effective ideology that benefited Japanese society. Shintō's monistic character enabled a smooth and noncompeting process of joining Shintō and Buddhist ideals in Japanese Buddhism. Shintō aspects and the worship of *kami* enabled Buddhism to gain popular support, and attention to Buddhist figures, such as Kannon, Chinese and Indian patriarchs, Hui-ssu, and Śrī-mālā, who would have been more of an obscure figure since Buddhism was a foreign religion, came to take central place in the Shintō-Buddhist character of Japanese Buddhism through the *honji suijaku* phenomenon.

We may be criticized by religious followers who are sensitive to the inclusion of nonsectarian elements, such as the *kami* worship, in their Pure Land Buddhist tradition. There is cognitive dissonance here, but no need for real concern. Since all branches of Buddhism in Japan came from the same tree, there is no need for doctrinal disputes, especially in regard to the Shōtoku worship or other forms of *kami* worship that have been part of the religiosity and mythology of Japanese Buddhism from its inception. Sectarian scholars may find this problematic because of their concern with heretical teachings, and also because of their belief in the superiority of their school of thought or idealized understanding of their founder. However, different branches of Buddhism in Japan should be regarded as siblings, children of the same parental form of Buddhism. This includes the aspect of Shōtoku worship, which is not only one of the salient characteristics of Shinran's Buddhism, but of all Japanese Buddhism. Another related point is the importance of understanding Buddhism within the context, the *honji suijaku* culture, in which it arose. For many years, the Japanese had to recognize the syncretic nature of Japanese Buddhism, but now Buddhists can begin to think about the true meaning of Buddhism that transcends any cultural adaptations.

Through Shōtoku worship, Shinran provided a distinctive bridge between the old and new Buddhist forms. Although he did not quite achieve the status of a Buddhist divinity, Prince Shōtoku was widely regarded as the father of Japanese Buddhism. Because of his charismatic persona that was captured in the Shōtoku sources, both old and new Buddhist forms acknowledged him as their spiritual forefather who was attributed *kami* status by virtue of his significant contributions made as prince regent and promoter of Buddhism in Japan. Again, the key issue is not whether Shōtoku was a true historical figure, but that Shōtoku was a legendary figure in the minds of all Japanese people. Also, if one adheres to the theory that new Buddhist forms were merely an expression of old Buddhist forms, then Shōtoku worship remained a constant presence in the sangha. The distinction of "old" and "new" Buddhist forms strongly suggests that the emergence of the new forms of Buddhism during the Kamakura period—Pure Land, Zen, and Nichiren—were rather revolutionary, independent, and grassroots movements in response to the alleged corruption of the old Buddhist forms. However, as Kuroda and Satō reinterpret such sectarian interpretations, these new forms were actually an outgrowth of the continuous and sustaining presence of the *kenmitsu taisei* or mainstream Buddhism, where all the founders of the new Buddhist forms—Hōnen, Shinran, Dōgen, Eisai, and Nichiren—received their spiritual training and ordination on Mount Hiei. Out of their concern for excluding nonsectarian aspects, modern Shin Buddhists tended to deemphasize the important role that Prince Shōtoku played in Shinran's teachings. But given the ample references made by Shinran and other prominent medieval figures—emperors, retired emperors, shōguns, Saichō, Kūkai, and others—one must seriously consider the fact that Prince Shōtoku was indeed the common denominator not only for the Buddhist sangha but also for all of Japanese society. With this in mind, we may reenvision the Kamakura period not as a time when new Buddhist forms developed separate and sectarian movements, but as a "blossoming" period of Buddhist expression within the fabric of the *honji suijaku* culture of the medieval period in Japan. It is also important to keep in mind that Zen, Nichiren, and Pure Land Buddhism originated from the Tendai center at Mount Hiei. Although he was not the central character, Prince Shōtoku, as a legendary and charismatic figure, played an important role in maintaining a sense of unity among differing factions as well as providing legitimacy.

# Appendix A

## Selected Sources
## on Shōtoku Legends

For primary sources, I examine the complete collection of Shinran's writings: *Kōtaishi Shōtoku hōsan* (Hymns in Praise of Prince Shōtoku), *Dai Nihon koku zokusan ō Shōtoku Taishi hōsan* (Hymns in Praise of Shōtoku Taishi, minor ruler of the great kingdom of Japan), *Jōgū Taishi gyoki* (Account of Prince [Shōtoku] of the upper palace), which are compiled in the five-volume work, *Shinshū shōgyō zensho;* the *Kyōgyōshinshō* (Teaching, Practice, and Realization), which is a compilation of passages from the sutras and Pure Land writings of India, China, and Korea; *Jōdo monrui jushō* (Passages on the Pure Land Way), his second systematic prose work, and *Tannishō* (A Tractate Deploring Heresies Against True Faith).

Primary sources for understanding the evolution of Shōtoku legends in Japan are divided into two categories: ancient and medieval. For ancient sources, two important sources provide historical facts regarding the life of Shōtoku Taishi: the *Nihon shoki* (Chronicles of Japan, 720) and the *Jōgū Shōtoku hōō teisetsu* (The Imperial Record of Shōtoku, Priestly-Prince of the Upper Palace). The *Nihon shoki* was commissioned by imperial authorities and compiled by members of the court and aristocracy about one hundred years after the death of Shōtoku.

Also written by imperial command during the Heian period, *Jōgū Shōtoku hōō teisetsu* is another early biographical source on Shōtoku Taishi. This text is the oldest biography of Shōtoku Taishi; it was composed mostly during the eighth century by an unknown author. The *Jōgū Shōtoku hōō teisetsu* reveals the importance of Shōtoku as both ruler and Buddhist and is primarily a Buddhist biography because it emphasizes Shōtoku's Buddhist activities, such as temple building and sutra study.

Although these two biographical sources were both written at imperial command, in part to legitimize claims of the imperial family's right to rule, they remain significant because they have served as the foundation for subsequent interpretations of Shōtoku's life and times. Consequently, since both sources were written at least one hundred years after Shōtoku's death, we must be mindful not to confuse claims about historical facts with the glorification of Shōtoku's political and religious achievements. Still, for the purpose of this study, these two sources help us to better understand the meaning of Shōtoku's image in different historical periods, and how that image was utilized to promote state Buddhism and the political interests of the ruling authorities during ancient and medieval Japan.

The *Jōgū kōtaishi bosatsuden* is another ancient source on the biography of Prince Shōtoku. This text is an important source because it is a more objective account. This is because Shitaku, a disciple of Chien-chen, did not write it by Imperial command but out of his personal initiative.

Another primary source is the *Hōryūji kondō shakasanzonzō* that describes Shōtoku's family and folklore. This source tells us that, during the reign of Go-Sanjo, the place for Shōtoku worship had already been established.

Shōtoku also wrote commentaries on three main sutras, otherwise referred to as the *Sangyōgisho* that can help us to understand Shōtoku's philosophy and knowledge of Buddhism. The *Sangyōgisho* consists of the *Shōmangyō* (*Śrīmālā simhanada sutra*), *Yuimagyō (Vimalakīrti nirdesa sutra)*, and *Hokekyō (Lotus sutra)*.

Other ancient sources regarding the worship of Shōtoku Taishi are the various *engis* (temple records) from the temples that Shōtoku built during his regency. It has been documented that Shōtoku erected a total of forty-six temples, including the famous Shitennōji and the Hōryūji, to promote Buddhism. These temples that were associated with Shōtoku worship kept historical records concerning the founding of their temples, called *engi*, which often included mystical accounts of Shōtoku as the incarnation of bodhisattva Kannon for the sake of legitimization. Closer examination of *engis* helps us to understand the nature of Shōtoku worship and rituals during the ancient and medieval period and explains how Shōtoku legends continued to evolve in mythical proportions with embellishments that served to legitimize the establishment and authority of temple establishments. For instance, I examine the *Zenkōji engi, Goshuin engi*, and *Gangōji engi*, which give us a better understanding of Shōtoku worship by Buddhist institutions.

Edited by Takeuchi Rizo, the *Hōryūji Shaka sanzon zō yakushi nyorai zō kohaimei* records how the temple was founded by Shōtoku and describes those artifacts and treasures related to Shōtoku, which became main objects for rituals performed there. Two other primary sources on Shōtoku Taishi are located at Hōryūji. First, the *Hōryūji garan engi narabini ruki shizaichō* (Lists of Accumulated Treasures from the Hōryū Temple) is the official temple record that explains the origins of the temple and gives us information about how the temple was financed and supported by the state. In addition, at the east pagoda hall of Hōryūji, a more detailed account on the official record of its property is found in the *Hōryūji Tōin engi shizaichō*.

In the *Hōryūji engi*, relics related to Shōtoku were brought by Gyōshin, Tachibana Michiyo, and Kōmyō. In the *Jōgū ōin (Tōin)*, there is an image of the child Shōtoku, which shows how Shōtoku was worshiped simultaneously as a *kami* and as a Buddhist divinity, since the child was a symbolic figure of worship because it possessed the power of potential. Another important relic for ancient study of Shōtoku Taishi is the *Tenjukoku mandara shūchomei*. This is a famous mandara with inscriptions that were dedicated to Shōtoku by his wife and discovered by one of Shinran's disciples. For ancient sources that are more objective and scholarly, we turn to *Shōtoku Taishi den*, which was composed by Myoiji, one of the important scholars of the Nara period at Tōdaiji. Also, there are additional notes on *Shōtoku Taishi den* written in *Shōtoku Taishi heishiden zōkanmon*.

*Sanbōe* is a collection of Buddhist legends in three volumes, compiled for and presented to an imperial princess, Sonshi Naishoinno, who had recently taken vows as a nun. Shōtoku Taishi, whose three different names help us to understand how Shōtoku was worshiped in different ways during his time, is mentioned in the second volume. It is an insightful text that explains how the legend of Shōtoku evolved in different ways to serve the needs of various ruling authorities who used Shōtoku worship to legitimize their authority.

*Shōtoku Taishi denryaku*, edited in 917 by Fujiwara Kanesuke (877–933) and also called *Heishiden*, is a two-fascicle biography of Prince Shōtoku considered to have been written during the middle of the Heian period. The *denryaku* is one of the most important sources to help us to understand medieval worship of Shōtoku Taishi. Many of the key elements in his biography were modeled on those of Shaka (Śākyamuni). For instance, the Buddha's birth was foretold by his mother's auspicious dream of a white elephant, Shōtoku's by that of a golden-hued monk. Shaka was born in a park in the vicinity of his parents' palace, Shōtoku in the equally unlikely setting of the palace stable. Immediately after birth, Shaka took seven steps and declared himself the master of heaven and earth. Shōtoku, at the equally precocious age of two, joined his hands in prayer and, turning to the east, called the Buddha's name, whereupon a tiny vessel containing a relic of the Buddha miraculously appeared in his hands. The appearance of the relic signaled Shaka's recognition of the prince. Like Shaka's seven steps, this moment marked the beginning of Shōtoku's spiritual career. Its compendium, written in the beginning of the Heian period and based on Kashiwadero Ōmi's family diary, *Jōgū Shōtoku Taishi den hoketsuki*, is an important medieval source that describes Shōtoku Taishi's reincarnation as the Chinese patriarch Hui-ssu and Kannon. This is an authoritative source on Shōtoku Taishi, which contains many legends of Shōtoku Taishi and was used as the basis for more legends, or *edens*. This is an addendum to the earlier biography of Shōtoku. Concerning *honji suijaku*, the *Jōgū Taishi shūiki* gives much information. *Kenshin tokugō uketsu* is another good source on *honji suijaku*; so is, *Taishi hon gyoku renshō*. In the *Shōtoku Taishi den shiki*, we learn about the private account of Shōtoku Taishi and the rituals performed around Shōtoku worship during the medieval period.

*Shōtoku Taishi denreki* is one of the most important sources for understanding the medieval worship of Prince Shōtoku. It contains historical accounts of Shōtoku Taishi and images of Shōtoku worshiped as both a superhuman being and a Buddhist saint. I will translate several key sections that give accounts of the evolution of Shōtoku worship through *honji suijaku*.

Another interesting text, in which legends of Shōtoku Taishi are conveyed through pictures and hanging scrolls, is *Shōtoku Taishi eden*, the earliest surviving example of which was painted for Hōryūji in 1069. The *Namubutsu Taishi*, independent statues of the infant Shōtoku calling the Buddha's name, was not created until the early thirteenth century. (The first reference to these statues appears in Azuma Kagami, under the date Jōgen 4 (1210), 11, in *Kuroita Katsumi*, ed., Shintei Zōho Kokushi Taikei, Yoshikawa, 1932, 32, p. 653.) It describes Shōtoku's discovery of the Hōryūji through various drawings on hanging scrolls. It also shows how each religious school during the Kamakura period worshiped Shōtoku Taishi.

Eizon, a reformer within *kenmitsu* Buddhism, wrote a ritual manual called *Taishi kōshiki* to establish the Shingonji School of Saidaiji Nara. Through this manual, we can learn how Shōtoku was worshiped among Shinran's contemporaries in medieval Japan. Another medieval source, the *Jōgū bosatsu hiden*, was composed by Eizon's nephew and tells us about Shōtoku worship in the medieval period.

Another important medieval source on Shōtoku worship is *Kōtaishi godan tantoku*, the ritual manual composed by one of the leading monks of *kenmitsu* Buddhism and a contemporary of Shinran's, Jien, and used as the textual basis for rituals at Shitennōji during medieval Japan. It describes certain rituals on Prince Shōtoku that were conducted at Shitennōji. This source is significant because Jien was a representative of *kenmitsu* Buddhism and the monk who drafted the petition to ban the *senju nenbutsu* teaching of Hōnen and Shinran on the accusation of heresy. Significantly, Jien's own worship of Shōtoku as described in this ritual manual does not seem to differ from Shinran's worship of Shōtoku Taishi, which suggests that the worship of Shōtoku as a manifestation of Kannon was consistent among all Buddhists in medieval Japan.

*Shōbōrinzō* is the compendium of Shōtoku worship composed by the priest Senku, who was the fourth generation abbot of Takada school of Shinshū. Closer examination of the *Shōbōrinzō* reveals a structure that is identical to that found in Shinran's devotional hymns to Shōtoku. One can tell that in the Takada tradition based in the Kanto region, Shinran's way of understanding Shōtoku, and its relationship with Amida Buddha is well preserved. In the year 1325, there is another manual called *Shōtoku Taishiken naimandara*, which is also a text transmitted from Takada school. Finally, *Shinshū shōgyō zensho* was a text, of course, compiled by Shin scholars. It contains all his hymns on Shōtoku Taishi whom he believed to be a manifestation of Kannon and *guze* Kannon.

The close examination of these primary sources represents the first exhaustive study on the Shōtoku cult and will dramatically alter the way Shinran is presently understood.

# Appendix B

---

## A Translation of Shinran's
### *Kōtaishi Shōtoku hōsan*
## (Hymns of Respect to Imperial Prince Shotoku), written in Kencho 7 [1255] at the age of Eighty-three

1

Give reverence to Prince Shōtoku of the country of Japan!
Out of his deep compassion,
Prince Shōtoku brought the profound Buddhist teachings to the people
And was responsible for the spread of Buddhism in Japan.

2

After he ordered the construction of the four sub-temples of Shitennōji,
Prince Shōtoku went into the mountainous forest
In Ōtagi (Kyoto) and made a proclamation.

3

Prince Shōtoku stated that the imperial capital
Would surely be established there sometime in the future.
To commemorate the event,
A hexagonal platform was built on that land.

4

Inside the hexagonal temple (Rokkakudō),
A three-inch-tall, Jambunada golden statue *guze* Kannon
Was placed there for security and protection.


5

After spending several decades in the imperial capital of Nanba
In the Settsu province,
Prince Shōtoku moved to Tachibana,
Where he built the Hōryūji.


6

From the capital of Tachibana, Prince Shōtoku moved again to Nara,
Where he built many more temples
And continued to spread the Buddha's teaching.


7

After the reign of four emperors in Nara,
The capital was moved to Nagaoka for fifty years
And then moved again to Ōtagi.


8

During the reign of Emperor Kammu, in Enryaku 6 (787),
When the capital was being built,
The world-saving bodhisattva of compassion (*guze* Kannon),
Performed miraculous signs for people to behold.


9

The Hōryūji was constructed on the first site,
Which marked the spread of Buddhism in Japan and
Prince Shōtoku's building of many temples and pagodas in various places.


10

In observance of Prince Shōtoku's orders,
The people, along with the imperial family and court officials,
Gave homage and paid their respects at the hexagonal temple.

11

Prince Shōtoku was born
As Queen Śrīmālā in India
And appeared as Master Hui-ssu (Jpn. Eshi) in China.


12

He appeared in China to help people;
He was reborn as both man
And woman five hundred times.


13

He appeared in the Hunan province at Mount Heng to spread the Buddhist
    teaching;
Having experienced tens of incarnations,
He proclaimed Śākyamuni Tathāgata's teaching.


14

He appeared as Master Hui-ssu to help people in attaining liberation;
He was referred to as Master of Southern Mountain
At the Mount Heng temple where the Wisdom sutras were proclaimed.


15

According to the record on his handprint seal,
Prince Shōtoku built a temple in eastern Kyoto
In order to benefit sentient beings.


16

Built in the spirit of dharma at Shitennōji,
The Kōryōji name was given to the temple
Because it was constructed in the Kōryō province.


17

In 593, after moving to the eastern section of the Kōryō region,
Prince Shōtoku built the Shitennōji
And spread the Buddhist teaching everywhere.

18

At this place, it was believed that the Tathāgata came in the past
And declared that he would turn the wheel of dharma
In order to spread the Buddhist teaching.

19

At that time, the honorable Prince Shōtoku made offerings to the
    Tathāgata.
Out of his devotion, he built the temple and pagoda
To honor the Tathāgata.

20

Constructing the statues of the Four Guardian Deities
And spreading the Buddhist teaching,
Prince Shōtoku built the Kyōden-in temple
As a place where enlightenment could be realized.

21

At this place, there is a body of pure water, which is called Kōryō pond.
An auspicious dragon lives there
And protects the Buddhist teaching.

22

In 597, Prince Shōtoku performed rituals for the dragon
On the banks of Tamatsukuri
To propagate the Buddha's teaching.

23

The place is adorned with the seven precious materials;
The dragon is always there.
The pure water, flowing to the east,
Is called "flowering water of white jade."

24

For those who drink the pure water with a heart of compassion,
It becomes a medicine of dharma.
Those who obey the words of Prince Shōtoku humbly draw from its
    flow.

25

The main hall and the pagoda stand in the center,
Facing the eastern gate of the Paradise.
All who make a pilgrimage there once
Will surely attain birth in the Pure Land.


26

Prince Shōtoku placed six grains of relics of the Buddha inside the pillar,
Which is erected in the center of the pagoda;
By doing this, Prince Shōtoku was bestowing benefits
To sentient beings of the six courses.


27

A gilt bronze statue of *guze* Kannon
Is enshrined in the Kyōden-in temple.
After the death of Prince Shotoku, King Seong Myong of Paekche


28

Built the sacred image to express his love and devotion,
And instructed Prince Ajwa, as a royal envoy,
To deliver it to Japan to be used as a memorial.


29

With his own hand, Prince Shōtoku laid gold on the base of the pagoda,
To symbolize the spread
And influence of Śākyamuni's teaching in Japan.


30

When Prince Shōtoku sent Buddhist statues,
Sutras, *vināyas*, treatises,
Robes, monks, and nuns to Japan
From Paekche,


31

It was the year 552,
During the reign of Emperor Kimmei.
For the first time, people in Japan were called upon
To take refuge in Śākyamuni Tathāgata's teaching.

32

The masters of *vināya*, meditation, dharani,
Including monks, nuns, Buddhist sculptors, and temple caretakers
Were brought in the year 577,
During the reign of Emperor Bidatsu.


33

Prince Shōtoku was born in the imperial family;
His edict was declared throughout the provinces.
He instructed the people to build many temples, pagodas, and Buddhist
    images,
To honor the Buddha.


34

Prince Shōtoku, a child of Emperor Yōmei,
Composed three major Mahāyāna commentaries:
The Lotus Sutra, the Śrīmālā Sutra, and the Vimalakīrti Sutra.


35

After the death of Prince Shōtoku,
Those who desire to spread the teaching of Śākyamuni Tathāgata
And help others toward enlightenment
Are to be regarded as manifestations of Prince Shōtoku.


36

Honoring the teachings of the six schools,
Prince Shōtoku helped people incessantly.
Always observing the five precepts,
Prince Shōtoku was called Śrīmālā.


37

When this queen was alive long ago,
Śākyamuni Tathāgata compassionately preached
The Śrīmālā Sutra.

38

Subsequently, Prince Shōtoku gave lectures on this sutra and also wrote a
　　commentary,
Which marked the beginning of the propagation of the Buddhist teaching
　　in Japan
For the benefit of all people here.


39

The Buddha's disciple, Queen Śrīmālā, states that
In Paekche, Koguryŏ, Ninna, and Silla,
Everyone is full of greed and immorality.


40

To conquer these countries and not yield to them
The Four Guardian Deities were sculpted
And enshrined facing westward.


41

The royal emissary, Prince Ajwa,
Brought the gilt bronze *guze* Kannon to Japan
And enshrined it inside the Kyōden-in temple.


42

Always take special care of this statue because
It is the body of Prince Shōtoku!
Worship this statue because
It is the transformed body of Amida Tathāgata!


43

The venerable disciple of the Buddha,
Queen Śrīmālā, entreated the buddhas of the ten quarters:
May Brahma, Indra, the Four Guardian Deities, the Dragon-god,
And other guardians of the dharma protect the Buddhist teaching!

44

Ilra of Silla proclaimed, "Give reverence to the *guze* Kannon,
The king of Zokusan who spread the light of dharma eastward,
And worship the Prince of eight ears."


45

Prince Ajwa of Paekche bowed down and said,
"Give reverence to the *guze* Kannon,
Who spread the wonderful dharma eastward to Japan,
And spread the light of dharma of forty-nine years."


46

In China, Prince Shōtoku's teachers were Master Hui-ssu and Master Hui-wen.
When he was the nun Śrīmālā,
His teacher was Master Hui-ssu.


47

In the thirteenth year of the presence of the dharma,
During the time of the Han Emperor Ming-ti,
The Indian monks Kāśyapamātanga and Dharmaraksa
Came to China, carrying Buddhist scriptures on a white horse.


48

About four hundred eighty years had passed
Since the Buddhist teachings came to Han China
And the "temple of the white horse" was built
On the western side of the capital.


49

During the reign of Emperor Kimmei,
The thirtieth ruler of the great country of Japan,
Buddhist statues and scriptures
Were brought to the court.


50

After more than five hundred years of the presence of the dharma,
During the time of Prince Shōtoku,
The Buddhist teaching spread, now during *mappō*,
The nembutsu is rampant.

51

According to the record on Shōtoku's handprint,
In the first year of Emperor Sushun's reign,
Relics of the Śākyamuni Buddha were presented to the court by
    Paekche.

52

Prince Shōtoku's words were,
"After my death, I will be reborn as the king and queen
Of this land and I will urge all regions and districts

53

To construct many great temples and pagodas
Containing great Buddhist statues.
Many sutras will be copied and
Wealth and land will be donated.

54

Manifesting myself as rich and poor persons,
I will spread the Buddhist teaching and build Buddhist statues;
And born as monks and nuns
I will save sentient beings.

55

This is not for any body else, but my own body."
Each word or expression of reverent praise
Is the golden word of Prince Shōtoku.

56

With regard to bestowing rank of imperial prince,
For the sake of spreading the Buddhist teaching,
He declined several times,
But the emperor would not accept his refusal.

57

When Prince Shōtoku was thirty-three years old,
He composed the Seventeen-Article Constitution
With his own hand
During the fourth month, in the beginning of summer.

58

After he composed the Seventeen-Article Constitution
Set it as the standard for imperial law,
It became the rule for peace and stability for the nation,
The treasure that makes this country flourish.

59

During the second year of Tenki (1054),
While excavating the earth with his hands in order to construct a pagoda,
Chūzen found a box of gilt bronze.

60

The inscription on the lid of the box read,
"This year, 621, an excellent site has been discovered at the Shinaga village,
At Ishikawa in the Kawachi province.

61

I have placed my tomb there
And after four hundred years following my death,
This record will be excavated."

62

In order to spread the Buddhist teaching and help people,
Prince Shōtoku left Mount Heng
And appeared here in Japan where the sun rises.

63

Emerging victorious from the wrong views of Moriya,
Prince Shotoku bestowed the gracious merits of the dharma.
The Buddhist teaching will soon spread all over
And many people will attain birth in the Land of Peace.

64

All those who doubt and reject the teaching given by the Tathāgata
And try to destroy it by using ill tactics
Are reincarnations of Moriya no Mononobe.
Do not be kind and become close to such people!

65

As Prince Shōtoku was proclaiming the Buddha's dharma
To teach and guide people,
Moriya no Mononobe, being the destructive enemy,
Followed him like his shadow.

66

Rebels of Moriya no Mononobe's clan harbored deep malice,
Attempted to destroy the Buddhist teaching by
Burning temples and pagodas.

67

In painful grief during the destruction of the dharma,
Prince asked the emperor with respect
To dispatch soldiers

68

Joining the soldiers with his bow of meditation and arrow of wisdom,
Prince Shōtoku subdued the rebel Moriya
For the sake of all people.

69

There are people who seek to destroy temples, pagodas,
Buddha's dharma and bring disaster and ruin to the nation and people;
Those people are reincarnations of Moriya; they should be rejected and cast aside.

70

The rebel Moriya no Mononobe,
Having gone through innumerable rebirths in the many realms of samsara,
Follows the Prince like his shadow
And is determined to destroy the dharma.

71

Those people who constantly slander the Buddha's dharma,
Lead people astray with their wrong views,
And seek to destroy the teaching of sudden attainment
Are reincarnations of the rebel Moriya.

72

Prince Shōtoku is known by the name, the "Prince of Eight Ears";
He is also known as Prince Umayado, of the "Stable Gate,"
And as Jōgū, meaning "Upper Palace."

73

The Second Article of the Constitution states,
"Revere the Three Treasures!
They provide refuge for all beings of the four modes of birth,
The beam that supports all nations."

74

What world, and what person, will not take refuge?
If they do not take refuge in the Three Treasures,
How can people in this world straighten and correct what is twisted and
    wrong?

75

The petition of the rich
Is like placing stones into water,
The plight of the poor
Is like placing water into stones.

# Notes

## Introduction

1. The second son of first Buddhist Emperor Yōmei, born in the third year of the reign of Emperor Bidatsu, Shōtoku Taishi, his ruling name, became the prince regent in 593 C.E. and helped his aunt Empress Suiko, who ruled from 592–628 C.E. Shōtoku's given name was Mumayado no Toyotomimi; "Mumayado" means stable door. *Nihon shoki* (Chronicles of Japan, 720), ed. Sakamoto Tarō et al., *Nihon koten bukkyō taikei* (68:148). In the *Kōtaishi Shōtoku hōsan* (Hymns in Praise of Prince Shōtoku) of the *Kyō-gyōshinshō* (Teaching, Practice, Faith, and Enlightenment), Shinran refers to Shōtoku Taishi with the following well-known descriptions: "Prince of Eight Ears" because he could listen to eight people at one time; "Prince of the Stable Gate" because the empress was at the stable when she gave birth to him; and "Prince of the Upper Palace" because Prince Shōtoku dwelled in a palace in Tsu province, on the cliff above the east pavilion at Watanobe. He is also known as Toyosatomimi or Kamitsumiyō. In the *Kojiki* (Record of Ancient Matters, 712), his name appears as Kamitsumiya no Umayado no Toyosatomimi no Mikoto and as Umayado no ōji in the *Nihon shoki*. The most popular name—Prince Shōtoku—first appeared in *Kaifuso*, written in 751, more than a hundred years after his death.

2. The concept of "mandate of heaven" *(t'ien-ming)* was used to support the rule of the kings of the Chou dynasty and later the Emperors of China. This political theory asserted that Heaven, *t'ien*, was primarily interested in the welfare of human beings. For this reason, it has established governors and rulers who assume the responsibility for the welfare of their people. It mandates that certain people be in charge; while they rule justly, fairly, and wisely, Heaven maintains that certain rulers or dynasties remain in power. If a dynasty or ruler ceases to rule justly or wisely and begins to rule only with its own self-interests at heart, then Heaven removes the mandate from that ruler and passes it on to another family, who are then required to revolt and overthrow the dynasty. The concept was first used by the Chou dynasty to justify their overthrow of the Shang dynasty and employed by many succeeding dynasties to justify their rule. One consequence of the idea of the Mandate of Heaven was that it was not necessary for a person to be of noble birth to lead a revolt and become a legitimate emperor. James Legge, trans., *The Sacred Books of China: The Texts of Confucianism*, in F. Max Mueller, ed., *The Sacred Books of the East*, 50 vols. (Oxford: Clarendon, 1879–1910), *Vol. 3*, 92–95.

3. *Kami* are sacred powers present throughout the cosmos (sometimes simply the sacredness present in an object), worshiped especially at shrines or *jinja*. In a famous definition, Motoori Norinaga (1730–1801) wrote: "I do not yet understand the meaning of the word *kami*. In its most general sense, it refers to all divine beings on earth or in heaven that appear in the classic texts. More specifically, the *kami* are the spirits abiding in, and worshiped at, shrines. In principle, humans, birds, animals, trees, plants, mountains, oceans, can all be *kami*. In ancient usage, anything that was out of the ordinary, or that was awe-inspiring, excellent, or impressive was called *kami* . . . evil and mysterious things, if they are extraordinary, are called *kami*."

4. 'One who observes the sound (of the World)'; Sk. Avalokiteśvara; one of the two bodhisattvas attending Amida and capable of manifesting thirty-three forms of incarnation to save people in different states of existence, hence attributed with the virtue of infinite compassion. In China and Japan, Kannon (Ch. Kuan-yin) is popularly worshiped as a female deity.

5. In his seminal work, *Nihon chūsei no kokka to shūkyō* (State and Religion in Medieval Japan, 1975), Kuroda Toshio coined the term "kenmitsu" to point out that at the core of what was referred to as "Old Buddhism" *(kyū Bukkyō)*, which consisted of the eight classical schools—the six exoteric schools of Nara (Sanron, Hossō, Kegon, Ritsu, Jōjitsu, and Kusha) and the two schools of Heian (Tendai and Shingon)—were the monasteries that all recognized as orthodoxy the combined study of both exoteric *(ken)* scriptures and esoteric *(mitsu)*, orally transmitted rituals that dominated the religious world in the Heian and Kamakura periods. Kuroda explained that the most prominent monasteries of the Kamakura period all belonged to Old Buddhism, and those monasteries continued to be the wealthiest landholders, while their political thought continued to be the ruling ideology for the shogunate in Kamakura, whose military rule was legitimized by the emperor and his court. Old Buddhism must therefore be considered as the religious mainstream of the Kamakura period. In this manner, the new Buddhist schools of Kamakura—Jōdo and Jōdo Shin schools of Pure Land Buddhism, the Rinzai and Sōtō schools of Zen, and the Nichiren school—are also identified as the mainstream Buddhism of medieval Japan, or *kenmitsu* Buddhism. Kuroda's argument seriously challenged the validity of the very idea of Kamakura New Buddhism. Ryūichi Abé, *The Weaving of Mantra: Kūkai and the Construction of Esoteric Buddhist Discourse* (New York: Columbia University Press, 1999), 406–407.

6. Traditionally, the term "medieval period" refers to the centuries covered by the Kamakura (1185–1333), Nambokuchō (1336–1392), and Muromachi (1333–1573). These four centuries are the "middle years" between the age of classical Japanese culture in the Heian period and the age of commercial townsmen in the Edo period. I use the term "medieval period" to include internal issues and developments within the sangha, particularly the inception of *honji suijaku* thought (i.e., in the latter half of the ninth century). See also note 17 for chapter 4.

7. *Shinjin* is a difficult word to translate with just one word, such as "faith." The key in understanding Shinran's concept of *shinjin* comes from analyzing his commentary on the Eighteenth Vow, which says: "If, when I attain Buddhahood, the sentient beings of the ten quarters, with sincere mind entrusting *(shinjin)* themselves, aspiring to be born in

my land, and saying my Name perhaps even ten times, should not to be born there, may I not attain the supreme enlightenment. Excluded are those who commit the five grave offenses and those who slander the right dharma." Ueda Yoshifumi and Dennis Hirota, *Shinran: An Introduction to His Thought* (Kyoto: Hongwanji International Center, 1989), 185. In Shinran's own words, *shinjin* is "hearing Amida's Vow and being free of doubt, believing deeply and without any double-mindedness that Amida Buddha's Primal Vow is true and real." Here, "hearing" refers to the receptivity and the unfolding of awareness that the practitioner experiences, "being free of doubt" refers to the non-clingingness to one's own calculations, "without any double-mindedness" refers to blind passions, and "believing deeply that Amida Buddha's Primal Vow is true and real" refers to the *shinjin*, described as the "entrusting with sincere mind." Shinran explains that entrusting oneself with sincere mind to the Vow and being free of all attachments to one's own efforts bring practitioners to realize *shinjin* in which Amida's mind and the practitioner's mind becomes one. In other words, *shinjin* is the awakening of the inherent Buddha's mind in beings by Buddha's activity. For further discussion and elucidation of the term, see Kenneth D. Lee, "The Comparative Analysis of Shinran's *shinjin* and Calvin's Faith" in *Buddhist-Christian Studies*, vol. 24 (Honolulu: University of Hawai'i Press, 2004), 171–190.

8. Alfred Bloom, *Shinran's Gospel of Pure Grace* (Ann Arbor: Association for Asian Studies, 1991), ix–xiv.

9. Iyenaga Saburō, *Chūsei bukkyō shisōshi kenkyu* (Tokyo: Hōzōkan, 1947); Sonoda Kōyū, "Heian bukkyō no seiritsu" in *Nihon bukkyōshi*, vol. I, *Kodaihen*, ed. Iyenaga Saburo (Tokyo: Hōzōkan, 1967), 175–240; Inoue Mitsusada, *Nihon kodai kokka no kenkyū* (Tokyo: Iwanami shoten, 1965).

10. Bloom, *Shinran's Gospel of Pure Grace*, 87–88.

11. Akamatsu Toshihide, *Zoku Kamakura bukkyōshi no kenkyū* (Kyoto: Heirakuji shoten, 1957); Shigematsu Akihisa, *Chūsei Shinshū shisō no kenkyū* (Tokyo: Yoshikawa kōbunkan,1974); Fujii Manabu, "Chūsei shūkyō no seiritsu" in *Kōza Nihon bunkashi*, vol. 3, ed. *Nihonshi kenkyūkai* (Tokyo: San'ichi shobō, 1962). The textbook depiction of Japanese history is largely grounded in sectarian historical narratives developed in the early modern and modern periods. This view interprets the development of Japanese Buddhism as a category representing a historical period rather than a classification of a particular type of Japanese Buddhism. In other words, the typological change in the Buddhist establishment—for instance, the new dominance established by Shingon and Tendai—directly corresponds to, or is perhaps even the natural outcome of, the change in political authority. That is, Japanese Buddhist history can be divided into separate periods by means of the periodization used in political history. Thus, according to Sonoda Kōyū, Heian Buddhism, comprising the Tendai and Shingon schools, was a form of Buddhism that flourished under the aegis of the Heian court and maintained its dominance during the historical period of Heian, which began with Kammu's transfer of the capital to Kyoto in 794 and ended when Minamoto no Yoritomo established the Kamakura shogunate in 1192. One of the criticisms of this approach is that it is simply a reductionistic approach, based on unfounded assumptions and a sweeping generalization of Japanese Buddhist history, not to mention its obvious insensitivity toward the internal issues and developments within the sangha. Sonoda Kōyū, "Heian bukkyō no

seiritsu" in *Nihon bukkyōshi*, vol. I, *Kodaihen*, ed. Iyenaga Saburō (Tokyo: Hōzōkan, 1967), 175.

12. Ishida argued that the revival in the studies of doctrine and precepts in the Nara schools, Tendai, and Shingon should be understood as internal developments within the old schools that had begun in the late Heian period. Ishida Yoshito, "Kyūbukkyō no chūseiteki tenkai" in *Nihon bukkyōshi chūseihen*, ed. Akamatsu Toshihide (Tokyo: Hōzōkan, 1967), 292–353. Imai refined Ishida's argument by dividing the Kamakura period into several historical stages and demonstrated that representatives of both New and Old Buddhism formulated their ideas as a means of resolving identical sociohistorical issues. Imai Masaharu, "Nichiren, Ippen, oyobi Eison: Kamakura kōki no bukkyō o megutte" in *Nichirenshū no shomondai*, ed. Nakao Yutaka (Tokyo: Yūzankaku, 1975), 24–27. Takagi conducted a comprehensive review of major Buddhist figures during the Kamakura period that indicated commensurate developments in both New and Old Buddhism. Takagi Yutaka, *Kamakura bukkyōshi kenkyū* (Tokyo: Iwanami shoten, 1982). Kuroda's work focused on the monastic institutions—especially their economic foundations—rather than on Buddhist doctrines. Kuroda Toshio, *Nihon chūsei no kokka to shūkyō* (Tokyo: Iwanami shoten, 1975).

13. "It is often overlooked that the progressive movements of the Kamakura [New] Buddhism at all their historical stages developed through confrontation with Exoteric-Esoteric Buddhism. Shinran, Dogen, Nichiren and other new leaders all advanced their movements not in isolation from Exoteric-Esoteric Buddhism but amidst a religious order that Exoteric-Esoteric Buddhism dominated. In sectarian history, naturally, the thoughts of Shinran and Dogen are explained in relation to their masters, Hōnen and Eisai, and then in the genealogical context of their Pure Land and Zen predecessors in Japan and China. However, in reality, their religions did not develop in such lineage successions. . . . The activities of Shinran, Dogen, Nichiren, Ippen, and all these progressive leaders were conditioned by their relationship to Exoteric-Esoteric Buddhism. That is, all of them began their careers with the traditional study of Buddhism within Exoteric-Esoteric Buddhism, raised doubts about it, and, struggling with words, phrases and logic of the scriptures of the orthodoxy, took their stand against it." Kuroda Toshio, *Nihon chūsei no kokka to shūkyō* (Tokyo: Iwanami shoten, 1975), 114.

14. The term "nembutsu" (Jpn. nenbutsu) has the general meaning of to meditate on a Buddha. In early Buddhism, nembutsu included the practice of contemplation on Śākyamuni Buddha. In the context of Pure Land Buddhism, nembutsu refers to the practice of invoking the name of Amida Budda with the phrase "Namu Amida Butsu" or "I take refuge in the name of Amida Buddha." Hōnen advocated the nembutsu as the one religious act that, when practiced exclusively, could lead any practitioner to be born in Amida's Pure Land during their next rebirth, and there they would achieve enlightenment quickly and easily. In order to assure one's rebirth in the Pure Land, Hōnen is known to have invoked the name of Amida Buddha, "Namu Amida Butsu," as much as 70,000 times per day. In contrast, Shinran advocated that it was not so much the outward practice of the vocal nembutsu that resulted in rebirth in the Pure Land as the state of mind lying behind it, namely, the state of 'sincere mind entrusting' *(shinjin)* in the Primal Vow.

15. Satō Hiroo, *Nihon chūsei no kokka to shūkyō* (Tokyo: Yoshikawa kōbunkan, 1987), 35–51. Taira Masayuki, *Nihon chūsei no shakai to bukkyō* (Tokyo: Hanawa shobō, 1992), 21–37.

16. Satō Hiroo, *Shinbutsu ōken no chūsei* (Tokyo: Hōzōkan, 1998).

17. *Mappō* refers to the degenerative era of Buddhism in the absence of Buddha's wisdom and practice; only the dharma (Buddha's teaching) is present. According to Tao-ch'o, second patriarch (562–645), the year 549 was 1,500 years after the Buddha's parinirvana (i.e., death) and marked the beginning of *mappō-ji*, the period of 'degenerating dharma' predicted in the *Lotus Sutra*, when no one can achieve enlightenment by their own effort *(jiriki)*, but must rely on the Other-power *(tariki)* of Amida Buddha.

18. *Jūshichijō kenpō*, *Nihon shoki*, kan 22, vol. 22, Suiko tennō, 12 nen, 4th month, *Shōtoku Taishi zenshū* 1; *Nihon shisō taikei* 2.

19. Py. Huisi; Ch. Hui-ssu (515–577); the second patriarch of the Chinese T'ien-t'ai (Tendai) sect; also called the Great Nan-yüeh (Nangaku Daishi) because he lived on Mount Nan-yüeh.

20. Also known as Anraku or Anraku-bō. At this time, the priests at Kōfukuji, Enryakuji, and other temples repeatedly petitioned the imperial court to outlaw the Pure Land school. In 1206, when the retired emperor Go-Toba was away from Kyoto on a pilgrimage to Kumano Shrine, Hōnen's disciples, including Gyōku (also known as Jūren) and Junsai held a Nembutsu ceremony at Shishigatani in Kyoto. Some court ladies in Go-Toba's service attended this ceremony and without consent renounced their secular life to become nuns. On learning of this incident when he returned, the retired emperor Go-Toba, angered by such insubordination and disrespect, immediately ordered Gyōku and Junsai to be executed, while Honen and Shinran were sent into exile.

## CHAPTER 1: SHINRAN AND SHŌTOKU

1. Shinran used several names during his lifetime, particularly after he began training as a Buddhist novice. His earliest name was Hannen, and he later called himself Shakku, Zenshin, Fujii no Yoshizane, and finally Gutoku Shinran. He also received the posthumous religious title of Kenshin Daishi, the "Great Master Kenshin," by imperial decree in the Meiji era. For the sake of clarity, his final and best-known name, Shinran, has been used throughout this study.

2. The Hino family was a minor branch of the Fujiwara clan, which dominated political and cultural life at the imperial court in Kyoto for two centuries. The Hino are said to have traditionally served as Confucian scholars. Shinran's father, Arinori, was a low-raking courtier in the office of the empress dowager, and his uncles were also active at court. Nothing is known of his mother, though she was no doubt similarly of aristocratic lineage. Ueda Yoshifumi and Dennis Hirota, *Shinran: An Introduction to His Thought* (Kyoto: Hongwanji International Center, 1989), p. 20.

3. It is said that Shinran received the name Hannen upon becoming a monk. Jien was the younger brother of Kujo Kanezane. He is noted for having been selected head of the Tendai denomination four times, as an outstanding poet, and as the author of *Gukanshō* (Notes of an Ignorant Observer). According to Kikumura, Jien was a religiously oriented politician, and his image as a Buddhist scholar is rather weak while his image as a man of letters is quite strong. Jien, however, had very little spiritual development since there is not even one mention of Jien's name in all of Shinran's writings. Norihiko Kikumura, *Shinran: His Life and Thought* (Los Angeles: The Nembutsu Press, 1983), 62.

4. Hayashima Kyōshō, *Shinran nyūmon* (Tokyo: Yūzankaku, 1979), 15.

5. Ueda Yoshifumi and Dennis Hirota, *Shinran: An Introduction to His Thought* (Kyoto: Hongwanji International Center, 1989), 29.

6. James Dobbins, *Jōdo Shinshū: Shin Buddhism in Medieval Japan* (Honolulu: University of Hawai'i Press, 2002), 14–15.

7. Ueda and Hirota, *Shinran*, 29.

8. In Shinran, the term "*shinjin*" signifies the central religious awakening in the Pure Land path, namely, the awakening of the Buddha's mind that is inherent in all sentient beings upon hearing the Name that embodies the Primal Vow. Shinran equates *shinjin* with the utterance of the Amitābha's name, "Namu Amida Butsu." Shinran explains that, by saying the name, one attains birth in the Pure Land on the basis of Amida Buddha's Primal Vow. Ueda and Hirota, *Shinran: An Introduction to His Thought* (Kyoto: Hongwanji International Center, 1989), 146.

9. The most important teaching of the *Larger Sutra* is the forty-eight vows of Amitābha (Jpn. Amida) Buddha as *Dharmākara* by which he perfects his Pure Land and saves sentient beings. These vows detail the bodhisattva's intention to achieve higher enlightenment and help others to attain birth in Amitābha's Pure Land. Particularly important for specifying the practice of birth in the Pure Land—faith, sincerity, *nembutsu*, and merit accumulation—are vows eighteen, nineteen, and twenty. The Eighteenth Vow became the most important because it provided the minimal requirement for birth, just the reciting of ten *nembutsu*: "If, when I attain Buddhahood, the sentient beings of the ten quarters, with sincere mind entrusting themselves, aspiring to be born in my land, and saying my Name perhaps even ten times, should not be born there, may I not attain the supreme enlightenment. Excluded are those who commit the five grave offenses and those who slander the right dharma." Ueda and Hirota, *Shinran*, 314.

10. *Yuishinshō mon'i* (Notes on Essentials of Faith Alone), *Ichinen tanen mon'i* (Notes on Once-calling and Many-calling), *Shinshū Shōgyō zensho*, vol. 2.

11. Ueda and Hirota, *Shinran*, 41.

12. A hall priest of the highest clerical rank, a *dōsō* practiced Pure Land rituals at Mount Hiei, such as the *Jōgyōdō* or 'Halls of Constant Practice.' Matsuno Junkō, *Shinran: Sono shōgai to shisō no tenkai katei* (Tokyo: Sanseidō, 1959), 2–3, 16–19.

13. In one of her letters to Kakushinni found in 1921, Eshinni writes: "This letter is to certify that your father was a *dōsō* at Mount Hiei, that he left the mountain and confined himself to the Rokkakudō for one hundred days, and that Prince Shōtoku

appeared and showed him the way, while praying for the salvation of all beings, in the dawn of the 95th day." *Eshinni* (Kyoto: Honpa Hongwanji, 1969–70), 34.

14. Takamichi Takahatake, *Young Man Shinran: A Reappraisal of Shinran's Life* (Waterloo: Wilfred Laurier University Press, 1973), 43.

15. *Shinran muki* (Record of Shinran's Dreams), *Teihon Shinran Shōnin zenshū*, vol. 4, pt. 2.

16. *Kyōgyōshinshō, Shinshū shōgyō zensho*, 2: 202; *Eshinni shōsoku, Shinshū shōgyō zensho*, 5: 104–105; and *Honganji no Shōnin Shinran denne, Shinshū shōgyō zensho*, 3: 640. There are two versions of the *Shinran muki*. The first, listing a total of three dreams, is reproduced in Furuta Takehiko, *Shinran shisō: Sono shiryō hihan* (Tokyo: Fuzanbō, 1975), 3–5. The second version, reproduced in *Shinran Shōnin senju kankokai*, ed., *Teihon Shinran Shōnin zenshū*, 9 vols. (Kyoto: Hōzōkan, 1969–70), vol. 4, pt. 2, 201–202, mentions only one dream. It contains a more detailed account of the third dream than the other *Shinran muki* does. One version of this last work describes three dreams that made a lasting impression on Shinran: one occurring in 1191, the second in 1200, and the third in 1201. There are two copies of Shinran's dream, one written by Shinran himself and the other by a disciple (dates of these texts unknown). Found in the Senjuji collection, Mie prefecture, and in *Shinran Shōnin zenshū*, vol. 4, 201–202.

17. *Shōzōmatsu wasan, Shinshū shōgyō zensho* 2: 526–529; *Kōtaishi Shōtoku hōsan, Shinshū shōgyō zensho* 2: 532–541; *Dai Nihon koku zokusan ō Shōtoku Taishi hōsan, Shinshū shōgyō zensho* 4: 23–42.

18. Tasurō Fujishima, "Shōtoku Taishi to Shinran Shōnin," *Nihon bukkyō gakkai nempō*, no. 29 (1963), 265–282.

19. *Kōtaishi Shōtoku hōsan, Shinshū shōgyō zensho*, vol. 2, 229.

20. Jpn. *Enbudangon*; Sk. *Jambū-nada-suvarna*; the purplish gold from the river running through the mango *(jambu)* forest in the *Jambudvīpa*, the southern continent of Mount Sumeru, in Buddhist cosmology.

21. *Taishi byōkutsu-ge, Shinran Shōnin zenshū*, 6: 213; the account of this dream is also in *Shōtoku Taishi denryaku*, 1:71, which contains an explicit identification of Prince Shōtoku as *guze bosatsu* (the world-saving bodhisattva).

22. Sk. *Tathāgata*; Jpn. *nyorai*; "thus-come," a term that is used synonymously with the Buddha, expressing the sense of the "one who has come from thusness."

23. *Kōtaishi Shōtoku hōsan, Shinshū shōgyō zensho*, vol. 2, 229.

24. *Eshinni monjo*, no. 3, *Shinran-Shōnin zenshū*, vol. 3, 186–187. In October 1921, Washio Kyōdō discovered in the archives of Nishi Hongwanji ten extant letters that Eshinni, toward the end of her life in Echigo, wrote to her youngest daughter, Kakushinni, residing in Kyoto. These letters not only document the historical existence of Shinran, but also confirm that a person named Eshinni existed historically and that she was Shinran's wife. See *Eshinni monjo*, no. 3, *Shinran-Shōnin zenshū*, vol. 3, 186.

25. *Shinran muki* (Shinran's Dreams) was discovered in *Senju-ji*, the head temple of the Takada Branch of Shin Buddhism, and, when the author was determined to be

Shinbutsu, a leading disciple of Shinran, the contents of his vision of Prince Shōtoku as a manifestation of bodhisattva Kannon were verified.

26. Reizō Hiramatsu, "Takada hoko shin hakken shiryō ni yoru shiron" in *Takada gakudō*, no. 46 (1959), 14–24.

27. *Shinran muki* ["Record of Shinran's Deram"], *Shinran Shōnin zenshū*, vol. 4, 201; *Honganji Shōnin Shinran denne, Shinshū shōgyō zensho* 3, 640; *Shinran yume no ki*, in *Shinran Shōnin zenshū Kankōkai*, ed., *Teihon Shinran Shōnin zenshū* (Kyoto: Hōzōkan 1969–1970), vol. 3, 640. Interestingly, supporting the legend that Shinran was married to Princess Tamahi, the daughter of the then prime minister, Kujō Kanezane, the expression "holy woman" *(gyokunyo)* is the basis for the name Tamahi (*gyoku* and *tama* in Japanese are identical characters read differently).

28. *Honganji Shōnin Shinran denne, Shinshū shōgyō zensho* 3, 640.

29. In her book, *Kuan-yin*, Yü explains that sexual transformation of Avalokiteśvara (Jpn. Kannon) occurred sometime between the T'ang and Sung dynasty. In the Sung period, the feminine incarnation of Kuan-yin (Perceiver of Sounds) was known as the Fish-basket Kuan-yin (Yu-lan Kuan-yin) or the Wife of Mr. Ma (Ma-lang-fu), discussed in chapter 8 in the story of Princess Miao-shan; Kobayashi Taichirō (1950:3–44) explains that the transformation to a feminine Kuan-yin was a result of the mixture between Buddhism and indigenous Chinese goddess worship during the T'ang and Sung dynasty. Chün-fang Yü, *Kuan-yin: The Chinese Transformation of Avalokiteśvara* (New York: Columbia University Press, 2001), 407–448.

30. Hattori Shisō, *Shinran nōto*, 1948; rpt. (Tokyo: Fukumura Shugppan, 1972). There is, however, some inconclusive discussion about the timing and number of the marriage(s). Legend says that Shinran married Lord Kujō Kanezane's daughter, Tamahime, in Kyoto, but there is no conclusive proof, especially since there is no such name found in the Kujō family geneology. Recent studies have shown that this legend originated from the Kantō community of Shinran's followers and first appeared in *The Secret Transmission of the Biography of Shinran* during the Muromachi period (1338–1573). There seems to be some shreds of evidence indicating that Shinran's marriage took place in Echigo, presumably with Eshinni. Compare, for instance, in the postscript of the *Kyōgyōshinshō*, the phrase "I am therefore neither monk nor layman" *(sō ni arazu zoku ni arazu)*, written about the fact of his exile, has the feeling of having been composed by a married person. It also implies that Shinran was not "neither monk nor layman" when he was training with Hōnen in Kyoto, which means that he continued to follow all the Buddhist precepts, including celibacy. The phrase "neither monk nor layman" also supports the theory that Shinran entered the married life after he was exiled as a common criminal and returned to lay status, no longer having to observe the precepts, especially celibacy. On the other hand, Kasahara believes that Shinran's marriage to Eshinni took place in Echigo, and that this was his second marriage; during the Kamakura period, it was a common practice for people to have several wives. Kasahara Kazuo, *Shinran to tōgoku nōmin* (Tokyo: Yamakawa Shuppansha, 1957). In any case, there is no conclusive evidence. Regarding an extensive study on Eshinni's background, see Hattori Shisō's *Zoku Shinran nōto*, 1950; rpt. (Tokyo: Fukumura Shuppan, 1970).

31. Although his teacher, Hōnen, never married, he advised: "People should always live by creating the proper condition for being able to say the nembutsu. If you cannot say the nembutsu as a celibate, say it by getting married. If you cannot say it by being married, say it as a celibate. If you cannot say it while remaining at one place, say it was you wander on your travels. If you cannot say it on your travels, say it at home. If you cannot say it while securing your daily necessities, say it by having others obtain them for you. If you cannot say it by others obtaining the necessities for you, say it by securing them yourself. If you cannot say it by yourself, say it with together with friends and comrades. If you cannot say it with other people, say it by yourself confined at home. Food, clothing, and shelter are necessary only in so far as they create the proper condition for people to say the nembutsu." Hōnen, 1133–1212, *Senjakushū: gendaigoyaku*/Hattori Eijun Yakuchū (Tokyo: Daitō Shuppansha, 1980), 102.

32. Kakunyo (1270–1351), the grandson of Shinran, played an important role in the formation of the early Jōdo Shinshū community at Honganji as one of the first interpreters of Shinran's thought, laying the foundation for later doctrinal interpretation.

33. *Eshinni monjo*, no. 3, *Shinran-Shōnin zenshū*, vol. 3, 186–187.

34. *Kōtaishi Shōtoku hōsan, Shinshū shōgyō zensho* 2:532–541, 526–527; *Dai Nihon koku zokusan ō Shōtoku Taishi hōsan, Shinshū shōgyō zensho* 4.23–42; Shinran's *Jogu Taishi gyoki, Shinshū shōgyō zensho* 4:5–21, which is dated 1257, is a transcription of the Shōtoku Taishi legend from Minamoto Tamenori's tenth-century work, the *Sanbōe* (Three Treasures).

35. Dennis Hirota, *The Collected Works for Shinran*, Vol. II (Kyoto: Jōdo Shinshū, 1997), 100. Nāgājuna (Jpn. Ryūju), a second- or third-century Mahayana scholar of southern India and founder of the Mādhyamika (Middle Way) doctrine, who is revered in Japan as the "founder of the eight school"—Kusha (Dharma Analysis Treasury), Jōjitsu (Establishment of Truth), Ritsu (Precepts), Hossō (Dharma Characteristics), Sanron (Three Treatises), Kegon (Flower Garland), Tendai, and Shingon (True Word); Vasubandhu (Jpn. Seshin or Tenjin), a fourth- or fifth-century Buddhist scholar in India, who wrote a thousand works, consisting of five hundred Hinayana and five hundred Mahayana works; T'an-luan (Jpn. Donran, 476–542), founder of the Chinese Pure Land school, who received the Amitāyus sutra from Bodhiruchi at Lo-yang; Tao-ch'o (Jpn. Dōshaku, 562–645), second patriarch in the Pure Land school in China, known to have lectured on the *Amitāyus sutra* two hundred times; Shan-tao (Zendō, 613–681), third patriarch of the Pure Land school in China, who disseminated the chanting of Amida Buddha's name at the capital Ch'ang-an; Genshin (Eshin, 942–1017), originally a priest of the Tendai school in Japan, who practiced nembutsu on Mount Hiei; Hōnen (Genkū; 1133–1212), founder of the Pure Land (Jōdo) school in Japan.

36. *Shōzōmatsu wasan* (Hymns of the Dharma-Ages), 1258, *Teihon Shinran Shōnin zenshū*, vol. 2 (Kyoto: Hōzōkan, 1969).

37. *Kōsō wasan* (Hymns of the Pure Land Masters), 1248, *Teihon Shinran Shōnin zenshū*, vol. 2 (Kyoto: Hōzōkan, 1969).

38. Ibid.

39. *Kōtaishi Shōtoku hōsan* (Hymns in Praise of Prince Shōtoku), *Shinshū shōgyō zensho*, vol. 2, Hymns 11–14.

40. Ibid., Hymn 30.

41. Ibid., Hymns 32–38.

42. Ibid., Hymn 11.

43. Ibid., Hymns 41–46.

44. Ibid., Hymn 66.

45. Ibid., Hymns 62–71.

## CHAPTER 2: THE LEGENDS OF SHŌTOKU

1. Yōmei was the fourth child of Emperor Kimmei (540–571). Prince Shōtoku's mother, Anahobe Hashihito was also a daughter of Kimmei, by a daughter of Soga Iname; she was Yōmei's half-sister. *Nihon shoki, Nihon koten bukkyō taikei* (68:148).

2. *Nihon shoki, Nihon koten bukkyō taikei* (68:148). Soga no Umako put his niece Suiko on the throne after he murdered his own reigning nephew. Suiko (554–628) was a daughter of Kimmei, a full sister of Yōmei, and Bidatsu's consort. Umako chose her to replace Sushun, and Shōtoku Taishi's selection as regent was also based on close family ties: the prince's grandmothers on both sides were Umako's sisters, and one of his wives was Umako's daughter. Sakamoto Tarō, *Shōtoku Taishi* (Tokyo: Yoshikawa kōbunkan, 1979), 37–39.

3. The body of law adapted from the T'ang administrative *(ritsu)* and penal *(ryō)* codes. The core of the *ritsuryō* regime consisted of literati—officials of the imperial court who were trained in the Confucian educational curriculum at the Daigaku, or state college. These officials treated the Buddhist clergy as if it were a government bureaucracy subordinate to their own, in accordance with a division of the *ritsuryō* termed the *Soniryō*, or Rules for Priests and Nuns. Ryūichi Abé, *The Weaving of Mantra: Kūkai and the Construction of Esoteric Buddhist Discourse* (New York: Columbia University Press, 1999), 4.

4. Composed in Chinese in 604 C.E., the Seventeen-Article Constitution is the first major work of political theory in Japan. The only source of the Seventeen-Article Constitution, the *Nihon shoki* (*Nihon koten bukkyō taikei* 68) tells us that Prince Shōtoku, the imperial consort, was its author. While some Western scholars question this attribution, there is little reason to doubt the Japanese account of their history. The seventeen articles are as follows:

    I.    Harmony is to be valued, and an avoidance of wanton opposition to be honored. All men are influenced by class-feelings, and there are few that are intelligent. Hence there are some who disobey their lords and fathers, or who maintain feuds with the neighboring villages. But when those above are harmonious and those below are friendly, and there is concord in the discussion of business, right views of things spontaneously gain acceptance. Then what is there which cannot be accomplished!

II.    Sincerely revere the three treasures. The three treasures, Buddha, the Law and the Priesthood, are the final refuge of the four generated beings, and are the supreme objects of faith in all countries. What man in what age can fail to revere this law? Few men are utterly bad. They may be taught to follow it. But if they do not betake them to the three treasures, how shall their crookedness be made straight?

III.    When you receive the imperial commands, fail not to obey them scrupulously. The lord is Heaven, the vassal is Earth. Heaven overspreads, and Earth upbears. When this is so, the four seasons follow their due course, and the powers of Nature obtain their efficacy. If the Earth attempted to overspread, Heaven would simply fall in ruin. Therefore when the lord speaks, the vassal listens; when the superior acts, the inferior complies. Consequently, when you receive the imperial commands, fail not to carry them out scrupulously. Let there be a want of care in this matter and ruin is the natural consequence.

IV.    The ministers and functionaries would make decorous behavior their leading principle, for the leading principle of the government of the people consists in decorous behavior. If the superiors do not behave with decorum, the inferiors are disorderly; if inferiors are wanting in proper behavior, there must necessarily be offenses. Therefore it is that when lord and vassal behave with propriety, the distinctions of rank are not confused; when the people behave with propriety, the Government of the Commonwealth proceeds of itself.

V.    Ceasing from gluttony and abandoning covetous desires, deal impartially with the suits that are submitted to you. Of complaints brought by the people there are a thousand in one day. If in one day there are so many, how many will there be in a series of years? If the man who is to decide suits at law makes gain his ordinary motive, and hears causes with a view to receiving bribes, then will the suits of the rich man be like a stone flung into water while the complaints of the poor will resemble water cast upon a stone. Under these circumstances the poor man will not know where to take his complaints. Here too there is a deficiency in the duty of the minister.

VI.    Chastise that which is evil and encourage that which is good. This was the excellent rule of antiquity. Conceal not, therefore, the good qualities of others, and fail not to correct that which is wrong when you see it. Flatterers and deceivers are a sharp weapon for the overthrow of the state, and a pointed sword for the destruction of the people. Sycophants are also fond, when they meet, of dilating to their superiors on the errors of their inferiors; to their inferiors, they censure the faults of their superiors. Men of this kind are all wanting in fidelity to their lord and in benevolence towards the people. From such an origin great civil disturbances arise.

VII.    Let every man have his own charge and let not the spheres of duty be confused. When wise men are entrusted with office, the sound of praise arises.

If unprincipled men hold office, disasters and tumults are multiplied. In this world, few are born with knowledge: wisdom is the product of earnest meditation. In all things, whether great or small, find the right man, and they will surely be well managed. On all occasions, be they urgent or the reverse, meet but with a wise man, and they will of themselves be amenable. In this way will the state be lasting and the Temples of the Earth and of Grain will be free from danger. Therefore did the wise sovereigns of antiquity seek the man to fill the office, and not the office for the sake of the man.

VIII. Let the ministers and functionaries attend the court early in the morning and retire late. The business of the state does not admit of remissness and the whole day is hardly enough for its accomplishment. If, therefore, the attendance at court is late, emergencies cannot be met. If officials retire soon, the work cannot be completed.

IX. Good faith is the foundation of right. In everything let there be good faith, for in it there surely consists the good and the bad, success and failure. If the lord and the vassal observe good faith one with another, what is there which cannot be accomplished? If the lord and the vassal do not observe good faith toward one another, everything without exception ends in failure.

X. Let us cease from wrath and refrain from angry looks. Nor let us be resentful when others differ from us. For all men have hearts, and each heart has its own leanings. Their right is our wrong, and our right is their wrong. We are not unquestionably sages, nor are they unquestionably fools. Both of us are simply ordinary men. How can any one lay down a rule by which to distinguish right from wrong? For we are all, one with another, wise and foolish, like a ring that has no end. Therefore, although others give way to anger, let us on the contrary dread our own faults, and though we alone may be in the right, let us follow the multitude and act like them.

XI. Give clear appreciation to merit and demerit and deal out to each its sure reward or punishment. In these days, reward does not attend upon merit nor punishment upon crime. All you high functionaries, who have charge of public affairs, let it be your task to make clear rewards and punishments.

XII. Let not the provincial authorities or the Kuni no Miyako levy exactions on the people. In a country there are not two lords; the people cannot have two masters. The sovereign is the master of the people of the whole country. The officials to whom he gives charge are all his vassals. How can they, as well as the government, presume to levy taxes on the people?

XIII. Let all persons entrusted with office attend equally to their functions. Owing to their illness or to their being sent on missions, their work may sometimes be neglected. But whenever they become able to attend to business, let them be as accommodating as if they had had cognizance of it from before, and not hinder public affairs on the score of their not having had to do with them.

XIV. All you ministers and functionaries! Be not envious. For if we envy others, they in turn will envy us. The evils of envy know no limit. If others excel us in intelligence, it gives us no pleasure; if they surpass us in ability, we are envious. Therefore it is not until after a lapse of five hundred years that we at last meet with a wise man, and even in a thousand years we hardly obtain one sage. But if we do not find wise men and sages, how shall the country be governed?

XV.    To turn away from that which is private and to set our faces toward that which is public—this is the path of a minister. Now if a man is influenced by private motives, he will surely feel resentments, and if he is influenced by resentful feelings, he will surely fail to act harmoniously with others. If he fails to act harmoniously with others, he will surely sacrifice the public interests to his private feelings. When resentment arises, it interferes with order, and is subversive of law. Therefore in the first clause it was said that superiors and inferiors should agree together. The purpose of that first clause is the same as this.

XVI.    Let the people be employed (in forced labor) at seasonable times. This is an ancient and excellent rule. Let them be employed, therefore, in the winter months, when they are at leisure. But from Spring to Autumn, when they are engaged in agriculture or with the mulberry trees, the people should not be so employed. For if they do not attend to agriculture, what will they have to eat? If they do not attend to the mulberry trees, what will they do for clothing?

XVII.   One person should not make decisions on important matters alone. They should be discussed with many. But small matters are of less consequence. It is unnecessary to consult a number of people. It is only in the case of the discussion of weighty affairs, when there is a suspicion that they may miscarry, that one should arrange matters in concert with others so as to arrive at the right conclusion. [Translated by W. G. Aston, *Nihongi* (London: Kegan, Paul, Trench, Trubner, 1896); *Nihon koten bukkyō taikei* 68:117.]

5.  What the *kami* consists of is hard to pin down. *Kami* first of all refers to the *kamis* of heaven, earth, and the underworld, of whom the most important are creator *kamis*— all Shintō cults, even the earliest, seem to have had an extremely developed creation mythology. But *kami* also are all those things that have divinity in them to some degree: the ghosts of ancestors, living human beings, particular regions or villages, animals, plants, landscape—in fact, most of creation, anything that might be considered wondrous, magnificent, or affecting human life. This meant that the early Japanese felt themselves to be under the control not only of the clan's principal *kami*, but by an innumerable crowd of ancestors, spiritual beings, and divine natural forces. As an example of the potential for divinity, there is a story of an emperor who, while traveling in a rainstorm encountered a cat on a porch that waved a greeting to him. Intrigued by this extraordinary phenomenon, the emperor dismounted and approached the porch. As soon as he reached the porch, a bolt of lightening crashed down on the spot his horse was standing and killed it instantly. From that point on, cats were, in Shintō, worshipped as beneficent and protective *kami*. R. Tsunoda et al., *Sources of Japanese Tradition*, vol. I (New York: Columbia University Press, 1958), 22.

6. The term *tennōsei* is used by contemporary scholars, Futaba Kenkō in his *Tennōsei to shinshū* (Kyoto: Nagata bushodō, 1991) and Kobayashi Toshio in his *Kodai tennōsei no kisoteki kenkyū* (Tokyo: Azekura shobō, 1994). The *Tennō* or emperor is a member of the clan descended from the Sun Goddess *Amaterasu*; all divinities owe their origin to *Amaterasu* for she gave birth to them. Since the *Tennō* clan is derived from the first of the *kamis*, it is only natural that they should have dominion over other clans, just as *Amaterasu* has precedence over other *kami*. The *Tennō* himself is directly descended from *Amaterasu*, and so is a "manifest *kami*," or *kami* on earth; it is this *kami*-nature that legitimizes his personal rule. The *Tennō* rules the state as the medium between the clans and *Amaterasu*. Part of the *Tennō*'s functions is to attend the shrines of the sun goddess and receive her judgments on government through oracles, dreams, and so forth. The clans remain semiautonomous, but the word of the *Tennō* represents the will of *Amaterasu* and is to be obeyed by all. Allan G. Grapard, *The Protocol of the Gods: A Study of the Kasuga Cult in Japanese History* (Berkeley and Los Angeles: University of California Press, 1992), 59. Thus, the Seventeen-Article Constitution exhorted people to lay aside partisan differences and accept imperial rule to achieve social harmony.

7. Grapard explains that Heaven, as exemplified by the regular procession of the heavenly bodies, represented an unvarying order, which served as the norm for life on earth. Grapard, *Protocol of the Gods*, 62.

8. Article II of the Seventeen-Article Constitution. W. G. Aston, trans., *Nihon shoki: Chronicles of Japan from the Earliest Times to A.D. 697* (London: George Allen & Unwin, 1956); *Nihon koten bukkyō taikei* 68:117.

9. Jātaka tales are the stories of the previous lives of the Śākyamuni Buddha. The Pali canon contains a collection of 547 such stories, which describe the benevolent acts carried out by Śākyamuni in previous lifetimes, which enabled him to be reborn as the Buddha in India.

10. Satō Hiroo, *Nihon chūsei no kokka to shūkyō* (Tokyo: Yoshikawa kōbunkan, 1987), 23–25.

11. The underlying spiritual theme of these three sutras is the *Mahāyāna* concept of the universality of the Buddha nature and the collective practice of developing this common potential for Buddhahood into a progressive enlightenment for all beings (known as the *ekāyāna* or "singular vehicle" doctrine)—a theme also present in such noted *Mahāyāna sutras* as the *Prajñāpāramitā* literature, the *Avatamsaka sutra*, the *Aparimitāyus* ("Larger *Sukhāvatī-vyūha*") sutra and the *Mahāparinirvāna sutra*. This singular-vehicle doctrine (Japanese: *ichiji shishō*) stressed the universality of the Buddha nature, which means that all beings possess the inherent capability to achieve enlightenment, not by mere practice for each individual effort, but by practice as dedication of merit and action for mutual benefit of the collective human effort to achieve enlightenment. *Nihon koten bukkyō taikei* (68:189); *Shōtoku Taishi denryaku* in *Dai Nihon bukkyō zensho*, vol. 1 (Tokyo: Suzuki Gakujutsu Zaidan, 1972), 95.

12. Preserved in the *Tenjukoku shuchō* or *Tenjukoku mandara* of the Chūgūji Temple; *Shōtoku Taishi denryaku* (1:112).

13. These *engi*s were important documents that temples used to associate themselves with state-sponsored temples, which was important for various reasons. For one, state-sponsored temples received financial support from the government to pay for their maintenance. The *engi* was an important source not only for the temple's identity and history to be passed on to later generations but also for justifying their karmic connection to Prince Shōtoku and bodhisattva Kannon.

14. *Taisho shinshū Daizōkyō* 3:1–52, 85 vols., Takakusu Junjirō, Watanabe Kaigyoku, et al., eds. (Tokyo: Taishō issaikyō kankōkai, 1924–1934).

15. Kimmei 13, *Shōtoku Taishi denryaku* 1:113. Gangōji, the Soga temple founded by Prince Shōtoku and Empress Suiko, was known as Asukadera and Hōkōji. According to legend, the Gangōji was the first Buddhist monastery ever established in Japan. The original site, now a Shingon temple, is in Asuka-son, Takaishi-gun, Nara-ken. "Shin" Gangōji, in Nara proper, was founded in 718, in conjunction with the building of the capital city, and was regarded as one of the Seven Great Nara Temples.

16. Fujii Yukiko, *Shōtoku Taishi no denshō: imēji no saisei to shinko* (Legend of Shōtoku Taishi: Belief and Reincarnation of the Image) (Tokyo: Yoshikawa kōbunkan, 1999), 317.

17. He first published his two books in 1913 and 1919, then revised by other people and published as three new books based on his two, *Nihon Jōdaishi no kenkyū* (Research of Japanese History) in 1947 and *Nihon koten no kenkyū* (Research of Japanese Classical Literature) in 1948 for volume one and 1950 for volume two with Iwanami shoten as the publisher.

18. Tsuda Sōkichi, *Nihon koten no kenkyū* (Research of Japanese Classical Literature), vol. 2 (Tokyo: Iwanami shoten, 1950), 26.

19. Ibid., 27.

20. Ōyama Seiichi, *Nihon shoki no kōn* (Tokyo: Heibonsha, 2003), 19–20.

21. Ibid., 408.

22. Ibid., 211.

23. Ibid., 229.

24. Ibid., 231.

25. Ibid., 238.

26. Fujii, *Shōtoku Taishi no denshō*, 318.

27. Ibid., 319.

28. Ibid., 323.

29. Ibid., 358.

30. Ekisai Kariya, "Awaharāji rohanmei" in *Kokyō ibun* (1818), *Kokuritsu kokkai toshokan shozōbon* (Tokyo: Hōbundō, 1893), 361.

31. Akamatsu Toshihide, *Shitennōji no shoseki* in *hihō*, vol. 3 (Tokyo: Kōdansha, 1968), 364.

32. Yoshida Kazuhiko, *Nihon kodai shakai to bukkyō* (Tokyo: Yoshikawa Kōbunkan, 1995), 96.

33. Fukuyama Toshio, *Nihon kenchikushi kenkyū* (Tōkyō: Bokusui Shobō, 1968–1971), 98.

34. Ōyama, *Nihon shoki no kōsō*, 213.

35. Ibid., 214.

36. Ibid., 13.

37. Ibid., 224.

38. Ibid.

39. Ōta Masahiro, *Jōgū Shōtoku hōō teisetsu yume monogatari*, vol. 2 of *Ōta Masahiro Chōsakushū* (Tokyo: Sanage jinjashi kankōkai, 1966), 94.

40. Ibid., 231–233.

41. Ibid., 237–238.

42. Hori Ichirō, "Mysterious Visitors from the Harvest to the New Year," in Richard Dorson, ed., *Studies in Japanese Folklore* (Bloomington: University of Indiana Press, 1963), 76–77; Robert S. Ellwood, *The Feast of Kingship: Accession Ceremonies in Ancient Japan*, *Monumenta Nipponica* monograph 50, 1973, 3.

## Chapter 3: Images of Shōtoku in Early Japan

1. There were two leaders of the coup d'état in 645. One was Nakatomi Kamatari, whose family was Fujiwara. The other was a prince of the reigning family who occupied the throne only briefly from 668 to 671 under the name of Tenchi. Edwin O. Reischauer, *Japan: The Story of a Nation*, 3rd. ed. (New York: Alfred A. Knopf, 1981), 20–24.

2. When the court recognized the stranglehold the Nara schools were beginning to assume and planned the move of the capital to Kyoto, the institutionalized forms of existing Buddhism suffered a defeat. The Nara schools had depended on the court for financial roots. The institutionalized forms of Buddhism had reached a certain impasse and thus a second period of Buddhism arose in Japan. In view of the development of the religious ideals of Buddhism, the transfer of the court to Kyoto was actually a blessing in disguise. (Interestingly, this move of the capital was predicted by Shōtoku who supposedly had supernatural attributes to have foreknowledge of the future.) If Buddhism was to survive, it had to make contact with the common people and win their support. This was difficult for the Nara schools, for with the exception of the Kegon school, they represented monastic-like institutions with little ability to appeal to the aspirations of the common people.

3. One of the main reasons the emperor sent Saichō to many missions to China was to gain the legitimacy through Chinese forefathers in order to establish state Bud-

dhism on Mount Hiei. Consequently, Saichō personally venerated Shōtoku Taishi as the incarnation of bodhisattva Kannon and relied on Shōtoku Taishi as an important source for legitimizing the new Tendai center at Mount Hiei. Saichō's effort to legitimize his Tendai faction through Shōtoku Taishi was encouraged by the imperial authorities who attempted to promote state Buddhism. Yuki Yoshifumi, *Shōtoku Taishi shinkō in nihon tendai* (Tokyo: Kokusho kankōkai, 1986), 142.

4. Alicia and Daigan Matsunaga, *Foundation of Japanese Buddhism. Vol. I: The Aristocratic Age* (Los Angeles: Buddhist Books International, 1974), 110.

5. *Shōtoku Taishi denryaku* (1:106–107). This belief was first disseminated by one of Ganji's disciples during the Nara period. Hui-ssu died in 577, three years after *Shōtoku* Taishi's birth.

6. *Shōtoku Taishi denryaku* (1:106–107).

7. Yuki, *Shōtoku Taishi shinkō no nihon tendai*, 142.

8. The sections on Shōtoku Taishi in the *Nihon shoki* in *Nihon koten bungaku taikei*, vol. 68 (Tokyo: Iwanami shoten, 1965), are placed in the historical context, which narrates the history of Japan, beginning with the Shintō mythological creation accounts to the reign of Empress Jitō in 697 C.E. Shōtoku is placed within the larger context of the political and religious struggles occurring during the Asuka period (538–710). It is also important to keep in mind that the *Nihon shoki* was compiled at imperial command about one hundred years after Shōtoku's death in 622, allegedly, in part to legitimize claims of the Fujiwara family's right to rule, so the accounts of Prince Shōtoku's life and achievements represent an "authorized biography." In contrast, the *Jōgū Shōtoku hōō teisetsu* in *Dai nihon bukkyō zensho*, vol. 71 (Tokyo: Suzuki Gakujutsu Zaidan, 1972) also reveals the importance of Shōtoku as imperial regent and founder of Buddhism in Japan but is primarily a Buddhist biography because it emphasizes Shōtoku's Buddhist activities, such as temple building and sutra study. William E. Deal, "Hagiography and History: The Image of Prince Shōtoku" in George J. Tanabe, Jr., ed., *Religions of Japan in Practice* (Princeton: Princeton University Press, 1999), 318.

9. *Nihon shoki*, 593 C.E. Summer, 4th Month, 10th Day, *Nihon koten bukkyō taikei* (68:172–173); *Shōtoku Taishi denryaku* (1:71–72).

10. *Jōgū Shōtoku hōō teisetsu*, *Dai Nihon bukkyō zensho*, 101.

11. *Shōtoku Taishi denryaku* (1:72). This description of Shōtoku's quick understanding of the dharma points to his inherent Buddha-nature. Tamenori, in his *Sanbōe*, later added that "by the age of four months he (Shōtoku) spoke with great skill. At dawn on the fifteenth day of the second month of the following year, without any encouragement, he seated himself, placed his palms together, faced the east, and prayed, chanting 'Nam-butsu' (I call upon the name of Buddha)." Edward Kamens, *The Three Jewels: A Study and Translation of Minamoto Tamenori's Sanbōe* (Ann Arbor: Center for Japanese Studies, 1988).

Another point to consider is the title of *hōō* or 'dharma-emperor' given to Shōtoku. The title of *hōō* refers to the Indian title of *cakravartin* (Py. *cakkavatti*) or "wheel-turner" or "ideal virtuous ruler" who possessed Buddha-nature. The *hōō* is a sacred figure whose charisma is second only to the Buddha's. His personal charisma not only calls forth the wheel from the depths of the ocean, but also draws other classic treasures, which crystallize his rule, such as the elephant, the horse, the jewel, the banker, and the general. (Dialogues of the Buddha III. Vol. IV of Sacred Books, p. 60: *Digha Nikaya* III, xxvi, 2–3). His authority is also established by a kind of heroic conquest, which is carried out by the power of dharma rather than by military force, meeting with the enthusiastic approval of earthly kings and admiration of the people. Frank Reynolds, *The Two Wheels of Dhamma: A Study of Early Buddhism* (Chambersburg: American Academy of Religion, 1972), 20–21.

12. Hori Ichirō explains that *hijiri* (holy men) began to appear in large numbers from the eleventh century and played an important role in spreading Buddhist teachings and practices beyond temple walls and in areas outside the urban centers. Some of these men had abandoned their positions within the major temples, dissatisfied with their practice or disillusioned by the worldliness that pervaded the ecclesiastic institutions; Others had never been formally ordained to begin with, having shaved their heads, donned monk's robes, and pursued their activities without government authorization. Many such wandering monks withdrew to secluded temples or huts where they meditated, chanted sutras, and performed austerities, sometimes adopting Shintō and native folk religious practices to cultivate spiritual powers. Often, however, they went down to the cities or traveled the countryside, guiding laypeople by giving sermons and leading worship and chanting. Those who followed a mendicant life lived by begging, stopping before houses to recite passages from sutras or incantations for warding off misfortune. At times they performed rites for the dead or to cure illness, and some collected contributions for temples they had formed affiliations with, to be used for construction or for an image or bell. Hori Ichirō, "On the Concept of Hijiri (Holy-Man)," *Numen* 5, 2–3 (1958): 128–160; 199–232.

13. This story appears in *Nihon shoki* (*Nihon koten bukkyō taikei* 68: 198-200), dated 613, in *Shōtoku Taishi denryaku* (1:102–103), and in both *Jōgū Taishi hōō teisetsu* and *Shōtoku Taishi den hoketsuki*, and also in *Nihon ryōiki*. Each of the versions is slightly varied in form.

14. The following section is a summary of Sey Nishimura's "The Prince and the Pauper: The Dynamics of a Shōtoku Legend" in *Monumenta Nipponica*, Vol. 40, no. 3 (Autumn, 1985), 299–310.

15. Tsuda Sōkichi, *Nihon Koten no kenkyū* (Tokyo: Iwanami shoten, 1972), 118. Tsuda's view is supported in Tamura Enchō, "Shōtoku Taishi Kataokayama Kisha Setsuwa" in *Bukkyō bungaku kenkyū*, April 1965, 28, and Sakamoto Tarō, "*Nihon shoki* to Shōtoku Taishi no denki" in *Koten no rekishi* (Tokyo: Yoshikawa kōbunkan, 1972), 48.

16. Sekiguchi Shindai, *Daruma no kenkyū* (Tokyo: Iwanami shoten, 1973), 208–209.

17. Kuranaka Susumu, "Shōtoku Taishi Kataoka Setsuwa no Keisei" in *Man'yo*, 10 (1966), 23.

18. Kōjō, "Denjutsu Isshin Kaimon" in *Taishō shinshō daizokyō* (Tokyo: Taishō issaikyō kankōkai,1964), 653.

19. Ryōyo, "Kashima Mondo" in *Zoku gunsho ruijū* (Tokyo: Zoku gunsho ruijū kanseikai, 1941), 33, 140.

20. *Shinran Shōnin zenshū*, vol. 3 (Tokyo: Shinran Shōnin zenshū kankōkai, 1957), 269–270.

21. *Genkō shakushō, Shintei zoho kokushi taikei* (31:27); Ogisu Jundo, "Shōtoku Taishi to datsuma nihon dorai no densetsu o megutte" in *Shōtoku Taishi kenkyū*, ed. Nihon bukkyō gakkai (Kyoto: Heirakuji shoten, 1964), 297–309.

22. *Jōgū Taishi hōō teisetsu, Dai nihon bukkyō zenshū*, 101.

23. Sakamoto Tarō, *Shōtoku Taishi ronshū* (Tokyo: Hyakuji shoten, 1971).

24. Sonoda, *Shōtoku Taishi* (*Bukkyo gakkai*, 28th year of the Meiji period).

25. Kumei Kunitake, *Jōgū Taishi jitsuroku* (*Heigo Shuppansha*, 38th year of the Meiji period).

26. Karitani and Tsuda Sayukichi, *Nihon jōdaishi kenkyū* (Tokyo: Iwanami shoten, 1930).

27. Naoki Kojirō, *Nihon kodai kokka no kōzō* (Tokyo: Aoki shoten, 1958); Inoue Kaoru, *Nihon kodai kokka no kenkyū* (Tokyo: Iwanami shoten, 1965); Inoue Kaoru, *Naracho bukkyōshi no kenkyū* (Tokyo: Yoshikawa kōbunkai,1966).

28. Sakamoto Tarō, *Nihon zenshi* (Tokyo: Tokyo daigaku shuppankai, 1959); Ishio Yoshihisa, *Nihon kodai no tennōsei to taiseikan seido* (Tokyo: Yūhikaku, 1962); Tamura Encho, *Asuka bukkyōshi kenkyū* (Tokyo: Hanawa shobō, 1969).

29. Tanaka Tsuguhito, *Shōtoku Taishi shinkō no seiritsu* (Tokyo: Yoshikawa kobunkan, 1983).

30. Sakamoto Tarō, *Taika no kaishin no kenkyū* (Tokyo: Shibundō, 1938).

31. Sakamoto Tarō, *Shōtoku Taishi* (Tokyo: Yoshikawa kōbunkan, 1979).

32. Ōkada Masada, *Kenpō jūshichijō ni tsuite* (*Shigaku zasshi*, 5th year of Taisho); *Omi narachō no kanbungaku* (Tokyo: Toyo bunkō, 1929).

33. The year of *kasshi* which according to Yin-Yang thought, is a year of turbulence in need of reformation.

34. Kojima, *Kanbun gaku* in *Zusetsu nihon bunkashi taikei* (Tokyo: Shogakukan, 1957).

35. Naoki Kojirō, *Nihon no rekishi* (Tokyo: Chūō kōronsha, 1973).

36. Takigawa, *Ritsuryō kakushiki no kenkyū* (Tokyo: Kakugawa shoten, 1967).

37. Kojima, *Kenpō jūshichijō no kundoku o megutte* in *Shōtoku Taishi ronshū*, vol. 2 (Kyoto: Heirakuji Shoten, 1971).

38. Sakamoto Tarō, *Shōtoku Taishi, Nihon shoki*, vol. 2 (Tokyo: Iwanami shoten, 1965); *Shōtoku Taishi shū* (Tokyo: Iwanami shoten, 1975).

39. Anezaki Masashi, *Jōgū Taishi Shōtoku o mon* (Nara: Hōryūji, 1941).

40. This publication led to the *hikka* incident because its content angered the public, the government office, and the imperial court.

41. Tsuda Sayukichi, *Nihon koten no kenkyū* (Tokyo: Iwanami shoten, 1950).

42. Hanayama Nobukatsu, *Shōtoku Taishi gyōsei hokke gishō no kenkyū* (Tokyo: Sankibo shorin, 1978); *Shokankyō gishō no Jōgū o sen ni kansuru kenkyū* (Tokyo: Iwanami shoten, 1944).

43. Shōtoku's invocation of the Four Guardian Deities may be based on a passage in *Konkomyo saishokyō* in which they promise to protect Buddhism from its enemies. Hiraoka Jokai, "Shitennō shinkō ni tsuite" in *Shōtoku Taishi kenkyū, Nihon bukkyō gakkai* (Kyoto: Heirakuji shoten, 1964), 65–81.

44. *Nihon shoki*, 586 C.E. Spring, 1st Month, 1st Day, *Nihon koten bukkyō taikei* (68:150ff); *Shōtoku Taishi denryaku* (1:78).

45. In classical Pure Land paintings, the Amida triad consists of Amida Buddha sitting in a glorified yogic position, flanked by his two bodhisattva attendants, bodhisattva Seishi (Wisdom) on his right and bodhisattva Kannon (Compassion) on his left.

46. Donald F. McCallum, *Zenkōji and Its Icon: A Study in Medieval Japanese Religious Art* (Princeton: Princeton University Press, 1994), 48. Also, in the *Kōtaishi Shōtoku hōsan* (Hymns in Praise of Prince Shōtoku) of the *Kyōgyōshinshō*, Shinran wrote several devotional hymns to hail Prince Shōtoku as the champion defender of Buddhism against the armies of Moriya of Yuga who sought to destroy the Buddhist teachings.

47. The first actual historical appearance of *shinbutsu-shūgō* can be found in *Zoku-nihongi* listed under the second year in the reign of Emperor Mommu (698) when the Taki-daijinguiji was moved. *Zoku-nihongi* in *Kokushi taikei*, II (Tokyo: Yoshikawa kōbunkan, 1935).

48. Alicia Matsunaga, *The Buddhist Philosophy of Assimilation: The Historical Development of the Honji Suijaku Theory* (Tokyo: Charles E. Tuttle Company, 1969), 230.

49. During the Nara period, the native *kami* began to assume two different attitudes toward Buddhism; the first was as the role of guardians to the dharma, whereby they maintained their independence as *kamis*. The complex process of uniting the *kami* with Buddhism must have evolved from the local conception of the role of each *kami*, as well as the degree of Buddhist influence present. Second was the role of suffering sentient beings seeking to escape their present conditions and attain Enlightenment. The clearest example is the role of Hachiman as guardian of the Tōdaiji. Ross Bender, "The Hachiman Cult and the Dōkyō Incident" in *Monumenta Nipponica* 34, no. 2 (1978): 125–152.

50. Alicia and Daigan Matsunaga, *Foundation of Japanese Buddhism, Vol. II: The Mass Movement* (Los Angeles: Buddhist Books International, 1974), 3.

51. Alicia and Daigan Matsunaga, *Foundation of Japanese Buddhism. Vol. I: The Aristocratic Age* (Los Angeles: Buddhist Books International, 1974), 201.

52. One of the reasons for such a development was the fact that the traditional method of selecting abbots had been wiped away with the collapse of the *ritsuryō* government.

53. This was the war of succession in 587 in which the Soga clan, supported by the military Ootomo clan, destroyed the power of the great Mononobe and Nakatomi clans, who had both opposed Buddhism. The Nakatomi were a clan of Shintō ritualists. Edwin O. Reischauer, *Japan: The Story of a Nation*, 3rd. ed. (New York: Alfred A. Knopf, 1981), 20.

54. *Nihon shoki, Nihon koten bukkyō taikei* 68:188.

55. Nabata Takashi, *Shōtoku Taishi to Asuka bukkyō* (Kyoto: Hōzōkan), 435.

56. Takahashi Kotohisa, *Shinran shisō no rekishiteki tenkai* (Kyoto: Nagata Bunshōdo, 1969), 142.

57. Kimmei 13, *Nara ibun* I: 380a.

58. However, the *engi* is considered to be a false one since it was obviously composed for the political purpose of legitimizing Michinaga's rule. According to Nabata, there is no evidence that Michinaga called himself an incarnation of Shōtoku, but he did worship Shōtoku deeply since he often visited Shitennōji and other temples related to Shōtoku. Nabata, *Shōtoku Taishi to Asuka bukkyō*, 425. Tanaka Shigehisa argues that Michinaga's worship of Shōtoku was related to his belief that Shōtoku was the guardian of temples.

59. Nabata, 446.

60. Among other temples that Shōtoku founded, Shitennōji was especially respected because the bone of the Buddha inside the temple had a special *kudoku* or religious merit. Nabata, 425.

61. The *Goshuin engi* describes that Shōtoku was worshiped as the king of secular and sacred law. In the letters of Enjo-ji, it is written that Shōtoku Taishi predicted that if secular powers neglected Buddhist law, then the state and king's law would be ruined. Nabata, 448. This prediction is also recorded in the *Goshuin engi*. As a result of Shōtoku's concern for upholding both Buddhist law and king's law as recorded in the Seventeen-Article Constitution, many Japanese emperors turned to Buddhism, even retiring early from their secular roles and entering the Buddhist monastery to follow Shōtoku's example as an ideal Buddhist king.

62. Minamoto Tamenori who was the provisional governor of the province of Mikawa wrote *Sanbōe* or The Three Jewels during the winter of 984. *Sanbōe* was an illustrated collection of Buddhist tales in three volumes, compiled for and presented to an imperial princess, Sonshi Naishinno, who had recently taken vows as a nun; it was written to serve as her guide to Buddhism. *Sanbōe* is an important text that helps us to understand lay attitudes toward tenth-century Japanese Buddhism, especially the Tendai tradition.

63. Apparently, in 986, Tamenori added the biography of Shōtoku Taishi and Gyoki in the second volume after being directed to do so by Prince Kaneakira, his

patron, who had seen these two "bodhisattvas" in a dream. *Nihon shisō taikei* (Tokyo: Iwanami shoten, 1970), 7:19.

64. An example of depiction of *jātaka* subjects in a Japanese artifact can be found at "Tamamushi no zushi," a miniature shrine dated to about 600 C.E. that is one of the great treasures of the Hōryūji monastery. Two of the shrine's panels are painted with scenes from the "Himalaya Boy" and Mahasattva *jātakas,* and the paintings emphasize the motif of sacrifice in both stories. The "Himalaya Boy"'s fall out of a tree toward the arms of the demon and Prince Mahasattva's fall into the pit of starving tigers are both depicted with figures of the young men plummeting in similar postures toward the beasts that wait to devour them. It is also important to point out, however, that the stories of these two self-sacrificing heroes were known in early Japanese Buddhism not as *jātaka,* as such, but rather because they figured in sutras that were particularly prominent in the earliest phase of the religion's propagation in Japan. The "Himalaya Boy"'s story occurs in *Daihatsu nehangyo,* and Mahasattva's is featured in *Konkomyo saishōokyō.* Both texts were the basis of rites that were among the first to be sanctioned and sponsored by the state. Although other sutras were to have greater significance for Japanese Buddhism, the rites based on these two continued to be observed long after their central role had come to an end. Edward Kamens, *The Three Jewels* (Ann Arbor: University of Michigan Press, 1988), 56.

65. A Japanese envoy between *Paekche* and the Asuka court.

66. *Shōtoku Taishi denryaku* also contains the explicit identification of the prince as *guze bosatsu. Shōtoku Taishi denryaku* 1:71, *Dai Nihon bukkyō zenshū* 68.

67. The story of Nichira's encounter with the prince is based on *Shōtoku Taishi denryaku* 1:76, a work of Fujiwara Kanesuke (877–933) and is dated to 917. Originally recorded in Chinese, the last five characters of Nichira's salutation literally mean "king of this nation in the east that is like scattered millet," that is, a disordered, fractious state; the terminology is found in early Chinese documents referring to Japan (Morohashi, *Dai kanwa jiten* 8, 896a). In the *Jōgū Taishi gyoki,* the salutation continues with two more five-character lines that mean: "You come from the west; you are born here to deliver all the wondrous teachings and save all sentient beings." Shusei, Koizumi, Hiroshi, and Takahashi Nobuyuki, eds. *Shohon taishō Sanbōe shusei* (Tokyo: Kasama shoin, 1980), 118.

68. *Nihon shoki* records his visit in the fourth month of 597 (*Nihon koten bungaku taikei* 68:175). The account of his praise for the prince and the accompanying sign is based on *Shōtoku Taishi denryaku* 1:88.

69. This section follows a passage in the *Nihon ryōiki* tale cited in *Nihon koten bungaku taikei* 70:77. Sakamoto, in his *Shōtoku Taishi,* 10–18, has a discussion of the prince's various names; Naganuma, *Shōtoku Taishi ronko,* 143–152.

70. Shirai Shigenobu, *Shōtoku Taishi gosen sangyo gishō no rinrigakuteki kenkyū* (Kyoto: Hyakkaen, 1970), 9.

71. This account is also recorded in *Shōtoku Taishi denryaku* (1:96–98). Mount Heng (Kozan), in Hunan, was the site of a number of monasteries associated with Hui-

ssu and other Buddhist figures. Mochizuki Shinkō, *Bukkyō daijiten*, vol. 2, rev. ed. (Tokyo: Sekai seiten kanko kyōkai, 1958–1963, 1044a–1045a.).

## CHAPTER 4: IMAGES OF SHŌTOKU IN MEDIEVAL JAPAN

1. During this time, Kannon veneration as a cult practice reached such popularity that special Kannon-do or "halls of Kannon veneration" were constructed at many temples. Takamichi Takahatake, *Young Man Shinran: A Reappraisal of Shinran's Life* (Waterloo: Wilfrid Laurier University Press, 1987), 31.

2. Max Weber, *The Theory of Social and Economic Organization*, ed. by Talcott Parsons, trans. by A. M. Henderson and Parsons (New York: Free Press, 1947), 328–329.

3. Ibid., 359.

4. Ibid., 363ff.

5. Kuroda Toshio coined the term "*kenmitsu taisei*," the exoteric esoteric system, which is named after the exoteric *(ken)* scriptures and the esoteric *(mitsu)* rituals that pervaded the sangha in medieval Japan. He argued that the *kenmitsu taisei*, with its strong financial base of the *shōen* system, was not affected by the political instability of the government during the late Heian and early Kamakura periods. Kuroda Toshio, *Nihon chūsei no kokka to shūkyō* (Tokyo: Iwanami shoten), 1975.

6. Weber pointed out that legitimacy may be ascribed to an order by those acting subject to it by tradition, a belief in the legitimacy of what has always existed. Ibid., 329.

7. Nabata Takashi, "Jodo Shinshū no Shōtoku Taishi no sūkei: Kyōgi to rekishi ni kanshite" in *Shinshū Jūhō shūei*, vol. 7, 116.

8. The *honji suijaku* theory refers to "the original forms of deities and their local traces," which defines local deities as manifestations of universal deities. Read Satō Hiroo's "Wrathful Deities and Saving Deities" in *Buddhas and Kami in Japan: Honji Suijaku as Combinatory Paradigm*, eds. Mark Teeuwen, Fabio Rambelli (New York: Routledge, 2003), 95–114.

9. Satō Hiroo, *Shinbutsu oken no chūsei* (Tokyo: Hōzōkan, 1998), 1–14.

10. The earliest surviving lists of *kami* identified with their *honji* Buddhas and bodhisattvas date back to the early twelfth century. The *honji suijaku* theory was propagated as a general philosophy and the actual application that was made by local priests and devotees, based on such factors as the regional popularity of the various cults, similarities in character, and attributes. Many mixed motives were involved, such as gaining access to new areas, extending the hegemony of existing schools, and creating harmony on the temple *shōen*. Efforts were made by Shintō shrine priests to become associated with popular Buddhist cults.

11. Satō Hiroo, *Shinbutsu oken no chūsei* (Tokyo: Hōzōkan, 1998), 24–31.

12. *Śrāvaka* is a disciple who hears the dharma from a teacher; *prateyekabuddha* is a person who, like the Buddha, attains enlightenment on his own without the help of any teacher.

13. The Japanese practical application of the *honjaku* theory to the relationships between Buddhist deities and the indigenous *kami* is unique, although quite in the Buddhist tradition of assimilation. Its singularity lies in the fact that, with the *honjaku* application, the *kami* or *suijaku* is afforded a philosophical equality with its Buddha or bodhisattva *honji*. The germ of the *honji suijaku* concept was latent in early Buddhism, however, both in the attitude toward the deva as temporarily elevated mortals and in the popular teaching to the laity that Indra, the king of the deva, had been converted to Buddhism. If the deva were mortals capable of being converted, they were also capable of attaining enlightenment. The Japanese immediately grasped such an idea, and by the end of the eighth century certain *kami* converted to Buddhism had attained the title of "bodhisattva." The first to receive this honor was Hachiman, but Tado and others soon followed suit. Satō, *Shinbutsu oken no chūsei*, 24–31.

14. An example of *honji suijaku* is found in *Ryōjin hishō* (Treasured Selections of Superb Songs), a collection of songs compiled personally by Emperor Go-Shirakawa (1127–1192) in 1179: "Kannon's original body remains forever on Mount Potalaka; to save all the living, he has been revealed as a great *kami* for all the cycles of time." *Ryōjin hishō* 275, *Nihon koten bungaku taikei*, 73; *Nihon koten bungaku zenshū*, 25.

15. Shintō, god of war, and divine protector of Japan and the Japanese people. The name Hachiman means god of eight banderoles. His symbolic animal and messenger is the dove.

16. *Jōgū Shōtoku Taishi den hoketsuki, Dai Nihon bukkyō zensho*, 112.

17. In contrast to the sectarian textbook approach to the study of Japanese Buddhist history, my distinction of the ancient and medieval period is based on my understanding of the development of Japanese Buddhism within the context of *honji suijaku*, which first appeared in texts from the latter half of the ninth century and became the basis for the combinations and associations of Shintō and Buddhist divinities. Kuroda Toshio, "Historical Consciousness and Hon-jaku Philosophy in the Medieval Period on Mount Hiei" in *The Lotus Sutra in Japanese Culture*, eds. George Tanabe Jr. and Willa Jane Tanabe (Honolulu: University of Hawaii Press, 1989), 144. Indeed, it is difficult to make a clear distinction between the ancient and medieval period because of the uncertainty of determining exactly when *honji suijaku* thought began to influence the development of Japanese Buddhism. My interpretation follows the ancient and medieval period distinction that is made by modern scholars, Kuroda Toshio, in his "Chūsei ni okeru kenmitsu taisei no tenkai" in *Nihon chūsei no kokka to shūkyō* (Tokyo: Iwanami shoten, 1975), Satō Hiroo, in his "Chūsei kenmitsu bukkyō no kokkakan" in *Kokka to shūkō Nihon shisōshi ronshū*, ed. Minamoto Ryoen (Kyōto: Shibunkaku, 1992), and Taira Masayuki, in his *Nihon chūsei no shakai to bukkyō* (Tokyo: Hanawa shobō, 1992).

I prefer to follow their categorization of the ancient and medieval period because their studies are more sensitive toward the internal issues and developments within the sangha. Thus, by "ancient period," I am referring to the era before the inception of *honji suijaku* thought (i.e., before the latter half of the ninth century); and by "medieval period" as the era after the latter half of the ninth century until the end of the Muromachi period in 1573. Furthermore, according to Kuroda, the *honji suijaku* theory was taken beyond the stage of being merely a general principle in the second half of the eleventh century. It was systematically used to establish relations between *kami* and buddhas by associating specific Shintō deities with specific buddhas and bodhisattvas; for example, it viewed the deity Hachiman as a *suijaku* of Amitabha, and the deity Amaterasu of Ise as a *suijaku* of Mahavairocana. Kuroda, "Historical Consciousness and Hon-jaku," 144. Regarding my discussion on *Taishi shinkō*, upon examination of primary sources available on Prince Shōtoku, I refer to the ancient period as the era when Shōtoku was primarily depicted as a superhuman being, manifestation of Tendai Eshi and bodhisattva Kannon, in ancient sources such as the *Nihon shoki* and *Jōgū Shōtoku hōō teisetsu*; and the medieval period as the era when Shōtoku was worshiped both as a *kami* and manifestation of bodhisattva Kannon as described in medieval sources, *Shōtoku Taishi denryaku* and *Shōtoku Taishiden*, as a result of the inception and development of *honji suijaku* thought from the latter half of the ninth century and onward.

18. *Jōgū Taishi bosatsu den, Dai Nihon bukkyō zensho* 71:112.

19. *Shōtoku Taishi denryaku* 1:106–107. Eshi is the Japanese name for the Chinese Hui-ssu (515–577), the second patriarch of the Chinese T'ien-t'ai (Tendai) school and the teacher of Chih-i (Chigi) who systematized the T'ien-t'ai teaching. He is also called the Great Master Nan-yüeh (Nangaku Daishi) because he lived on Mount Nan-yüeh. A native of the Honan Province (Kananshō, Henansheng), Nan-yüeh entered the priesthood when he was very young; he studied the T'ien-t'ai Buddhism under Hui-wen (Emon) and received its essence from him; he reputedly realized the Lotus Samadhi (Hokke zanmai). He was the first to hold an acute sense that the time was that of the last dharma period—the period of Decadent Dharma *(muppo)*, and so he is said to have faith in Amida and Maitreya (Miroku). While dwelling in Mount Ta-su (Daisōzan), he received a visit from Chih-i (Chigi), to whom he transmitted the essentials of the T'ien-t'ai teaching. His works include the *Rissei-ganmon* (Proclamation of Vows), the *Hokekyō-anrakugyōki* (Rules of the Practice of Peace and Bliss of the Lotus Sutra), and the *Shōho-mujo-zanmai* (Samadhi of No dispute regarding All Existence).

20. *Tōdaiwajō tōseiden-in gunshōruiju*, IV (1893), 511. For a slightly variant version see *Honcho kōsōden* in *Dai Nihon bukkyō zensho*, vol. 102, 72. Supposedly this original theory was fabricated by one of Ganjin's disciples to make his master's teachings appear orthodox in the face of criticism from the entrenched Nara Buddhism. Shōtoku Taishi was easily used in correlation with Nangaku, otherwise known as Hui-ssu, the second T'ien T'ai patriarch, because of his own commentary on the Lotus Sutra, the basic T'ien T'ai text. Cf. Ōgura Hobun, "*Shōtoku Taishi to honji suijaku shisō*," *Ikaruga*, First Series, I (1926), 10.

21. *Eizandaishiden* of *Dengyō Daishi zenshū bekkan*, 197–198. The same story is related in the earlier *Keikokushū* contained in *Gunshoruiju*, vol. 8, 509, but here *ojin (nirmana-kaya)* is used in place of *goshin*.

22. Another section of the *Eizandaishiden* (87) even states that Emperor Kammu referred to Shōtoku Taishi as the *suijaku* of Nangaku. Since this text has had many revisions until fairly recent times, it is most likely that the term "*suijaku*" was added at a later period to replace *goshin* or a similar concept.

23. *Shōtoku Taishiden, Shōtoku Taishi zenshū* 3; *Nihon koten bukkyō taikei* (68:163).

24. Imabori Taitsu, "Chūsei no Taishi shinkō to jingi" in *Honji suijaku shintō to nenbutsu* (Kyoto: Hōzōkan, 1999), 80–83.

25. Ibid., 84–88.

26. *Shōtoku Taishi denreki; Shōtoku Taishi denryaku* (1:89); *Dai Nihon bukkyō zensho*, 112.

27. Imabori, "Chūsei no Taishi shinkō to jingi," 90.

28. *Shōtoku Taishiden, Shōtoku Taishi zenshū* 3; *Nihon koten bukkyō taikei* (68:163).

29. *Shōtoku Taishi denreki, Dai Nihon bukkyō zensho*, 112.

30. Rigen Daishi, biography in *Honcho-kosoden* in *Dai Nihon bukkyō zensho*, vol. 102, 141.

31. The *Taishi-wasan* was written by Shinran in 1257.

32. The *Taishi-koshiki* was written in the seventeenth through eighteenth centuries.

33. *Shōtoku Taishi denryaku* in *Dai Nihon bukkyō zensho*, vol. 71 (Tokyo: Suzuki gakujutsu zaidan, 1972), 155.

34. Ibid., 158.

35. Ibid.

36. Imabori, "Chūsei no Taishi shinkō to jingi" in *Honji suijaku shintō to nenbutsu*, 94–97.

37. Ibid., 97.

38. This section is a summary of Tatsuguchi Myōsei's article, "Namu Butsu Taishi-zō kō" in *Shūgakuin ronshū* 52 (October 1981): 71–100.

39. Takada Ryūshin, *Shōtoku Taishi shinkō no tenkai* (Tokyo: Shōgakkan, 1995), 398.

40. A standing icon doll, with a childlike face, made of rock. Jizō Bosatsu-zō was regarded as a bodhisattva who protected children. It is usually placed at gravesites of children who died young or at birth.

41. Takada, 400.

42. The earliest work to mention the involvement of women in relic veneration is Minamoto no Tamenori's *Sanbōe-kotoba*. The section on the relic assembly *(shari-e)* of Enryakuji ends with the comment that "people who attend the relic assembly are exuberant about approaching and seeing [the relics]. Yet women, who do not [are not permitted to] climb the mountain [Hiei], sadly hear of the matter only distantly. I have

heard that a relic assembly begun by Chien-chen is conducted annually in the fifth month at Tōshōdaiji and also sometimes in the third month at Kazan[ji] following a practice established by Bishop Henjo. Ladies from all manner of families and places are permitted to make a pilgrimage to these two temples and make obeisance to the relics." Tamenori's explanation suggests that the relic assemblies at Tōshōdaiji and Kazanji offered women their only access to relics since Mount Hiei, the Tendai center, was designated a sacred space forbidden to women (nyonin kekkai). Shohon Taishō Sanbōe shūsei, 285–286; Kamens, Three Jewels, 303–304. Furthermore, Prince Shōtoku's two commentaries, Shōmangyō and Hokekyō, on which he reportedly lectured at court, promoted women. Queen Śrīmālā had been a brilliant and pious Buddhist queen in India whose understanding of the Buddha's teachings astounded even the Buddha, while the Lotus sutra (Hokekyō) proclaimed that a bodhisattva might inhabit even a female body.

43. Another ancient source that dramatized the legend of Shōtoku is Jōgū Taishi bosatsu den, in which Shōtoku Taishi is described not only as a reincarnation of Tendai Hui-ssu but also of the bodhisattva Kannon.

44. Shinaga is in the present town of Minami Kawachi in Ōsaka prefecture. In that area there are many funerary mounds, such as the ones assigned to the Asuka period sovereigns Yōmei, Bidatsu, and Suiko. The funerary mound of Prince Shōtoku is a multiple burial, which also includes coffins for the prince's mother, Empress Anahobe no Hashihito, and one of the prince's consorts, Princess Kashiwade. Haga Noboru, Sogi no rekishi (Tokyo: Yūzankaku, 1987), 24–27; Saito Tadashi, Higashi Ajia so, bosei no kenkyū (Tokyo: Daiichi shobō, 1987), 179–182.

45. Masamune Atsuo et al., eds., Engishiki, vol. 24 of Nihon koten zenshū (Tokyo: Nihon koten zenshū kankōkai, 1927–1929), 169.

46. Archaeologists are discussing the origins of the corridor tomb. Some of them argue that this type originated in the Southern Dynasties, whereas others believe that it began in Koguryo, was then transmitted to Silla and Paekche, and finally appeared in Japan. Nagashima Kimichika, "Yokoanashiki sekishitsu no denba" in Higashi ajia no naka no kofun bunka, vol. 13 of Kofun jidai no kenkyū, ed. by Ishino Hironobu et al. (Tokyo: Yūzankaku, 1993), 108–118.

47. "Eifukuji" in Ōsaka fu no chimei.

48. Kurokawa Katsumi, ed., Fuso ryakki in Shintei zōhō kokushi taikei, vol. 12 (Tokyo: Yoshikawa kōbunkan, 1931), 46.

49. Abe Yasurō, "Shōtoku Taishi shinkō" in Shōtoku Taishi jiten, Imabori, ed. (Tokyo: Yoshikawa, 1994), 450.

50. Lady Tachibana, one of the four consorts of Prince Shōtoku, was the granddaughter of Empress Suiko since her father, Prince Ōwari, was one of the children born to the empress and Emperor Bidatsu. Takioto Yoshiyuki has suggested that the marriage of Prince Shōtoku and Lady Tachibana was for political reasons because she was a descendant of Empress Suiko's lineage, and so the marriage would have strengthened the relationship between the empress and the prince. That was also the case of another consort, Princess Uji no Kaidako, who was the daughter of Empress Suiko and

Emperor Bidatsu. It is known that the prince had four consorts: Ujinokaidako no himemiko, Hokikimi no iratsume, Tojiko no iratsume, and Inabe no Tachibana no Ōkimi. Takioto Yoshiyuki, "Shōtoku Taishi no Tsumatachi," in *Shōtoku Taishi jiten*, 80–84.

51. María del Rosario Pradel, "The Fragments of the Tenjukoku shūchō mandara Reconstruction and Iconography and the Historical Contexts." Ph.D. diss., University of California, Los Angeles, 1997.

52. Ōashi Katsuaki. *Tenjukoku shūchō no kenkyū* (Tokyo: Yoshikawa kōbunkan, 1995).

53. Japanese scholars find it significant that the imperial genealogy presented in the first part of the inscription begins with Emperor Kimmei because it was during his reign that Buddhism was officially introduced to Japan with the famous envoy from King Song of *Paekche* in 552, according to *Nihon shoki. Nihon shoki* 2, vol. 68 of *Nihon koten bungaku taiskei* (Tokyo: Iwanami shoten, 1965), 100. W. G. Aston, *Nihongi: Chronicles of Japan from the Earliest Times to A.D. 697* (Rutland and Tokyo: Charles E. Tuttle Co., 1988), 65.

54. Leon Hurvitz, tr., *Scripture of the Lotus Blossom of the Fine Dharma* (New York: Columbia University Press, 1976), 200–201.

55. Hurvitz, 1976: 300; William E. Deal, "Women and Japanese Buddhism: Tales of Birth in the Pure Land" in George J. Tanabe Jr., ed., *Religions of Japan in Practice* (Princeton: Princeton University Press, 1999), 176–184; Inoue Mitsusada and Ōsone Shōsuke, eds., *Ōjōden Hokke genki, Nihon shisō taikei* 7 (Tokyo: Iwanami shoten, 1982).

56. Toshihide Akamatsu, *Zoku-kamakura bukkyō no kenkyū* (Kyoto: Heirakuji shoten, 1966), 32.

57. Hayashi Mikiya, *Taishi shinkō no kenkyū* (Tokyo: Yoshikawa kōbunkan, 1980), 21.

58. Other books that record the tale of Hui-ssu reincarnation are: Shitaku's *Jōgū Kōtaishi bosatsu den* (Jōgū Prince Bodhisattva story) and *Dai to denkaishisō aruiwa meiki daiwajō ganjin den* (referred to as Ganjin den); Mahito Genkai's *Todaiwajō tōsei den* (referred to as Tosei Den); Myōitsu's *Dai to koku koshū Kōzan dōjō shakuji-zenji shichidaiki*; Kōjō's *Hui-ssu shichidaiki* in *Denjutsu isshin kaimon* 6. Ōmi no Mifune's *Keiun gannen sangatsu tennō junko shoji jūga Shōtoku Taishi dera isshū*; and, Saichō's *Konin nana-nen shitennō-ji jōgū-byō kyūden hokke-shū shi narabini zō*.

59. Fujii Yukiko, *Shōtoku Taishi no denshō* (Tokyo: Yoshikawa kōbunkan, 1999), 160–162.

60. Ibid., 165–166.

61. Ibid., 171–172.

62. Ibid., 173.

63. Kōjō composed the following eulogy on Nangaku: "He left his image as a *zenji* in Japan while keeping his real body in the Western T'ang in China. His real body fol-

lowed Buddhist practices at the temple while I heard his manifestation. His disciple Chigan sat on his left side and Socho sat close to his right side. The Chin dynasty enjoyed great pleasure while the Taishaku [Indra and his attendants] stood in line in the fragrant garden. He had three thousand devotees and four wise men. Footsteps on the scattered colorful flowers, the *kamis* enjoying the wonderful sutra—the truth is preached at the quiet temple and the tenets of Buddhism flow down into the realm of truth. Auspicious flowers remind me of his image and people worship his sacred spirit of Mount Eigaku." *Honcho-kōsō den, Dai Nihon bukkyō zensho*, vol. 102–107.

64. Ennin had a dream in which the following personages appeared and safely escorted him: Dharma, Hoshi, Nangaku, Tendai, Sokei, Prince Shōtoku, Gyogi bosatsu, and Dengyō Daishi.

65. *Shoreishi* in *Kōbō Daishi zenshū*, III, 457.

66. Fujii, *Shōtoku Taishi no denshō*, 175–177.

67. Ibid., 177–178.

68. Ibid., 179–180.

69. Christine Guth, "The Divine Boy in Japanese Art" in *Monumenta Nipponica*, Vol. 24, No 1 (Spring, 1987), 1–23

70. H. Minamoto, "Tapestry Representing Tenjukoku or the Heavenly World" in *Bukkyō Bijutsu*, XIII, 1929, special number on the Asuka period, 60.

71. Alexander Soper, "Notes on the Hōryūji and the Sculpture of the Suiko Period" in *The Art Bulletin*, Vol. 33, No. 2 (June 1951), 77–94.

72. Aston, trans., *Nihongi*, 148–149.

73. Takada Ryōshin, *Shōtoku Taishi shinkō no tenkai* (Tokyo: Shōgakukan, 1995), 395.

74. Ibid., 12.

75. According to *Nihon shoki*, construction of the palace at Ikaruga began in 601, *Nihon koten bungaku taikei* (68:177). The site was eventually incorporated into the monastery that became Hōryūji, and the Yumedono, an octagonal structure, is now part of Hōryūji. It houses the revered *guze* Kannon image, said to resemble the prince's own features. Kuno Takeshi et al., *Nihon no bijutsu 3: Hōryūji* (Tokyo: Shōgakukan, 1971), 105, 207–208.

76. Ibid., 189–191.

77. Gyōshin was the main person responsible for the construction of Uenomiyo ōin *(Jōgū oin)*. After its completion, Gyōshin made *Jōgū ōin* a sacred place for Shōtoku worship. Takada believes that Gyōshin and his followers were responsible for creating Prince Shōtoku myths and legends. Takada, *Shōtoku Taishi shinkō no tenkai,* 392.

78. A statue of Taishi as a child, which was constructed with the influence of esoteric Buddhism and *Denryaku*. Ibid., 395.

79. Ibid., 405.

80. Ibid., 395.

81. Also, an image of Shōtoku was drawn on the reverse side of *Shomangyō*, which indicates that Shōtoku was thought to be like a Buddha in the Nara period.

82. John Rosenfield, "The Sedgewick Statue of the Infant Shōtoku Taishi," in *Archives of Asian Art*, 22 (1968–1969): 56–79.

83. The worship of Nyorin Kannon, which is similar to the *honji* of Shōtoku and Kobo Daishi's *goshin* (Kukai's after-body), was based on the notion that something was tied to Shōtoku worship.

84. Tanaka Tsuguhito, *Shōtoku Taishi shinkō no seiritsu* (Tokyo: Yoshikawa Kōbunkan, 1983), 197.

## CHAPTER 5: SHŌTOKU AND SHINRAN'S BUDDHISM

1. During the *insei* or "cloistered-government" period (1086–1156), influential emperors abdicated and influenced the political power structure from the position of retired emperor. Emperor Shirakawa was the first to abdicate in favor of his son Horikawa. However, Shirakawa continued to take an active role in government decision making. The influence of the Fujiwara clan, which had dominated court decisions, was much reduced by Go-Sanjō's efforts to increase the power of the imperial house. As a result, Shirakawa was able to exercise much more control over court matters, particularly the regulation of *shōen* holdings. Despite this increase in imperial authority, it seems that Shirakawa wished to make the imperial house even more of a political force, and one in which his direct descendants could accede to the throne. The emperors who abdicated their thrones in favor of their sons during the *insei* period are: Shirakawa (1072–1086), Horikawa (1086–1107), Toba (1107–1123), Sutoku (1123–1141), Konoe (1141–1155), Go-Shirakawa (1155–1158), Nijō (1158–1165), Rokujō (1165–1168), Takakura (1168–1180), Antoku (1180–1185), and Go-Toba (1185–1198). Cameron Hurst III, *Insei: Abdicated Sovereigns in the Politics of Late Heian Japan 1086–1185* (New York: Columbia University Press, 1976), 130.

2. Mikail Adolphson, *The Gates of Power: Monks, Courtiers, and Warriors in Premodern Japan* (Honolulu: University of Hawai'i Press, 2000), 17.

3. Ibid., 83.

4. Ibid., 57.

5. Adolphson explains that the *gōso* may be seen as the embodiment of three important concepts in medieval Japan: (1) they illustrate the practical aspect of the *honji suijaku* idea. Native gods protected Buddhism and its physical representations, while the carrying of divine symbols to the capital provided convincing evidence of the important role played by the *kami*. Although the *shinmoku* (the holy *sakaki* branch) was the preferred symbol from Kasuga, portable shrines (*shin'yō* or *mikoshi*), which were used by most other shrines, provided the most apparent symbolism, with mirrors representing

the *kami* and a phoenix often placed on top. The efficiency of these protests attests to the power of these symbols and the *kami* themselves. Moreover, the use of *kami*, symbolized by either a *sakaki* branch or sacred palanquins, is one of the most intriguing aspects of the *gōso*. The native deities played an important role in protecting the interests of the temple-shrine complexes in Nara as well as on Mount Hiei; (2) the *gōso* show that the *ōbō-buppō sōi* concept of mutual dependence of the imperial law and Buddhism provided the theoretical and religious base for the state's dominant ideology. The secular powers needed the support of Buddhism and thus were required to underwrite it financially and politically. The reconstruction of damaged palanquins at the court's expense and the punishments of warriors who incurred such damages effectively prove this point; and, (3) the *gōso* provide indisputable support for the idea of shared rulership *(kenmon taisei)*. Protesting in the capital was the prerogative of the most prestigious religious elites and their responsibilities as spiritual supporters for the leaders of the state gave them the right to both economic and judicial privileges. The *gōso* themselves thus represent the symbiosis of religious and political doctrines and the larger political history of the era. Mikail Adolphson, *The Gates of Power: Monks, Courtiers, and Warriors in Premodern Japan* (Honolulu: University of Hawai'i Press, 2000), 352.

6. Ibid., 351.

7. Ibid., 5.

8. "*Kamogawa no mizu, sugoruku no sai, yama hosshi, sorezore chin ga kokoro ni shitagawau mono.*" *Genpei seisuiki*, volume 1 (Tokyo: Miyai shoten, 1994), 124; *Heike monogatari*, volume 1, in *Shinkō Nihon koten shūsei*, edited by Mizuhara Hajime (Tokyo: Shinkōsha, 1979), 93.

9. A document from the imperial court in the late tenth century contains one of the earliest known references to the mutual dependence, stating that a violation of the imperial law was also a crime against the divine law of Buddhism, which in turn served to protect the state. Hirata Toshiharu, *Sōhei to bushi* (Tokyo: Nihon kyōbunsha, 1965), 124.

10. Adolphson, *The Gates of Power*, 210.

11. *Shinshū shōgyō zensho*, 1: 378–379; see also Jan Nattier's *Once Upon a Future Time: Studies in a Buddhist Prophecy of Decline* (Berkeley: Asian Humanities Press, 1991).

12. Buddhist tradition maintains that as the world moves farther and farther away from the time of the historical Buddha, understanding of his teachings grows increasingly distorted and the people's capacity to practice and benefit from those teachings accordingly declines, until eventually Buddhism is lost. In the age of True Dharma *(shōbō)*, lasting 500 (some say 1,000) years, the Buddha's teaching is properly practiced and enlightenment can be attained; in the age of Counterfeit Dharma *(zōbō)*, lasting 1,000 (some say 500) years, the teaching is practiced but enlightenment is no longer possible; and in the age of degenerating Dharma *(mappō)*, lasting 10,000 years, only teaching remains—one finds neither practice nor proof. Edward Kamens, *The Three Jewels: A Study and Translation of Minamoto Tamenori's Sanbōe* (Ann Arbor: Center for Japanese Studies, 1988), 44–46.

13. Salvation here was often conceived of in a worldly rather than a religious sense. Many nobles in the late Heian period seem to have looked upon rebirth in the Pure Land as an extension of their elegant lifestyle into the next world, without any fundamental questioning of the values that lifestyle presupposed.

14. *Introduction to Mirror for the Moon: A Selection of Poems by Saigyō*, trans. by William R. LaFleur (New York: New Directions, 1977), xviii–xix.

15. *Shōzōmatsu wasan, Shinshū shōgyō zensho*, vol. II, Hymn 13, 105–106.

16. Norihiko Kikimura, *Shinran: His Life and Thought* (Los Angeles: The Nembutsu Press, 1983), 65.

17. Ibid.

18. In *Heike monogatari* there is a passage in the section titled "Account of the Destruction of the Temple," which says, "A *dōsō* is a child who has just attained the status of a student and is in the lowest ranks of the monks." The *dōsō* thus could not be considered a very important monk. Often they were attracted to the monkhood because there was no other means of livelihood open to them. Their primary motivation seems to have been physical rather than spiritual, and it is not surprising to learn that there were frequent conflicts between the scholarly but physically weak *gakushū* and the brawny *dōsō*, with the *dōsō* usually winning. According to *Heike monogatari*, those who supported the *dōsō* were: "thieves, robbers, highwaymen, and pirates in the various provinces, greedy rascals all, who are not concerned about living or dying." The *dōsō* may almost be regarded as a lawless brigade.

19. Sokusui Murakami, *Shinran dokuhon* (Kyoto: Hyakkaen, 1968), 16.

20. See "Hyohan-ki" entry for September 24, 1167, in *Shiryo-taisei*, vol. 20 (Kyoto: Rinsen shoten, 1965), 265. Satō Tetsuei, "Eizan Jōdokyō no tenkai to Shinran Shōnin," in *Shinran taikei, Rekishiben*, vol. 2, ed. Kashiwahara Yūsen, Kuroda Toshio, and Hiramatsu Reizō (Kyoto: Hōzōkan, 1988), pp. 262–278.

21. Haruki Kageyama, *Hieizan* (Tokyo: Kadokawa shoten, 1960), 104. Saichō developed the practice of cessation and realization as study and meditative practice of such Mahāyāna scriptures as the *Lotus sutra*, the *Suvarnaprabhāsa sutra* ("Sutra of the Golden Radiance", Jpn. *Konkōmyō-kyō*), the Sutra of the Benevolent Emperor. He also developed the Tendai bodhisattva morality *(ekayāna śila)* and Chih-I's fundamental "cessation [of delusion] and realization [enlightenment]" *(shikangyō)*. It is within Chih-I's systematization that the four kinds of Tendai *samādhi* or meditative ecstasies *(shishū-zanmai)* are found: (i) "constant sitting *samādhi*" for ninety days, singularly meditating on the name of the Buddha to the exclusion of all other activity, as explained in the *Saptsatika-prajñāpāramitā sutra*; (ii) "constant moving *samādhi*," which involves ninety days of circumambulation around the central Buddha figure of the Buddha hall while chanting the name of the Buddha Amida, as described in the *Pratyutpanna-samādhi sutra*; (iii) "half-sitting, half-moving *samādhi*," which consists of several *samādhi* of seven, twenty-one, or thirty-seven days of sitting and circumambulatory meditation around the central Buddha figure; (iv) "neither sitting nor moving *samādhi*," which encompasses all other meditation. The practice of meditation on the Buddha *Mahāvairocana (shanagō)* is the

second category of meditative practices, which are basically several levels of esoteric Buddhist awareness and action based on the *Mahāvairocana sutra*. Paul Groner, *Saichō—The Establishment of the Japanese Tendai School* (Berkeley: Berkeley Buddhist Studies Series, 1984), 65–76.

22. In his book *Letters of Eshinni*, Dobbins suggests that Shinran abandoned his monastic activities on Mount Hiei *after* he received the revelation, but I contend that Shinran left Mount Hiei *before* his revelatory experience at Rokkakudō. James Dobbins, *Letters of Eshinni: Images of Pure Land Buddhism in Medieval Japan* (Honolulu: University of Hawai'i Press, 2004), 100. My thesis is that Shinran left Mount Hiei because he wanted to distance himself from the saturated religiopolitical atmosphere on Mount Hiei and to practice Buddhism elsewhere. Shinran's decision to continue his religious practice under the tutelage of Hōnen confirms the fact that Shinran was not abandoning his Buddhist precepts, but merely wanted to sever ties with his institutional affiliation at Mount Hiei.

23. Tamura Enchō, *Nihon bukkyō shisōshi kenkyū: Jōdokyō hen* (Kyoto: Heirakuji shoten, 1959), 10–14.

24. There was a growing sense of corruption and materialism on Mount Hiei, especially among the upper strata of Hiei priests. Priests became sons of the secular world and sought position and fame. High births and social connections implied importance, which was contrary to Buddhist tenets. In later Jōdo Shinshū development, Rennyo (1415–1499), the pivotal leader of Jōdo Shinshū at Honganji (also known as Ikkoshū), tried to centralize political and religious power through politically motivated marriages with members of the imperial family and other high officials. The lower strata of priests became *sōhei* or "warrior-priests," whose job was to guard the temporal interests of Enryakuji, the main temple at Mount Hiei. Kōshō Yamamoto, *An Introduction to Shin Buddhism* (Tokyo: Karinbunko, 1963), 21–23.

25. Hee-Sung Keel, *Understanding Shinran* (Fremont: Asian Humanities Press, 1995), 36.

26. Abé, *Weaving of Mantra*, 408.

27. Kuroda Toshio, "Chūsei ni okeru kenmitsu taisei no tenkai," in *Nihon chūsei no kokka to shūkyō* (Tokyo: Iwanami shoten, 1975), 413–457.

28. *Mida nyorai myogōtoku, Shinshū shōgyō zensho*, 2: 733.

29. Nāgārjuna did not teach the attainment of nonretrogression in the present life, but he did not teach birth in the Pure Land. In his *Treatise on the Pure Land*, Vasubhandhu did not state whether birth occurs in the present life or the next. The first clear statement of birth after death in this world occurs in T'an-luan's commentary on the *Treatise on the Pure Land*; the *Larger Sutra* teaches birth after death also.

30. Kuroda Toshio, *Nihon chūsei no kokka to shūkyō* (Tokyo: Iwanami shoten, 1975), 68.

31. As the center of Tendai Buddhism, Mount Hiei was originally established through the patronage of the imperial court at the beginning of the Heian period so that the monks there always enjoyed close ties to the court. One piece of evidence that serves

to confirm this fact is the petition that was drawn by the powerful Kōfukuji temple in 1205 to ban the spread of *senju nenbutsu* teaching. When we look at the nine points of sacrileges and crimes committed by the *senju nenbutsu* followers, the basis of the accusations not surprisingly revolve around the theme that the *senju nenbutsu* teaching challenged the emperor's authority. For instance, the first article states, "Error of establishing a new sect without imperial edict," and the last article read, "Error of bringing confusion to the nation since the nembutsu practice was not based upon the harmony of the dharma of the emperor and Buddha." In essence, the petition's purpose was to upset the emperor (as it did) so that it would be approved. Nonetheless, the underlying reason for the petition stemmed from the jealousy among the leaders of *kenmitsu taisei* concerning the growing number of *senju nenbutsu* followers and the popularity of Hōnen and Shinran.

32. Adolphson, *Gates of Power*, 3.

33. Takahashi Kotohisa, *Shinran shisō no rekishitei tenkai* (Tokyo: Nagata bunshōdo, 1981), 112.

34. Postscript in *Kyōgyōshinshō, Nihon koten bungaku taikei*, vol. 82 (Tokyo: Iwanami shoten, 1964); *Shinshū shōgyō zensho*, vol 2 (Kyoto: Oyagi kōbundo, 1941). In publications before World War II, the Japanese government censored this direct accusation against the emperor in the postscript. For example, many of the versions of Shinran's *Kyōgyōshinshō* in which he accuses "the emperor and his ministers, acting against the dharma and abandoning all integrity" omit the word "emperor" as a way of protecting the dignity of the emperor. A legacy of this prohibition carried over into postwar printings of *Shinshū shōgyō zensho*. In a 1967 printing, *Shinshū shōgyō zensho*, 2: 201, there are two blank spaces for the characters *shūjo*; in a 1977 printing, the characters are back in place. However, it is clear that Shinran was speaking against the unjust punishment to *senju nenbutsu* followers, the imperial decree to ban the *senju nenbutsu* teaching, and unfair exile of the leaders of the *senju nenbutsu* teaching. Futaba Kenkō, *Shinran no kenkyū: Shinran ni okeru shin to rekishi* (Kyoto: Hyakkaen, 1962), 367.

35. *Shūi shinseki goshōsoku, Shinshū shōgyō zensho* 2: 727–729.

36. Chiba Jōryu, Kitanishi Hiromu, and Takagi Yūtaka, *Bukkyōshi gaisetsu* in *Nihon hen* (Kyoto: Heirakuji shoten, 1969), 94–95.

37. Buddhism was incorporated into the central government by the provincial temple *(kokubun-ji)* system so that it might bestow its blessings and protection on the state. This continued to be Buddhism's official role long into the Heian period, though the Tendai and Shingon sects that predominated during that time were established independently of the court. Jacqueline Stone, "Seeking Enlightenment in the Last Age: Mappō Thought in Kamakura Buddhism" in *The Eastern Buddhist*, The Eastern Buddhist Society, vol. 18, no. 1, Spring 1985, 32.

38. Tamaru Noriyoshi, "Buddhism in Japan" in *Buddhism and Asian History*, ed. J. Kitagawa and M. Cummings (New York: Macmillan, 1989), 167.

39. Hayashima Kyōshō, *Shinran nyumon* (Tokyo: Yūzankaku, 1972), 141–142.

40. The *senju* or "exclusive" *nenbutsu* teaching specifically refers to the act of invocation of the name of Amida Buddha to bring rebirth in the Pure Land. The Pure Land

teaching is described as being exclusive because the invocation of the Amida Buddha was one among the five traditional nembutsu practices. The term "*nenbutsu*" literally means "to think of the Buddha." According to Pure Land Buddhist tradition, nembutsu practice consists of five practices, otherwise known as "the five practice-gates of mindfulness," for attaining birth in the Pure Land. In the *Jōdo-ron*, Vasubandhu describes the five practices as: (1) *raihai*, worshiping Amida; (2) *sandan*, praising his virtue by invoking his name; (3) *sagan*, aspiration for birth in the Pure Land; (4) *kanzatasu*, contemplation on Amida, the Pure Land, and Bodhisattva dwelling there; and (5) *ekō*, transferring merit to other sentient beings to save them from suffering. These five practices were undertaken by monks as part of larger programs of practice in the monastic community. Hisao Inagaki, *A Dictionary of Japanese Buddhist Terms*, School of Oriental and African Studies (Heian: University of London, 1988), 77. Hōnen singled out the nembutsu practice of invoking Amida Buddha's name from the context of other nembutsu practices in order to provide an easy path for common people to attain rebirth in the Pure Land.

Although the proponents of the *senju nenbutsu* teaching did not deny that enlightenment was possible through other nembutsu practices, they emphasized the invocation of the Amida Buddha as being the only necessary nembutsu practice for attaining enlightenment. The main thrust of the *senju nenbutsu* teaching was that individual salvation was made possible not by self-power *(jiriki)* or merit accumulation *(ekō)*, but on the basis of Amida Buddha's Other-power *(tariki)* and vow to save all people. In other words, salvation was available through Amida's merit *(ekō)* or grace. Hence, Shinran claimed that salvation was possible for even the worst of sinners as long as the individual invoked the name of Amida Buddha with *shinjin* (sincere mind entrusting).

41. In the *Tannisho*, Shinran said that "if even a good man can be born in the Realm of Purification, much more so an evil man." *Tannisho* ("A Tractate Deploring Heresies Against True Faith") in *Shinshū shōgyō zensho*, 2:786.

42. Ueda Yoshifumi and Dennis Hirota, *Shinran: An Introduction to His Thought* (Kyoto: Hongwanji International Center, 1989), 148.

43. In the ninth month in 1205 the powerful Kōfukuji temple of Nara presented a petition to the now retired emperor Go-Toba to stop the *senju nenbutsu* movement. This document, known as the *Kōfukuji sōjō*, was believed to have been composed by Jōkei of Kasagi and contained nine points of alleged sacrileges and crimes committed by *senju nenbutsu* followers. Many of the following articles touched on issues of vital political importance to the established temples: (1) error of establishing a new sect without imperial edict. This was the first time a sect had risen among the masses or lower segments of society rather than being officially established by the higher authorities. By this time, Buddhism in Japan was subjugated by the political authorities and was only allowed to exist for the sake of serving the nation and the emperor; (2) error of drawing new Buddhist images, in particular the *Sesshū Fusha Mandara*, in which the nembutsu followers were directly illuminated by Amida's light but followers of other sects were not. There are no existing representations of this mandara, but, according to contemporary accounts, it featured Amida in the center, issuing rays of light to illumine the ten directions. A number of laymen, priests, and worshipers were drawn surrounding Amida, and the rays issuing forth from the central image managed to directly touch

only nembutsu followers. Some versions even went so far as to depict the nembutsu followers taking the life of living creatures and still receiving illumination while pious monks of other sects chanting the sutra failed to receive it. The mandara irritated the established temples for two reasons: first, it appeared to lack proper scriptural basis, although Hōnen claimed it was inspired by a statement found in the Meditation Sutra. More important, the mandara proved to be a most effective and popular means of instructing the laity, who could gain hope for salvation from it despite their situation in life. Consequently, the notion of "licensed evil" would become one of the major criticisms against the *senju nenbutsu* teaching; (3) error of treating Śākyamuni Buddha improperly. Since the emphasis of the sect was solely on chanting the name of Amida, critics interpreted the "neglect" of Śākyamuni as an insult to the founder of Buddhism; (4) error of neglecting good deeds other than the nembutsu. The author of the *Kōfukuji sōjō* took the nembutsu creed to an extreme by asserting that its followers despised or even condemned to hell the practice of other devotions such as chanting the *Lotus* Sutra, building temples, or creating images. He also declared that the sect had abandoned the Mahāyāna tradition by refusing to chant other sutras; (5) error of rejecting the Shintō *kamis*. This was an interesting criticism because it was actually aimed at Hōnen's alleged refusal to worship at famous historical shrines. As the *ritsuryō* system was collapsing, respect toward these famous shrines, instituted and supported by the government with close alliances to the established temples, had diminished; (6) error of abandoning practices other than the nembutsu that properly lead to the Pure Land. Here the author cited the traditional combination of practices believed to result in the attainment of the Pure Land; (7) error of misunderstanding the significance of the nembutsu. Hōnen's followers did not practice the traditional forms of meditation or visualization of the Pure Land in conjunction with the chanting of the nembutsu. The criticism here was that chanting alone represented an inferior form of physical practice; (8) error rejecting the *vināya* and compromising with the lay life. According to this criticism, nembutsu priests neglected to follow monastic discipline while claiming that those who worried about such sins as gambling or meat eating failed to place total reliance on the power of Amida; (9) error of bringing confusion to the nation since the nembutsu practice was not based on the harmony of the dharma of the emperor and Buddha. This criticism blamed the decline of the eight sects of established Buddhism and the resulting failure of the *ritsuryō* government solely on the rise of the *senju nenbutsu* movement. The true meaning of this criticism was that a religion rising from the masses naturally upset the existing authoritarian control, and the author used the existing state of political and social confusion as proof of his contention. Finally, this petition also requested that Gyōku and Junsai be especially singled out for punishment. Kamāta Shigeo and Tanaka Hisao, eds., *Kamakura kyū bukkyō* in *Nihon shisō taikei*, no. 15 (Tokyo: Iwananmi shoten, 1971), 31–42.

44. Akamatsu Toshihide, *Kamakura bukkyō no kenkyū* (Kyoto: Heirakuji shoten, 1957), 105–106.

45. Gyōku (also known as Jūren) advocated the *ichinen ōjō* (one-calling attainment), which by its simple appeal quickly gained popularity among the poor and uneducated lower classes, while Junsai (also known as Anrakubō) was a dynamic, handsome young preacher and extremely attractive to court ladies.

46. Takahatake explains that sexual relations had taken place between the two condemned Pure Land adherents Gyōku and Junsai and Emperor Go-Toba's ladies-in-waiting during the emperor's absence from the court. Takahatake Takamichi, *Young Man Shinran: A Reappraisal of Shinran's Life* (Waterloo: Wilfrid Laurier University Press, 1987), 81.

47. Ibid.

48. For Shinran, nembutsu is not to be regarded as another way of storing merit for oneself. Traditionally, nembutsu was considered an act by which practitioners could accumulate merit and transfer it toward their birth in the Pure Land. But Shinran changed this notion completely by explaining that *eko* is not our own act but Amida's, for we have nothing to "transfer." For Shinran, the goal of practice was not designed to rid oneself of blind passions, or to accumulate merit for oneself and others through virtuous acts. Shinran states that genuine practice must be the activity of the practitioner's mind in accord with reality, free of blind passions and delusions. Along with the belief in *mappō*, Shinran believed that human beings were too weak and depraved to conduct any true practice in order to earn their merits for birth in the Pure Land. For this reason, Shinran calls nembutsu "nonpractice" because it is actually the Great Practice that enables us to attain birth in the Pure Land by Amida Buddha's directing *eko* to us, his own true and real act. In short, Shinran believed that since salvation came from Other-power *(tariki)*, practice should come from there as well. Shinran sees nembutsu as essentially the cosmic activity of Amida Buddha that through faith becomes expressed as our practice.

Before Hōnen and Shinran, Buddhists were teaching people that "good behavior," for example, paying tax earnestly, would bring them closer to the realization of enlightenment. In other words, good behavior in the secular world was counted as religious merit. Taira argues that *kenmitsu* were using a merit-based system to dominate and exploit the common people. Taira labels Hōnen and Shinran's teaching as "heresy" because they were opposed to such a ruling system and offered a simple path toward enlightenment that was faith-oriented, not merit-oriented. In this sense, both Hōnen and Shinran were truly revolutionary because they struggled to emancipate people from the medieval ruling system. Taira Masayuki, *Nihon chūsei no shakai to bukkyō* (Tokyo: Hanawa shobō, 1992), 79.

49. The evangelistic success of the *senju nenbutsu* movement was actually consistent with the Buddha's life. In the scriptural accounts, the Buddhist community is depicted, from its inception, as a missionary community. A detailed and well-documented discussion of the early Buddhists is contained in Nalinaksha Dutt's *Early History of the Spread of Buddhism and the Buddhist Schools* (London: Luzac, 1925), 13. Very soon after the Buddha's first conversions, he sent those mendicants who had accepted his message out to convert others; their efforts contributed greatly to the expansion of the new sect. Throughout the canonical period, missionary preaching constituted one of the major functions of the Buddha's mendicant followers, including not only the *bhikkus* (members of the male order) but also the *bhikkunis* (members of the order of nuns). Moreover, the laity soon became involved in the missionary efforts and contributed mightily to its success. For example, it is said that the daughter of the famous lay disciple Anāthapindaka (Jpn. Gikkodoku: "giver of food to the poor") was responsible for the conversion of her

father-in-law's entire family, and through her success was instrumental in setting up a Buddhist center in the eastern country of Anga. Hendrik Kern, *Manual of Indian Buddhism* (Varanasi: Indological Book House, 1968), 26.

50. Tambiah describes the parallelism that existed between the sangha and the polity in Thailand. It is precisely because the recruitment of kings was contentious that whoever ascended the throne subsequently sought to be legitimized by the Buddhist sangha and divinized by court functionaries. Tambiah explains a three-tiered structure of polity of merit exchange that was composed of the king, the sangha, and the people. At the highest levels there is the old classical conception that links the king with the sangha as its protector, patron, and purifier. The sangha in turn, headed by its patriarch, is the protector and keeper of the Buddha's dharma and hence is the third refuge of the people. At the middle level of the polity the structure of the military dictatorship with its concentration of power corresponds to the centralization of the sangha and the concentration of power in the hands of the patriarch and the Council of Elders *(Mahātherasamakhom)*. The rulers are Buddhists and therefore their commitment to acts of merit making toward the sangha as ends in themselves cannot be separated from their political use or exploitation of them as national symbols. Finally, at the polity's base are the relatively autonomous settlements and households of the peasantry (and urban workers) that are matched by the innumerable relatively autonomous *wat* (monastic communities) and fraternities that constitute the basic components of the sangha. The dynamic link between them is by now all too familiar: a mutuality of merit making (which includes material support of monks) by the laity and of merit conferring (through recitations and rituals) by the monks. Stanley Tambiah, *World Conqueror and World Renouncer: A Study of Buddhism and Polity in Thailand Against a Historical Background* (Cambridge: Cambridge University Press, 1976), 503–507.

51. Futaba Kenkō, *Tennōsei to shinshū* (Kyoto: Nagata bunshodō, 1991), 37.

52. Ibid.

53. According to the account in *Aśokavadāna*, rightful kingship is attained according to the laws of karma. John S. Strong, *The Legend of King Aśoka* (Princeton: Princeton University Press, 1983), 57. In *Avadāna* literature, the Buddha in particular is seen as a vast and fertile field of merit *(punya-ksetra)* where devotees can "plant" their meritorious deeds. Thus any good (or bad) action directed toward him, no matter how petty it may seem, can have positive (or negative) karmic results beyond all expectations. In popular Buddhist literature, the *avadānas* (Jpn. *hiyu*: parables) and other stories are meant to illustrate the workings of karma. The focus is often on a single significant act that then sets a theme for the whole story of the person's subsequent lifetime and the development of his or her character.

In Aśoka's case, after making his gift of dirt to the Buddha, he then proceeds to formulate his *pranidhāna*: "By this root of merit," he declares, "I would become king, and, after placing the earth under a single umbrella of sovereignty, I would pay homage to the Blessed Buddha" *(Mukhopadhyāya, 31)*. The significance of this moment is then marked in the story by two closely related events: the Buddha's smile and his prediction *(vyakaraṇa)* pertaining to Aśoka. Having accepted the offering of dirt, the Buddha first displays his smile, which signifies a revelation of the entire cosmos and indicates Aśoka's future place in the scheme of things. Rays of light of different color shoot out in all directions from the Buddha's lips. Some illuminate the hells, where they bring relief to the suffering hell-beings; others penetrate the Pure Lands where they proclaim to the deities the impermanence inherent in their blissful state, but all the rays eventually return and are reabsorbed into the Buddha's body. In the case of Aśoka, the rays reenter the Buddha's left palm, signifying that he is to become a *balacakravartin*. John S. Strong, *The Legend of King Aśoka: A Study and Translation of the Asokavadāna* (Princeton: Princeton University Press, 1983), 60.

54. Py. *chakkavatti*; Jpn. *tenrinjōō*: wheel-turning king or dharma-emperor.

55. James C. Dobbins, *Jōdo Shinshū: Shin Buddhism in Medieval Japan* (Honolulu: University of Hawai'i Press, 2002), 60–61.

56. The idea of licensed evil *(hōitsu muzan)* is used by Shinran in *Mattoshō*, *Shinshū shōgyō zensho*, 2:682. Both *hōitsu*, self-indulgence, and *muzan*, remorselessness, are mental components which, according to classical Abhidharma Buddhism, obstruct the path to enlightenment. *Bukkyōgaku jiten*, 150. This expression denotes offensive or even malicious conduct stemming from the presumption that one is guaranteed birth in the Pure Land. Such conduct could range from simple haughtiness to violent behavior, but in each case the assurance of birth in the Pure Land, or at least the presumed assurance, is touted as canceling out the karmic consequences of evil deeds and as giving people liberty to do whatever they please. Shinran, Hōnen, and the traditional schools of Buddhism were united in their opposition to licensed evil, but they differed over what kinds of acts constitute licensed evil and what makes them heretical. Dobbins, *Jōd Shinshū*, 48.

57. Postscript in the *Kyōgyōshinshō*, *Shinshū shōgyō zensho* 2; *The Collected Works of Shinran: The Writings, Vol. I*. Trans. by Dennis Hirota (Kyoto: Jōd Shinshū Hongwanjisha, 1997), 289.

58. Ueda and Hirota, *Shinran*, 109.

59. Dobbins, *Jōd Shinshū*, 58.

60. Hattori Shisō, *Shinran nōtō* (1948; rpt. Tokyo: Fukumura Shuppan, 1970), 100.

61. *Goshōsokushū*, *Shinshū shōgyō zensho*, 2:700–701.

62. However, one of the serious criticisms that arose later against Shinran's Buddhism was the issue of licentiousness. People took for granted that their salvation was assured by faith in the Amida Buddha alone, so some used that as a way to justify their continuing evil deeds since the accumulation of merit was no longer needed. However, Shinran was very concerned that his teaching was being misinterpreted. In any case, there were suddenly a large number of adherents to Shinran's teaching as it swept through the outskirts of the capital.

Dobbins points out that one conspicuous form of licensed evil that irritated the authorities was the denigration of the Buddhas, bodhisattvas, and Shintō *kami* revered by mainstream religious groups. Respect for them was part and parcel of the concept of piety advanced by the orthodox Buddhist schools and upheld by the political establishment. Consequently, derision of these figures by nembutsu adherents was a symbolic act of defiance against civil and religious authority, provoking repressive measures. There are elements in Shinran's teachings that in some ways lent themselves to such inclinations. Specifically, Shinran believed that all forms of Buddhism outside of the true Pure Land teachings were merely provisional *(ke)* and should be superseded. Devotion to the true teachings, when carried to its logical end, entailed the rejection of all Buddhas and bodhisattvas besides Amida. This is intimated in a passage in the *Ichinen tanen moni* (Notes on the Single and the Repeated Nembutsu): "'Single-mindedly' *(ikkō)* means not to change to any beneficial religious practice other (than the nembutsu) and not to concentrate on any Buddha other (than Amida). . . . 'Exclusively' *(mohara)* means not to have any intention *(kokoro)* to change to other beneficial religious practices or to different Buddhas." Shinran did not dispute the existence of other Buddhas or bodhisattvas, but considered revering them to be superfluous for the true believer. Dobbins, *Jōd Shinshū*, 58.

63. *Genzeriyaku wasan, Shinshū shōgyō zensho*, vol. 2.

## CONCLUSION

1. Synchronic study model, which balances the diachronic (the ongoing development over time) study of religious phenomena with the synchronic (the setting and events that are simultaneous with specific developments); it is borrowed from structuralist discourse, which concentrates on elements within works of literature without focusing on historical, social, and biographical influences. Structuralism, however, is grounded in linguistics and developed by Ferdinand de Sausseure. Sausseure's work argues that language is a complete, self-contained system and should be studied as such. Sausseure also claimed that language is a system of signs. When applied to literature, this form of criticism is generally known as semiotics. Ferdinand de Saussure, *Course in General Linguistics*, tr. Roy Harris (LaSalle: Open Court, 1986), 83.

As explained by Umberto Eco, a synchronic perspective provides an awareness of both the context (i.e., related texts), and circumstance (e.g., the historical, social, and economic settings) of a text. Umberto Eco, *A Theory of Semiotics* (Bloomington: Indiana University Press, 1976). In Eco's usage, context is the rest of the text and other texts that in some way go with the text in question, while circumstance refers to the other aspects of a historical moment: social, economic, religious, and so on. Thus, this balanced approach seeks to understand events, institutions, individuals, and practices in relation both to their times and their place in the ongoing processes of historical change.

2. James C. Dobbins, "Envisioning Kamakura Buddhism" in *Re-Visioning "Kamakura" Buddhism*, ed. by Richard Payne (Honolulu: University of Hawai'i Press, 1998), 27.

3. An alternative name for Hachiman is Yawata (god of eight banderoles). His symbolic animal and messenger is the dove. Since ancient times, Hachiman was worshipped by peasants as the god of agriculture and by fishermen who hoped he would fill their nets with much fish. In the Shintō religion, he became identified by legend as the deified emperor Ōjin, son of the Empress Jingo, from the third to fourth century C.E. However, after the arrival of Buddhism in Japan, Hachiman became a syncretistic deity,

a harmonization of the native Shintō religion with Buddhism. In the Buddhist pantheon in eighth century C.E. he was associated with the great bodhisattva Daibosatsu. Hachiman also was noted as the guardian of the Minamoto clan of samurai. Minamoto no Yoshiie, upon coming of age at Iwashimuzu Shrine in Kyoto, took the name Hachiman Tarō Yoshiie and through his military prowess and virtue as a leader became regarded and respected as the ideal samurai through the ages. After his descendant Minamoto no Yoritomo became shōgun and established the Kamakura shogunate, he rebuilt Tsurugaoka Hachiman Shrine in Kamakura, Japan and started the reverence of Hachiman as the guardian of his clan.

4. Shiren explains that this deity is in fact one of the manifestations of Izanagi, the male protagonist in the primordial divine couple of Japanese mythology. Bernard Faure, *Visions of Power: Imagining Medieval Japanese Buddhism*. Trans. by Phyllis Brooks (Princeton: Princeton University Press, 1996), 105.

5. Robert E. Morrell, trans., *Sand and Pebbles (Shasekishū): The Tales of the Mujū Ichien, A Voice for Pluralism in Kamakura Buddhism* (Albany: State University of New York Press, 1985).

# Selected Bibliography

## COLLECTIONS

*DNBZ*  *Dai Nihon bukkyō zensho.* 151 vols. Tokyo: Bussho kankōkai, 1911–1922.

*GSZ*  *Gendaigoyaku Shinran zenshū.* 10 vols. Tokyo: Futsūsha, Shōwa 34–36 [1959–1961].

*NI*  *Nara ibun.* 3 vols. Takeuchi Rizō, ed. Tokyo: Tōkyōdō shuppan, 1962.

*NKT*  *Nihon koten bungaku taikei.* 100 vols. Tokyo: Iwanami shoten, 1958–1968.

*NKZ*  *Nihon koten bungaku zenshū.* 60 vols. Tokyo: Shōgakukan, 1970–1976.

*NST*  *Nihon shisō taikei.* 67 vols. Tokyo: Iwanami shoten, 1970–1982.

*SSZ*  *Shinshū shōgyō zensho.* 5 vols. Shinshū shōgyō zensho hensanjo, ed. Kyoto: Ōyagi kobundō, 1969–1970.

*TD*  *Taishō shinshū Daizōkyō.* 85 vols. Takakusu Junjirō, Watanabe Kaikyoku et al., ed. Tokyo: Taishō issaikyo kankōkai, 1924–1934.

*TSSZ*  *Teihon Shinran Shōnin zenshū.* 9 vols. Teihon Shinran Shōnin zenshū kankōkai, ed. Kyoto: Hōzōkan, 1976.

## PRIMARY SOURCES

*Azuma kagami* (Mirror of the Eastern region). Vol. I. Katsumi Kuroita, ed. Tokyo: Kokushi taikei kankōkai, 1932.

*Dai Nihon koku zokusan ō Shōtoku Taishi hōsan* (Hymns to Prince Shōtoku, Monarch of the Millet-Scattered Islands of Japan). *SSZ*, vol. 4.

*Engishiki* (Procedures of the Engi Era). *NKZ*, vol. 24.

*Eshinni shōsoku* (Letters of Eshinni). *SSZ*, vol. 5.

*Eshinni monjo* (Letters of Eshinni). *Eshinni monjo*, ed. Miyazaki Enjun.

*Fusō ryakki, Shintei zōhō kokushi taikei,* vol. 12. Tokyo: Yoshikawa kōbunkan, 1965.

*Gaijashō* (Notes Rectifying Heresy). *SSZ,* vol. 3.

*Gangōji garan engi narabi ni ruki shizaichō. NST,* vol. 20.

*Gobunshō* (The letters of Rennyo). *SSZ,* vol. 3.

*Godenshō* (A biography of Honganji's Master Shinran). *SSZ,* vol. 3.

*Goshosokushū* (Collection of [Shinran's] letters). *SSZ,* vol. 2.

*Gutokushō* (Shinran's notes). *SSZ,* vol. 2.

*Haja kenshōsho* (Notes Assailing Heresy and Revealing Truth). *SSZ,* vol. 3.

*Hyakurenshō* in *Kokushi taikei,* vol. 11, rev. ed. Tokyo: Yoshikawa kōbunkan, 1965.

*Hokekyō gisho. TD,* vol. 9.

*Honchō kōsōden. DNBZ,* vol. 113.

*Honganji Shōnin Shinran denne* (An Illustrated Biography of Honganji's Master Shinran). *SSZ,* vol. 3.

*Hōonkō shiki* (A Service of Thanksgiving for Shinran's Virtues). *SSZ,* vol. 3.

*Hōryūji betto shidai, Zoku gunsho ruiju,* vol. 4, Honinbu. Tokyo: Zoku gunsho ruiju kanseikai, 1930.

*Hōryūji garan engi narabini ruki shizaichō* (Lists of Accumulated Treasures from the Hōryū Temple). *DNBZ,* vol. 85.

*Hōryūji shaka sanzon zō, Kigakushin nyoraizō kōhaimei. NI, vol. 1.*

*Hōryūji shaka sanzon zō, Yakushi nyoraizō kohaimei. NI,* vol. 1.

*Hōryūji Tōin engi shizaichō. DNBZ,* vol. 85.

*Ichinen tanen mon'i* (Notes on the Single and Repeated Nembutsu). *SSZ,* vol. 2.

*Jūshichijō kenpō* (Seventeen-Article Constitution in *Nihon shoki,* kan 22, vol. 22, Suiko Tennō, 12 nen, 4th month; *Shōtoku Taishi zenshū* 1). *NST,* vol. 2.

*Jōdo wasan* (Hymns on the Pure Land). *SSZ,* vol. 2.

*Jōgū bosatsu hiden. DNBZ,* vol. 71.

*Jōgū kōtaishi bosatsuden* (Biography of the Priestly-Prince of the Upper Palace). *DNBZ,* vol. 71.

*Jōgū Shōtoku hōō teisetsu* (The Imperial Record of Shōtoku, Priestly-Prince of the Upper Palace). *NST,* vol. 2.

*Jōgū Shōtoku Taishi den hoketsuki. DNBZ,* vol. 112.

*Jōgū Taishi gyoki* (Account of the Prince of the Upper Palace). *SSZ,* vol. 4.

*Kanmuryōjukyō* (Sutra on the Contemplation of the Buddha of Boundless Life). *TD,* vol. 12; *SSZ,* vol. 1.

*Kechimyaku monju* (Collection of Writings from the Lineage). *SSZ,* vol. 2.

*Kōfukuji sōjō* (Kōfukuji's Petition to the Emperor). *NST,* vol. 15.

*Kōji ruien kankōkai.* Tokyo: Koji Ruien Kankōkai, 1931.

*Kōsō wasan* (Hymns of the Pure Land Masters). *SSZ,* vol. 2.

*Kōtaishi Shōtoku hōsan* (Hymns in praise of Prince Shōtoku). *SSZ,* vol. 2.

*Kyōgyōshinshō* (A Collection of Passages Revealing the True Teaching, Practice, and Realization of the Pure Land Way). *SSZ,* vol. 2.

*Mattōshō* (Lamp for the Latter Ages). *SSZ,* vol. 2.

*Muryōjukyō* (Sutra of the Buddha of Boundless Life). *TD,* no. 360, vol. 12.

*Nihon bukkyō gakkai,* ed., Shōtoku Taishi kenkyū. Kyoto: Heirakuji Shoten, 1964.

*Nihon ryoiki* (Record of Miraculous Events in Japan). *NKT,* vol. 70.

*Nihon shoki* (Chronicles of Japan). *NKT,* vol. 68.

*Nyobonge* (Verse on Making Love to a Woman). *TSSZ,* vol. 4, pt. 2.

*Rennyo Shōnin Ofumi* (Letters of Master Rennyo). *TD,* vol. 83.

*Ryojin hishō* (Treasured Selections of Superb Songs). *NKT,* vol. 79.

*Sanbōe* (An Illustrated Account on the Three Treasures). Sanbōe, ed. Izumoji Osamu. Tōyō bunko, no. 513.

*Shinran muki* (A record of Shinran's dreams). *TSSZ,* vol. 4, pt. 2.

*Shinran Shōnin goin-en hidenshō* (A Selection of Hidden Notes on Circumstances in Master Shinran's Life). *Shinranden sosho,* ed. Sasaki Gessho. Tokyo: Mugasanbō, 1910.

*Shinran Shōnin goshosokushū* (A collection of Master Shinran's letters). *SSZ,* vol. 2.

*Shinran Shōnin senju kankōkai,* ed. *TSSZ,* vol. 4, pt. 2.

*Shinran Shōnin shōtōden* (The Orthodox Biography of Master Shinran). *GSZ,* vol. 4.

*Shiryō-taisei,* vol. 31. Kyoto: Rinsen shoten, 1965.

*Shitennōji goshuin engi. DNBZ,* vol. 112.

*Shitennōji rekidai bettō shumu jijo, Zoku gunsho ruijū,* vol. 4. Tokyo: Hideya, 1904.

*Shōmangyō* (Śrīmālā Sutra). *TD,* vol. 12.

*Shōtoku Taishiden. NKT,* vol. 68.

*Shōtoku Taishi denki, Yamato Kōji Taikan,* vol. 1. Tokyo: Iwanami shoten, 1977.

*Shōtoku Taishi denreki. DNBZ,* vol. 112.

*Shōtoku Taishi denryaku* (A Chronological Account of Shōtoku Taishi). *DNBZ,* vol. 112.

*Shōtoku Taishi denshiki.* Tokyo: Iwanami shoten, 1934.

*Shōtoku Taishi heishiden zokanmon. DNBZ,* vol. 71.

*Shōtoku Taishiden hoketsuki* (Supplementary Note on Shōtoku Taishi's Biography). Tokyo: Yoshikawa kōbunkan, 1980.

*Shōtoku Taishi hōsan. SSZ,* vol. 2.

*Shōtoku Taishi kokon mokuroku sho. DNBZ,* vol. 71.

*Shōtoku Taishi koshiki* (A Celebration of the Virtues of Prince-Regent Shōtoku). *SSZ,* vol. 5.

*Shōtoku Taishi to Nihon bunka.* Tokyo: Shunjūsha, Shōwa 49 [1974].

*Shōzōmatsu wasan* (Hymns on the Right, Semblance, and Last Dharma-Ages). *SSZ,* vol. 2.

*Shohon Taishō Sanbōe shūsei.* Eds. Shūsei, Koizumi, Hiroshi, and Takahashi Nobuyuki. Tokyo: Kasama Shoin, 1980.

*Taishi mandara koshiki, Yamato Koji Taikan,* vol. 1. Tokyo: Iwanami shoten, 1977.

*Tandokumon* (Passages in Praise of Shinran's Virtue). *SSZ,* vol. 3.

*Tannishō* (Notes Lamenting Deviations). *SSZ,* vol. 2.

*Tōdaiwajō tōseiden. DNBZ,* 113.

*Yuimagyō gisho. DNBZ,* vol. 4.

*Yuimagyō–Shomangyō ichiji sakuin.* Tokyo: Toyo Tetsugaku Kenkyūjo, 1979.

*Yuishinshō mon'i* (Notes on 'Essentials of Faith Alone'). *SSZ,* vol. 2.

*Zonkaku hōgo* (Zonkaku's Words on the Dharma). *SSZ,* vol. 3.

## ENGLISH TRANSLATIONS OF SHINRAN'S WORKS

*Essentials of Passages on the Pure Land Way: A Translation of Shinran's Jōdo monrui jushō.* Shin Buddhism Translation Series. Kyoto: Hongwanji International Center, 1982.

*Hymns of the Pure Land: A Translation of Shinran's Jōdo Wasan.* Shin Buddhism Translation Series. Kyoto: Hongwanji International Center, 1991.

*Hymns of the Pure Land: A Translation of Shinran's Kōsō Wasan.* Shin Buddhism Translation Series. Kyoto: Hongwanji International Center, 1992.

*The Jōdo Wasan: The Hymns on the Pure Land.* Ryūkoku Translation Series IV. Kyoto: Ryūkoku University Translation Center, 1965.

*The Kōsō Wasan: The Hymns on the Pure Land.* Ryūkoku Translation Series IV. Kyoto: Ryūkoku University Translation Center, 1974.

*The Kyō Gyō Shin Shō (Ken Jōdo Shinjitsu Kyōgyōshō Monrui): The Teaching, Practice, Faith, and Enlightenment (A Collection of Passages Revealing the True Teaching, Practice, and Enlightenment of Pure Land Buddhism).* Ryūkoku Translation Series V. Kyoto: Ryūkoku University Translation Center, 1966.

*Letters of Shinran: A Translation of Mattōshō.* Shin Buddhism Translation Series. Kyoto: Hongwanji International Center, 1978.

*Notes on "Essentials of Faith Alone": A Translation of Shinran's Yuishinshō-mon'i.* Shin Buddhism Translation Series. Kyoto: Hongwanji International Center, 1979.

*Notes on Once-calling and Many-calling: A Translation of Shinran's Ichinen-tanen mon'i.* Shin Buddhism Translation Series. Kyoto: Hongwanji International Center, 1980.

*Notes on the Inscriptions on Sacred Scrolls: A Translation of Shinran's Songo shinzo meimon.* Shin Buddhism Translation Series. Kyoto: Hongwanji International Center, 1981.

*The Shoshin Ge: The Gatha of True Faith in the Nenbutsu.* Ryūkoku Translation Series I. Kyoto: Ryūkoku University Translation Center, 1962.

*Shōzōmatsu Wasan: Shinran's Hymns on the Last Age.* Ryūkoku Translation Series VII. Kyoto: Ryūkoku University Translation Center, 1980.

*Tannishō: A Shin Buddhist Classic.* Trans. by Taitetsu Unno. Honolulu: Buddhist Study Center Press, 1984.

*Tannishō: A Primer.* Trans. by Dennis Hirota. Kyoto: Ryūkoku University Translation Center, 1982.

*The Tannishō: Notes Lamenting Differences.* Ryūkoku Translation Series II. Kyoto: Ryūkoku University Translation Center, 1962.

*The True Teaching, Practice and Realization of the Pure Land Way: A Translation of Shinran's Kyogyoshinshō.* 4 vols. Shin Buddhism Translation Series. Kyoto: Hongwanji International Center, 1983–1990.

## SECONDARY SOURCES

## Works in Western Languages

Abé, Ryūichi. *Weaving of Mantra: Kūkai and the Construction of Esoteric Buddhist Discourse.* New York: Columbia University Press, 1999.

Adolphson, Mikail. *The Gates of Power: Monks, Courtiers, and Warriors in Premodern Japan.* Honolulu: University of Hawai'i Press, 2000.

Akamatsu Toshihide. *Shitennōji no Shoseki* in Hihō, vol. 3, Shitennōji, Tokyo: Kōdansha, 1968.

———. "Medieval Tendai Hongaku Thought and the New Kamakura Buddhism; A Reconsideration" in *Japanese Journal of Religious Studies* 22 (2) (1995): 17–48.

Andreasen, Esben. *Popular Buddhism in Japan: Shin Buddhist Religion & Culture.* Honolulu: University of Hawai'i Press, 1998.

Anesaki Masaharu. *Prince Shōtoku, The Sage Statesman.* Tokyo: Shōtoku Taishi Hōsankai, 1948.

Aston, W. G., trans. *Nihongi: Chronicles of Japan from the Earliest Times to A.D. 697.* Rutland: Charles E. Tuttle Co., 1988.

Bandō Shōjun. "Myoe's Criticism of Hōnen's Doctrine" in *Eastern Buddhist*, n.s., 7, 1 (May 1971).

Bender, Ross. "The Hachiman Cult and the Dōkyō Incident" in *Monumenta Nipponica* 34, 2 (1978): 125–152.

Berger, Peter L. *The Sacred Canopy: Elements of a Sociological Theory of Religion.* Garden City: Anchor Books, 1983.

Bloom, Alfred. *Shinran's Gospel of Pure Grace.* Ed. Delmer M. Brown. Ann Arbor: Association for Asian Studies, 1965.

———. "The Life of Shinran Shōnin: The Journey to Self-Acceptance." *Numen* 15 (1968).

Bloom, Alfred. ed. *Living in Amida's Universal Vow: Essays in Shin Buddhism.* Bloomington: World Wisdom, 2004.

Como, Michael. "Ethnicity, Sagehood, and the Politics of Literacy in Asuka Japan." *Japanese Journal of Religious Studies* 30, 1–2 (2003): 61–84.

Cowell, E. B., ed. *The Jātaka, or Stories of the Buddha's Former Lives, Translated by Various Hands*, 6 vols. Cambridge: Cambridge University Press, 1895–1907.

De Bary, W. Theodore, ed. *Sources of Japanese Tradition*, vol. I. New York: Columbia University Press, 1958.

De Visser, M. W. *Ancient Buddhism in Japan: Sutras and Ceremonies in Use in the Seventh and Eighth Centuries A.D. and Their History in Later Times*, 2 vols. Leiden: E. J. Brill, 1935.

Deal, William E. "Hagiography and History: The Image of Prince Shōtoku" in *Religions of Japan in Practice*. George J. Tanabe Jr., ed. Princeton: Princeton University Press, 1999.

Dobbins, James C. "From Inspiration to Institution: The Rise of Sectarian Identity in Jōdo Shinshū" in *Monumenta Nipponica* 41/3 (Autumn 1986).

———. *Jōdo Shinshū: Shin Buddhism in Medieval Japan.* Indianapolis: Indiana University Press, 1989.

———. *Letters of the Nun Eshinni: Images of Pure Land Buddhism in Medieval Japan.* Honolulu: University of Hawai'i Press, 2004.

———. "The Concept of Heresy in the Jōdo Shinshū" in *Transactions of the International Conference of Orientalists in Japan* 25 (1980).

———. "The Biography of Shinran: Apotheosis of a Japanese Buddhist Visionary" in *History of Religions* 30, 2 (November 1990).

Dobbins, James C., ed. "The Legacy of Kuroda Toshio" in *Japanese Journal of Religious Studies* 23 (3–4), 1996.

Dutt, Nalinaksha. *Early History of the Spread of Buddhism and the Buddhist Schools*. London: Luzac, 1925.

Eco, Umberto. *Theory of Semiotics*. Bloomington: Indiana University Press, 1976.

Eliot, Sir Charles. *Japanese Buddhism*. London: Edward Arnold and Company, 1935.

Faure, Bernard. *Visions of Power: Imagining Medieval Japanese Buddhism*. Trans. by Phyllis Brooks. Princeton: Princeton University Press, 1996.

Foard, James H. "In Search of a Lost Reformation: A Reconsideration of Kamakura Buddhism" in *Japanese Journal of Religious Studies* 7, 4 (December 1980).

Fujii Masao. "Founder Worship in Kamakura Buddhism" in *Religion and the Family in East Asia*, ed. George A. de Vos and Sofue Takao. Berkeley: University of California Press, 1984.

Gomez, Luis O. "Shinran's Faith and the Sacred Name of Amida" in *Monumenta Nipponica*, 38/1 (Spring 1983), 73–84.

Grapard, Allan G. "The Shintō of Yoshida Kanemoto" in *Monumenta Nipponica* 47, 1 (1993).

———. *The Protocol of the Gods: A Study of the Kasuga Cult in Japanese History*. Berkeley and Los Angeles: University of California Press, 1992.

Groner, Paul. *Saichō: The Establishment of the Japanese Tendai School*. Berkeley: Berkeley Buddhist Studies Series, 1984.

Hall, John W. *Government and Local Power in Japan, 500–1700: A Study Based on Bizen Providence*. Princeton: Princeton University Press, 1966.

Hall, John W., and Jeffrey P. Mass, eds. *Medieval Japan: Essays in Institutional History*. Stanford: Stanford University Press, 1988.

Hall, John W., and Toyoda TakHuisi, eds. *Japan in the Muromachi Age*. Berkeley: University of California Press, 1977.

Hanayama Shinsho. "Prince Shōtoku and Japanese Buddhism" in *Philosophical Studies of Japan* 4 (1963): 23–48.

Hirota, Dennis, trans. *The Collected Works of Shinran. Volume I: The Writings*. Shin Buddhism Translation Series. Kyoto: Jōdo Shinshū, 1997.

———. *The Collected Works of Shinran. Volume II: Introductions, Glossaries, and Reading Aids*. Shin Buddhism Translation Series. Kyoto: Jōdo Shinshū, 1997.

Hurst, G. Cameron III. *Insei: Abdicated Sovereigns in the Politics of Late Heian Japan 1086–1185*. New York: Columbia University Press, 1976.

Inagaki Hisao. *A Dictionary of Japanese Buddhist Terms*. Heian: University of London, 1988.

Ito Kimio. "The Invention of *Wa* and the Transformation of the Image of Prince Shōtoku in Modern Japan" in *Mirror of Modernity: Invented Traditions of Modern Japan*, Stephen Vlastos, ed. Berkeley: University of California Press, 1998.

Kamens, Edward. *The Three Jewels: A Study and Translation of Minamoto Tamenori's Sanbōe*. Ann Arbor: Center for Japanese Studies, 1988.

Kanaji Isamu. "Three Stages in Shōtoku Taishi's Acceptance of Buddhism" in *Acta Asiatica: Bulletin of the Institute of Eastern Culture* 47. Takasaki Jikido, ed. Tokyo: Tōhō Gakka, 1985.

Kasulis, Thomas. "Letters of Shinran" in *Philosophy East and West*, 31/2 (1981).

Katz, Stephen. "Language, Epistemology, and Mysticism" in *Mysticism and Philosophical Analysis*. New York: Oxford University Press, 1978.

Keel, Hee-Sung . *Understanding Shinran*. Fremont: Asian Humanities Press, 1995.

King, Winston L. "An Interpretation of the Anjin Ketsujōshō" in *Japanese Journal of Religious Studies*, 13/4 (1986).

Kōshō Yamamoto. *An Introduction to Shin Buddhism*. Tokyo: Karinbunko, 1963.

Kuroda Toshio. "Historical Consciousness and *hon-jaku* Philosophy in the Medieval Period on Mount Hiei," trans. Allan Grapard, in *The Lotus Sutra in Japanese Culture*, ed. George J. Tanabe Jr. and Willa Tanabe. Honolulu: University of Hawai'i Press, 1989.

———. "Shintō in the History of Japanese Religion," trans. James C. Dobbins and Suzanne Gay, in *Journal of Japanese Studies* 7 (1981).

———. "The Development of the *Kenmitsu* System as Japan's Medieval Orthodoxy" in *Japanese Journal of Religious Studies*, special issue: The Legacy of Kuroda Toshio, 23, 3 and 4 (1996): 233–269.

———. "The Imperial Law and the Buddhist Law," trans. Jacqueline I. Stone, in *Journal of Japanese Studies* 23 (1996).

Kyōko Motomochi Nakamura. *Miraculous Stories from the Japanese Buddhist Tradition: The Nihon Ryōiki of the Monk Kyōkai*. Cambridge: Harvard University Press, 1973.

LaFleur, William R. "Tendai Buddhism in Japan," ed. Paul Swanson, in *Japanese Journal of Religious Studies* 14, 2–3 (1987).

LaFleur, William R, trans. *Introduction to Mirror for the Moon: A Selection of Poems by Saigyō*. New York: New Directions, 1977.

Lee, Kenneth Doo Young. "The Comparative Analysis of Shinran's *shinjin* and Calvin's Faith" in the *Buddhist-Christian Studies Journal* 24 (December 2004): 171–191.

Maraldo, John. "Hermeneutics and Historicity in the Study of Buddhism" in *Eastern Buddhist* 19 (I) (1986): 17–43.

Matsunaga Alicia, and Daigan. *Foundation of Japanese Buddhism. Vol. I: The Aristocratic Age*. Los Angeles: Buddhist Books International, 1974.

———. *Foundation of Japanese Buddhism. Vol. II: The Mass Movement*. Los Angeles: Buddhist Books International, 1976.

Matsuo Kenji, "What Is Kamakura New Buddhism" in *Japanese Journal of Religious Studies* 24, 1–2 (Spring 1997).

McCallum, Donald F. *Zenkōji and Its Icon: A Study in Medieval Japanese Religious Art.* Princeton: Princeton University Press, 1994.

McMullin, Neil. "Historical and Historiographical Issues in the Study of Pre-Modern Japanese Religions" in *Japanese Journal of Religious Studies* 16, 1 (1989).

———. "The Sanmon-Jimon Schism in the Tendai School of Buddhism: A Preliminary Analysis" in *The Journal of the International Association of Buddhist Studies* 7, 1 (1984): 83–105.

———. *Buddhism and the State in Sixteenth-Century Japan.* Princeton: Princeton University Press, 1984.

Meech-Pekarik, Julia. "The Flying White Horse: Transmission of the Valahassa Jātaka Imagery from India to Japan" in *Artibus Asiae* 42, 1 and 2 (1981–1982): 111–128.

Minoru Shinoda. *The Founding of the Kamakura Shōgunate 1180–1185.* New York: Columbia University Press, 1960.

Morrell, Robert E. "Shōtoku Taishi" in *Great Thinkers of the Eastern World*, ed. Ian P. McGreal. New York: HarperCollins, 1995.

———. *Early Kamakura Buddhism: A Minority Report.* Berkeley: Asian Humanities Press, 1987.

———. "The Buddhist Poetry in the Goshūishū" in *Monumenta Nipponica* 28, 1 (Spring 1973). 88–100.

———. *Sand and Pebbles (Shasekishi): The Tales of Mujū Ichien, A Voice for Pluralism in Kamakura Buddhism.* Albany: State University of New York Press, 1985.

Nakai Gendo. *Shinran and His Religion of Pure Faith.* Kyoto: Kanao Bunendō, 1946.

Nakamura Hajime. "The Ideal of a Universal State and its Philosophical Basis—Prince Shōtoku and His Successors" in *A History of the Development of Japanese Thought* I. Tokyo: Kokusai Bunka Shinkōkai, 1967.

Nakamura Hajime, trans. "The Seventeen-Article Constitution by Prince Shōtoku" in *Prince Shōtoku and Shitennōji Temple.* Ōsaka: The Hōsankai of Shitennōji Temple, 1970.

Nakamura Kyoko Motomochi, trans. *Miraculous Stories from the Japanese Buddhist Tradition: The Nihon ryōiki of the Monk Kyōkai.* Richmond: Curzon Press, 1997.

Nishimura Sey. "The Prince and the Pauper: The Dynamics of a Shōtoku Legend" in *Monumenta Nipponica* 40: 3 (Autumn 1985).

Norihiko Kikumura. *Shinran: His Life and Thought.* Los Angeles: Nenbutsu Press, 1983.

Ocho Enichi. "From the Lotus Sutra to the Sutra of Eternal Life: Reflections on the Process of Deliverance in Shinran" in *The Eastern Buddhist* 11, 1 (May 1978).

Ohtani, Lady Yoshiko. *The Life of Eshinni: The Wife of Shinran Shōnin.* Trans. by Taitetsu Unno. Kyoto: Honpa Hongwanji, 1970.

Ōsumi Kazuo. "Buddhism in the Kamakura Period" in *The Cambridge History of Japan*, vol. 3: *Medieval Japan.* Kōzō Yamamura, ed. Cambridge: Cambridge University Press, 1990.

Philippi, Donald L., trans., *Kojiki*. Princeton: Princeton University Press, 1968.

Piggott, Joan R. "Hierarchy and Economics in Early Medieval Tōdaiji" in *Court and Bakufu in Japan: Essays in Kamakura History*. Jeffrey P. Mass, ed. New Haven: Yale University Press, 1982.

———. *The Emergence of Japanese Kingship*. Stanford: Stanford University Press, 1985.

Pradel, María del Rosario. "The Fragments of the *Tenjukoku shūchō mandara* Reconstruction and Iconography and the Historical Contexts." Ph.D. diss., University of California, Los Angeles, 1997.

Reischauer, Edwin O. *Japan: The Story of a Nation*, 3rd. ed. New York: Alfred A. Knopf, 1981.

Rogers, Minor, and Ann. *Rennyo: The Second Founder of Shin Buddhism*. Berkeley: Asian Humanities Press, 1991.

Rogers, Minor Lee. "Rennyo and Jōdo Shinshū Piety: The Yoshizaki Years" in *Monumenta Nipponica*, 36/1 (Spring 1981).

———. "The Shin Faith of Rennyo" in *The Eastern Buddhist*, 15/1 (Spring 1982).

Ruppert, Brian D. *Jewel in the Ashes: Buddha Relics and Power in Early Medieval Japan*. Cambridge: Harvard University Press, 2000.

Sansom, George. *A History of Japan to 1334*. Stanford: Stanford University Press, 1958.

Sasaki Gesshō, and Suzuki Daisetz T., trans. "The Life of Shinran Shōnin *(Godenshō)*" in *Collected Writings on Shin Buddhism*, Daisetz Teitaro Suzuki, ed. Kyoto: Shinshū Ōtaniha, 1973.

Smith, Bardwell, ed., *The Two Wheels of Dhamma: Essays on the Theravada Tradition in India and Ceylon*. Chambersburg: American Academy of Religion, 1972.

Smith, Wilfred Cantrell. *Faith and Belief*. Princeton: Princeton University Press, 1979.

Snellen, J.B., trans. "Shoku Nihongi: Chronicles of Japan, Continued, A.D. 697–791 (Books I–VI)" in *Transactions of the Asiatic Society of Japan*, second series, 11 (1934), 14 (1937).

Solomon, Michael. "Honganji Under Rennyo: The Development of Shinshū in Medieval Japan" in *The Pure Land Tradition: History and Development*. Ed. by James Foard, Michael Solomon, and Richard K. Payne. Berkeley: Berkeley Buddhist Studies Series, 1996.

Stone, Jacqueline. "Seeking Enlightenment in the Last Age: *Mappō* Thought in Kamakura Buddhism" in *The Eastern Buddhist*, The Eastern Buddhist Society, 18, 1 (Spring 1985).

Strong, John S. *The Legend of King Aśoka: A Study and Translation of the Asokavadana*. Princeton: Princeton University Press, 1983.

Suzuki Daisetz T. *Collected Writing on Shin Buddhism*. Kyoto: Shinshū Ōtaniha, 1973.

Taira Masayuki. "Kuroda Toshio and the Kenmitsu Taisei Theory" in *Japanese Journal of Religious Studies*, special issue: The Legacy of Kuroda Toshio, 23, 3 and 4 (1996): 427–448.

Takahatake Takamichi. *Young Man Shinran: A Reappraisal of Shinran's Life*. Waterloo: Wilfrid Laurier University Press, 1987.

Tambiah, Stanley. "The Buddhist Conception of Kingship and its Historical Manifestations" in *Journal of Asian Studies* 37 (1978): 801–809.

————. *World Conqueror and World Renouncer: A Study of Buddhism and Polity in Thailand Against a Historical Background*. Cambridge: Cambridge University Press, 1976.

Tamura Enchō. "Japan and the Eastward Permeation of Buddhism" in *Acta Asiatica* 47 (1985): 1–30.

Tamura Noriyoshi. "Buddhism in Japan" in *Buddhism and Asian History*, ed. J. Kitagawa and M. Cummings. New York: Macmillan, 1989.

Tanabe, George Jr. *Myoe the Dreamkeeper: Fantasy and Knowledge in Early Kamakura Buddhism*. Cambridge: Harvard University Press, 1992.

Tanaka Eizo, trans. "Anjin Ketsujō Shō: On the Attainment of True Faith" in *The Pure Land*, 2/2–5/2 (December 1980–December 1983).

Teewen, Mark, and Rambelli, Fabio. *Buddhas and Kami in Japan: Honji Suijaku as Combinatory Paradigm*. New York: Routledge, 2003.

Terry, Charles S. "Legend and Political Intrigue in Ancient Japan: Shōtoku Taishi" in *Great Historical Figures of Japan*, ed. Murakami Hyōe and Thomas J. Harper. Tokyo: Japan Culture Institute, 1978.

Thurman, Robert. "Buddhist Hermeneutics" in *Journal of the American Academy of Religion* 46 (I) (1978): 19–39.

————. *The Holy Teaching of Vimalakīrti*. University Park: Pennsylvania State University Press, 1976.

Tsunoda Ryūsaku et al., eds. *Sources of Japanese Tradition I*. New York and London: Columbia University Press, 1958 and 1964.

Ueda Yoshifumi, ed. *Letters of Shinran: A Translation of Mattōshō*. Kyoto: Honganji International Center, 1978.

Ueda Yoshifumi, and Hirota, Dennis. *Shinran: An Introduction to His Thought*. Kyoto: Hongwanji International Center, 1989.

Unno Taitetsu, trans. *Tannishō: A Shin Buddhist Classic*. Honolulu: Buddhist Study Center Press, 1984.

Varley, Paul, trans. Kitabatake Chikafusa. *Jinno Shotoki: A Chronicle of Gods and Sovereigns*. New York: Columbia University Press, 1980.

Wayman, Alex, and Hideko, trans. *The Lion's Roar of Queen Śrīmālā*. New York: Columbia University, 1974.

Weinstein, Stanley. "Rennyo and the Shinshū Revival" in *Japan in the Muromachi Age*, ed. John Whitney Hall and Toyada Takeshi. Berkeley: University of California Press, 1977.

———. "The Concept of Reformation in Japanese Buddhism" in *Studies in Japanese Culture*, ed. Saburō Ōta. Tokyo: Japan Pen Club, 1973.

Yamaguchi, Susumu. "The Concept of the Pure Land in Nagarjuna's Doctrine" in *The Eastern Buddhist*, Eastern Buddhist Society, 1, 2 (September 1966).

Yamamoto Kōshō. *An Introduction to Shin Buddhism*. Ube: Karinbunko, 1963.

———. *The Private Letters of Shinran Shōnin*. Tokyo: Okazakiya shoten, 1946.

Yoshida Kazuhiko. "Revisioning Religion in Ancient Japan" in *Japanese Journal of Religious Studies* 30, 1–2 (2003): 1–26.

Yü, Chün-fang. *Kuan-yin: The Chinese Transformation of Avalokiteśvara*. New York: Columbia University Press, 2001.

## Works in Japanese

Abe Yasurō. "Hoshu to ōken: Chūsei ōken to mikkyō girei" in *Iwanami kozo toyo shisō*, vol. 16 (Nihon shisō 2), ed. Izutsu Toshihiko et al., 116–169. Tokyo: Iwanami shoten, 1989.

Abe Yasurō. "Taishakuhan no seiritsu" in *Kowaka bukkyō kenkyū*, vol. 4, ed. Ago Toranoshin, 80–195. Tokyo: Miai shoten, 1986.

Akamatsu Toshihide. "Chūsei bukkyō no seiritsu" in *Nihon bukkyōshi Chūseihen*. Tokyo: Hōzōkan, 1967.

———. *Kamakura bukkyō no kenkyū*. Kyoto: Heirakuji shoten, 1957.

———. *Shinran* in *Jinbutsu sosho*, no. 65. Tokyo: Yoshikawa kōbunkan, 1961.

———. *Shitennōji no Shoseki* in *Hihō*, vol. 3. Tokyo: Kōdansha, 1968.

———. *Zoku Kamakura bukkyō no kenkyū*. Kyoto: Heirakuji shoten, 1968.

Akamatsu Toshihide and Kasahara Kazuo, eds. *Shinshūshi gaisetsu*. Kyoto: Heirakuji shoten, 1963.

Chiba Jōryu. *Shinshū kyōdan no soshiki to seido*. Kyoto: Dobosha, 1978.

———. *Honganji monogatari*. Kyoto: Dobosha, 1984.

Chiba Jōryu, Kitanishi Hiromu, and Takagi Yutaka. *Bukkyōshi gaisetsu* in *Nihon hen*. Kyoto: Heirakuji shoten, 1969.

Dobosha Shuppan, ed. *Shinran ni deatta hitobito*, 5 vols. Kyoto: Dobosha, 1989.

Eiki Giken. "Shinran Shōnin, Zonkaku Shōnin no Hokke-kyo ni taisuru taido" in *Shinshūgaku*, no. 44, 1971.

Ekisai Kariya. "Awaharaji Rohanmei" in *Kokyō ibun* (1818) *Kokuritsu kokkai toshokan shozōbon* (Possession of the National Japanese Library). Tokyo: Hōbundō, 1893.

Enjun Miyazaki. "Anjo no Miei to sono igi" in *Shoki Shinshū no kenkyū*. Kyoto: Nagata bunshodō, 1971.

———. "Chūsei bukkyō ni okeru dendo no mondai—Shū to shite etoki ni tsuite" in *Kamakura bukkyō keisei no mondaiten*, ed. Nihon Bukkyō Gakkai. Kyoto: Heirakuji Shoten, 1969.

Fujieda Akira. "Kaisetsu, Shōmangyō-gishō" in *Nihon shisō taikei 2*, Shōtoku Taishi shū, Ienaga Saburō et al., eds., pp. 484–544. Tokyo: Iwanami shoten, 1975.

Fujii Manabu. "Chūsei shūkyō no seiritsu" in *Kozo nihon bunkashi*, vol. 3, ed. Nihonshi kenkyūkai. Tokyo: San'ichi shobō, 1962.

———. "Chūsei shoki no seiji shisō to kokka ishiki" in *Iwanami koza nishon rekishi kinsei*, vol. 2, ed. Iwanami nihon rekishi kenkyūkai. Tokyo: Iwanami shoten, 1975.

Fujii Yukiko, *Shōtoku Taishi no denshō*. Tokyo: Yoshikawa kōbunkan, 1999.

Fukui Kōjun. *Toyo shisōshi kenkyu*. Tokyo: Shoseki Bunbutsu Ryūtsūkai, 1961.

Fukuyama Toshio. *Nihon kenchikushi kenkyū*. Tokyo: Bokusui shobō, 1968–1971.

Furuta Takehiko. *Shinran shisō    Sono shiryō hihan* Tokyo: Fuzanbō, 1975.

Futaba Kenkō. "Nara jidai ni okeru risshū to kairitsu" in *Kairitusu no sekai*, ed. Mori Shōji. Tokyo: Keisuisha, 1993.

———. *Nihon bukkyōno kadai: mōhitotsu no hunka no kōchiku ni mukete*. Tokyo: Mainichi shimbunsha, 1986.

———. *Nihon kodai bukkyōshi no kenkyū*. Kyoto: Nagata bunshodō, 1984.

———. *Shinran no kenkyū: Shinran ni okeru shin to rekishi*. Kyoto: Hyakkaen, 1962.

———. *Shōtoku Taishi kara Shinran e*. Kyoto: Honganji Shuppan Kyōkai, 1972.

———. *Tennōsei to shinshū*. Kyoto: Nagata bunshodō, 1991.

———. "Umako no shari shinkō" in *Kodai bukkyō shisōshi kenkyū*, 70–80. Kyoto: Nagata bunshodō, 1962.

———. *Shinran no hiraita chihei*. Kyoto: Hyakkaen, 1975.

Futaba Kenkō and Satō Michio, eds. *Shinshū Kyōgaku kenkyū*. Kyoto: Nagata bunshodō, 1980.

Futaba Kenkō, ed. *Kokka to bukkyō*. Nihon bukkyōshi kenkyū, vol. 1. Kyoto: Nagata bunshodō, 1979.

———. *Shinran no subete*. Tokyo: Shinjinbutsu Juraisha, 1984.

Gorai Shigeru. *Zenkōji-mairi* (Pilgrimage to Zenkōji). Tokyo: Kadokawa shoten, 1988.

Hanayama Shinsho. "Gyobutsu Hokke gisho no sengo" in *Indotetsugaku no shomondai*. Tokyo: Iwanami shoten, 1951.

Hara Katsuro. "Tōzai no shūkyō kaikaku" (1911; reprinted in *Shinran taikei: Rekishihen*, vol. 1). Kyoto: Hōzōkan, 1989.

Hattori Shiso. *Shinran nōto*. Tokyo: Fukumura shuppan, 1948.

———. *Zoku Shinran nōto.* Tokyo: Fukumura shūppan, 1970.

Hayakawa Shōhachi. "Ritsuyosei to Tennō" in *Shigaku zasshi* 85, 3 (1976): 69–85.

Hayami Tasuku. *Heian kizoku shakai to bukkyō.* Tokyo: Kikkawa kōbunkan, 1975.

Hayashi Mikiya. *Taishi shinkō.* Tokyo: Hyoronsha, 1972.

———. *Taishi shinkō no kenkyū.* Tokyo: Yoshikawa kōbunkan, 1980.

———. *Taishi shinkō: Sono hassei to hatten.* Tokyo: Hyōronsha, 1980.

Hayashima Kyōshō. *Shinran nyumon.* Tokyo: Yūzankaku, 1979.

Hayashima Kyōshō and Bando Shōjun, eds. *Nihon bukkyō kiso koza* 5, Jōdo Shinshū. Tokyo: Yūzankaku, 1979.

Hiramatsu Reizō. *Shinshū-shi ronko* (Essays on the History of the Shin School). Kyoto: Dōbōsha, 1988.

Hirata Toshiharu. *Heian jidai no kenkyū.* Tokyo: Yamaichi shobō, 1943.

Hoshino Genpō, Ishida Mitsuyuki, and Iyenaga Saburō, eds. *Kyōgyōshinshō* in *Shinran, Nihon Shisō Taikei*, vol. 11. Tokyo: Iwanami shoten, 1971.

Iyenaga Saburo. *Chūsei bukkyō shisohi kenkyū.* Kyoto: Hōzōkan, 1947.

———. *Nihon shisōshi ni okeru hitei no ronri no hattatsu.* Tokyo: Shinsensha, 1969.

———. *Jōgū Shōtoku hōō teisetsu no kenkyū.* Tokyo: Sanseidō, 1972.

———. *Nihon bukkyō shi.* Kyoto: Hōzōkan, 1967.

Iyenaga Saburō et al. *Shōtoku Taishi shū.* Tokyo: Iwanami shoten, 1975.

Iyenaga Saburō, Akamatsu Toshihide, and Tamamuro Taijō, eds. *Nihon bukkyōshi.* 3 vols. Kyoto: Hōzōkan, 1967.

Imai Masaharu. *Ippen Shōnin to Jishū.* Tokyo: Yoshikawa Kōbunkan, 1981.

Inaba Masamaru, ed. *Rennyo Shōnin ibun.* Kyoto: Hōzōkan, 1937.

Inoue Mitsusada. *Nihon Jōdokyō seiritsu shi no kenkyū.* Tokyo: Yamakawa shuppansha, 1957.

———. *Nihon kodai kokka no kenkyū.* Tokyo: Iwanami shoten, 1965.

———. *Nihon kodai shisōshi no kenkyū.* Tokyo: Iwanami shoten, 1982.

Inoue Toshio. *Honganji.* Tokyo: Shibundō, 1962.

Ishida Mizumaro. *Nihon bukkyō shisō kenkyū.* Vol. I, *Kairitsu no kenkyū.* Tokyo: Hōzōkan, 1986.

———. "Shitennōji to shari shinkō" in *Shitennōji to Ōsaka/Hyōgo no Koji*, ed. Ishida Mizumaro, Miya Tsugio, et al., 66–75. Tokyo: Shueisha, 1985.

Ishida Shobō, ed. *Shōtoku Taishi jiten.* Tokyo: Kaishiwa Shobō, 1997.

Ishida Yoshito. "Kyūbukkyō no chūseiteki tenkai" in *Nihon bukkyōshi chūseihen*, ed. Akamatsu Toshihide. Tokyo: Hōzōkan, 1967.

Ishimoda Sho. *Kodai makki seijishi josetsu.* Tokyo: Iwanami shoten, 1964.

———. *Chūseiteki sekai no keisei.* Tokyo: Ito shoten, 1946.

Ishimura Kiei. *Nihon kodai bukkyō bunkashi ronko.* Tokyo: Sankibo busshōrin, 1987.

Itō Zuiei. "Shōtoku Taishi no *Bukkyō* shisō—Sono ichi, koto ni Tenjukoku o megutte." *Hokke bunka kenkyū* 4 (1978), 15–29.

Iwaki Takatoshi, ed. *Zoho Gangōji hennen shiryō,* vol. I. Tokyo: Yoshikawa kōbunkan, 1975.

Kamata Shigeo and Tanaka Hisao, eds. *Kamakura kyūbukkyō* in *Nihon shisō taikei.* No. 15. Tokyo: Iwananmi shoten, 1971.

Kamata Tōji. "Atarashii kami to shite no hotoke" in *Nihon no bukkyō,* vol. 3, ed. Ōkubo Ryōshun, Satō Hiroo, Sueki Fumihiko, et al. Tokyo: Shunjūsha, 1995.

Kamikawa, Michio. "Chūsei no sokui girei to bukkyō" in *Tennō daigawari gishiki no rekishitieki tendai,* ed. Iwai Tadakuma and Okada Seishi. Tokyo: Shinjusha, 1989.

Kanaji Isamu. "Sangyō gisho no seiritsu ni tsuite" in *Shōtoku Taishi kenkyū,* vol. 4. Ōsaka: Shōtoku Taishi Kenkyūkai, 1968.

Kaneko Daiei. *Shinran ni eizuru Shōtoku Taishi.* Tokyo: Meguro shoten, 1939.

Kasahara Kazuo. *Shinran to tōgoku nōmin.* Tokyo: Yamakawa shūppanha, 1957.

———. *Shinran kenkyu nōto.* Tokyo: Tosho shinbunha, 1965.

———. *Shinran to Rennyo: Sono kōdō to shisō.* Nihonjin no kōdō to shisō, no. 40. Tokyo: Hyoronsha, 1978.

Katsumata Shunkyō. "Kenmitsu taiben shisō no tenkai" in *Nihon meisō ronshū: Kūkai,* eds. Wada Shujo and Takagi Shingen. Tokyo: Sankibo busshōrin, 1982.

Kazue Kyōichi. *Nihon no mappō shisō.* Tokyo: Kōbundō, 1961.

Kishi Toshio. "Shūkke to Tennō" in *Matsurigoto no tenkai,* ed. Kishi Toshio. Tokyo: Chūo kōron, 1986.

Kobayashi Toshio. *Kodai Tennōsei no kisoteki kenkyū.* Tokyo: Azekura shobō, 1994.

Koizumi Hiroshi and Takahashi Nobuyuki, eds. *Shūsei, Shohon taisho Sanbōe schusei.* Tokyo: Kasama Shoin, 1980.

Kume Kunitake. "Jōgū Taishi Jitsuroku" in Fujiwara Yusetsu, ed., *Shōtoku Taishi zenshū.* Tokyo: Ryūginsha, 1942.

———. "Shōtoku Taishi no Kenkyū." *Kume Kunitake rebishi chosabushū* 1. Tokyo: Yoshikawa kōbunkan, 1988.

Kuroda Toshio. *Nihon chūsei no kokka to shūkyō.* Tokyo: Iwanami shoten, 1975.

———. *Chūsei ni okeru kenmitsu taisei no tenkai* in *Nihon chūsei no kokka to shūkyō.* Tokyo: Iwanami shoten, 1975.

———. *Jisha seiryoku.* Tokyo: Iwanami shoten, 1980.

————. *Ōbō to buppō: Chūsei no kōzu*. Kyoto: Hōzōkan, 1983.

Matsuno Junko. *Shinran—Sono kōdō to shisō*. Nihonjin no Kōdō to Shisō, no. 2. Tokyo: Hyōronsha, 1971.

Matsuo Kenji. *Kamakura shinbukkyō no tanjō*. Tokyo: Kōdansha, 1995.

Mino Hōyū. *Shōtoku Taishi to Shinran*. Kyoto: Nagata Bunshōdō, 1973.

Mochida Yasuhiko. "Shōtoku Tennōcho ni okeru tairyo joi to sono eikyo" in *Kodai oken to saigi*, ed. Mayuzumi Hiromichi. Tokyo: Yoshikawa Kōbunkan, 1990.

Mochizuki Kazunori. *Hokekyō to Shōtoku Taishi*. Tokyo: Dai'ichi shobō, 1975.

Mochizuki Shinko, ed. *Bukkyō daijiten*, 10 vols. Tokyo: Sekai seiten kankō kyōkai, 1958–1963.

Murai Yasuhiko. *Kodai kokka kaitai katei no kenkyū*. Tokyo: Iwanami shoten, 1965.

Murakami Sokui et al., eds. *Koza: Shinran no shisō*. Vol. 8, *Shinran shisō no shūyaku to tenkai*. Tokyo: Kyōiku Shinchōha, 1978.

Murayama Shuichi. *Honji suijaku*. Tokyo: Yoshikawa kōbunkan, 1974.

————. *Shinbutsu shugo shuchō*. Kyoto: Heirakuji shoten, 1957.

Nagahara Kenji. *Nihon hōkensei seiritsu katei no kenkyū*. Tokyo: Iwanami shoten, 1961.

Nabata Ōjun et al, eds. *Shinran-shū Nichiren-shū* in *Nihon koten bungaku taikei* 82. Tokyo: Iwanami shoten, 1964.

Nakamura Hajime et al., eds. *Bukkyōgo daijiten*, 3 vols. Tokyo: Tokyo shoseki, 1975.

Nakamura Hajime. "Shōtoku Taishi no goseishin to kongo no sekai" in Mochizuki Kazunori, ed., *Rekishi no nagare*. Kyoto: Sōgō rekishi kenkyūkai, 1964.

Nakano Takeshi. "Ryoiki izen no *engi* ni tsuite" in *Mauchi Kazuo hakase taikan kinen setsuwa bungaku ronshū*. Tokyo: Taishūkan shoten, 1981.

Nakao Shunbaku. *Nihon shokitendai no kenkyū*. Kyoto: Nagata bunshodō, 1973.

Nara Hiromoto. "Shōtoku Taishi no jōdokan ni tsuite." *Indogaku bukkyōgaku kenkyū* 17.1 (1968), 228–231.

*Nihon Daijiten Kankōkai*, ed. Kokugo daijiten, 20 vols. Tokyo: Shōgakukan, 1972–1976.

Ocho Enichi. "Shinran to Tendaigaku" in *Ōtani Gakuhō* 46, 4 (February 1967): 1–12.

Ohara Shojitsu. *Shinshū Kyōgaku no dentō to kōshō*. Kyoto: Nagata bunshodō, 1965.

Okada Seishi. "Daiō shūnin girei no genkei to sono tenkai" in *Tennō daigawari gishiki no rekishiteki tendai*, ed. Iwai Tadakuma and Okada Seishi. Tokyo: Kashiwa shobō, 1989.

Ono Genmyō, ed. *Busshō kaisetsu daijiten*. 12 vols. Tokyo: Daitō shūppansha, 1933–1936.

Ono Tatsunosuke. *Shinkō Nihon bukkyō shishoshi*. Tokyo: Yoshikawa kōbunkan, 1973.

————. *Shōtoku Taishi no kenkyū—sono bukkyō to seiji shisō*. 1970. Reprint, Tokyo: Yoshikawa kōbunkan, 1996.

Ōyama Seiichi. *Nihon shoki no kōsō*. Tokyo: Heibonsha, 2003.

———. *"Shōtoku Taishi" no tangō*. Tokyo: Yoshikawa kōbunkan, 1999.

Ozawa Tomio. *Mappō to masse no shisō*. Tokyo: Yūzankaku shūppan, 1974.

Sakamoto Tarō. *Shōtoku Taishi*. Tokyo: Yoshikawa kōbunkan, 1979.

———. *"Nihon shoki* to Shōtoku Taishi no denki" in *Koten no rekishi*. Tokyo: Yoshikawa kōbunkan, 1972.

Sakurai Tokutarō. "Engi no Ruikei no Tenkai" (Types of *Engi* and Their Development), in Sakurai et al., eds. *Jisha Engi*, vol. 20 of *Nihon Shisō Taikei*. Tokyo: Iwanami shoten, 1975.

Satō Hiroo. *Nihon chūsei no kokka to shūkyō*. Tokyo: Yoshikawa kōbunkan, 1987.

———. *Kamakura bukkyō*. Tokyo: Yoshikawa kōbunkan, 1985.

———. "Soniryo to jujutsu" in *Chingo kokka to jujutsu*, eds. Uehara Shoichi and Kanaoka Shūyu. Tokyo: Shūeisha, 1989.

———. "Kyū bukkyō to kamakura shin bukkyō no kankei o dou miruka" in *Soten nihon no rekishi*, vol. 4, ed. Minegishi Sumio. Tokyo: Shinjunbutsu ōraisha, 1991.

———. "Chūsei kenmitsu bukkyō no kokkakan" in *Kokka to shūkyo nihon shisōshi ron-shū*, ed. Minamoto Ryōen. Kyoto: Shibunkaku, 1992.

———. *Shinbutsu ōken no chūsei*. Tokyo: Hōzōkan, 1998.

Satō Shin'ichi. *Nihon no chūsei no kokka to shūkyō*. Tokyo: Iwanami shoten, 1983.

Sekiguchi Shizuo. "Wako dojin: Ryojin hisho to honji suijaku shisō" in *Nihon kayo kenkyū* 17 (April 1978): 10–15.

Shigematsu Akihisa. *Honganji hyakunen sensō*. Tokyo: Yoshikawa kobunkan, 1986.

———. *Kakunyo*. Jinbutsu Sosho. No. 123. Tokyo: Yoshikawa kōbunkan, 1966.

———. *Shinran shinshū shisōshi kenkyū*. Tokyo: Yoshikawa kōbunkan, 1990.

———. *Chūsei shinshū shisō no kenkyū*. Tokyo: Yoshikawa kōbunkan, 1986.

———. *Nihon jōdokyō seiritsu katei no kenkyū*. Kyoto: Heirakuji shoten, 1964.

Shigemitsu Kyoto. *Shōtoku Taishi no Eshi Zenshi Koshin-setsu ni tsuite*. Tokyo: Tenmon Gakuho, 1991.

Shimode Sekiyo. "Narajidai no siji to dōtoku" in *Narajidai no soryo to shakai*, ed. Nemoto Seiji. Tokyo: Yūzankaku, 1994.

Shinkawa Tokio. "Narajidai no dōkyo to *bukkyō*" in *Ronshū nihon bukkyō shi: Nara jidai*, ed. Hayami Tasuku. Tokyo: Yūzankaku, 1986.

———. "Shūtarashūron" in *Nara bukkyō no tendai*, ed. Hayami Tasuku. Tokyo: Yūzankaku, 1994.

Shiroyama Shūnsuke. "Shinbutsu shūgō no shinten" in *Ronshū nihon bukkyō shi: Nara jidai*, ed. Hayami Tasuku. Tokyo: Yūzankaku, 1986.

*Shōtoku Taishi Hōsankai Kanshū* in *Shōtoku Taishi zenshū*. 4 vols. Tokyo: Rinsen shoten, 1988.

So Nahata. *Kokushi kodokushi nit tsuite*. Kyoto: Otani Gakuho, 1979.

Sone Masato. "Heian shoki nanto bukkyō to gokoku taisei" in *Nara Heian jidaishi ronshū*, vol. 2, ed. Tsuchida Naoshige sensei kanreki kinenkdai. Tokyo: Yoshikawa kōbunkan, 1984.

Sonoda Kōyū. "Heian bukkyō no seiritsu" in *Nihon bukkyōshi*, vol. I, *Kodaihen*, ed. Iyenaga Saburō. Tokyo: Hōzōkan, 1967.

———. "Saichō to sono shisō" in *Saichō*, eds. Andō Toshio and Sonoda Kōyū. Tokyo: Iwanami shoten, 1974.

———. *Heian bukkyō no kenkyū*. Tokyo: Hōzōkan, 1981.

Sueki Fumihiko. *Nihon bukkyō shisōshi ronkō*. Tokyo: Shunjūsha, 1993.

———. "Chiko hannya shingyo jutsugi ni tsuite" in *Nara bukkyō no tenkai*, ed. Hayami Tasuku. Tokyo: Yūzankaku, 1994.

———. *Heian shoki bukkyō no kenkyū*. Tokyo: Shunjūsha, 1994.

———. "Kenmitsu taisei to hongaku shisō" in *Kuroda Toshio chosakushū geppō* 2 (December 1994): 1–3.

Suzuki Yasutami. "Nihon ritsuryō kokka to shiragi bokkai" in *Nihon ritsuryō kokka to higashi ajia*, ed. Inoue Mitsusada. Tokyo: Gakuseisha, 1982.

Taga Munehaya. *Jien no kenkyū*. Tokyo: Yoshikawa kōbunkan, 1970.

Taira Masayuki. "Jogo to Kamakura bakufu" in *Kodai Chūsei no shakai to kokka*, ed. Ōsaka daigaku bungakubu Nihonshi kenkyūshitsu, 427–444. Ōsaka: Seibunko, 1998.

———. *Nihon chūsei no shakai to bukkyō*. Tokyo: Hanawa shobō, 1992.

———. "Hōnen no shisō kōzō to sono rekishi teki ichi—Chūsei teki itan no seiritsu" in *Nihonshi kenkyū* 198 (February 1979).

———. "Chūsei shūkyō no shakai teki tenkai" in *Kōzō Nihon rekishi*. Tokyo: Tokyo Daigaku shūppankai, 1984.

Takada Jishō. "Shinran Shōnin no Hokekyōkan" in *Ryūkoku kyōgaku*, no. 12 (June 1977).

Takada Toshin. "Zenkōji Nyorai Gosho-bako no Roman" (The Story of the Letter Box of the Zenkōji Buddha), in *Hōryūji 1: Rekishi to Ko Bunken*, vol. 1, of *Nihon no Koji Bijutsu*. Tokyo: Iwanami shoten, 1987.

Takagi Yutaka. *Heian jidai hokke bukkyō shi kenkyū*. Kyoto: Heirakuji shoten, 1973.

———. *Kamakura bukkyōshi kenkyū*. Tokyo: Iwanami shoten, 1982.

Takahashi Kotohisa. *Shinran-shisō no rekishiteki tenkai*. Kyoto: Nagata bunshodō, 1985.

Takahashi Miyuki. "Chūsei ni okeru jingu sobyokan no seiritsu no tenkai" in *Kokka to shūkyō: Nihon shisō ronshū*, ed. Minamoto Ryoen, 95–114. Kyoto: Shibunkaku, 1992.

Takakusu Junjirō and Watanabe Kaigyoku, eds. *Taishō shinshū daizōkyo*, 85 vols. Tokyo: Taishō issaikyō kankōkai, 1924–1932.

Takeda Kenju. *Shinran Shōnin no Taishi shinkō no kenkyū*. Nagoya: Bunkōdō shoten, 1992.

Takeuchi Rizō. *Ritsuryō to kizoku seiken*, vol. 2. Tokyo: Ochanomizu shobō, 1958.

Takeuchi Rizō, Yamada Hideo, and Hirano Kunio, eds. *Kodai jinmei jiten*, 7 vols. Tokyo: Yoshikawa kōbunkan, 1958–1977.

Takinami Sadako. *Nihon kodai kyūtei shakai no kenkyū*. Kyoto: Shibunkaku, 1991.

Tamura Enchō. *Asuka bukkyōshi kenkyū*. Tokyo: Hanawa shobō, 1969.

———. *Hōnen Shōnin den no kenkyū*. Kyoto: Hōzōkan, 1972.

———. *Shōtoku Taishi*. Tokyo: Chūōkōronsha, 1964.

——— "Shōtoku Taishi Katakoyayama Kisha Setsuwa" in *Bukkyō bungaku kenkyū*, April 1965.

Tamura Encho, ed. *Shōtoku Taishi to Asuka bukkyō*. Tokyo: Yoshikawa kōbunkan, 1985.

Tamura Kōyū. "Tokuitsu chosaku ko" in *Dengyō daishi kenkyū*, ed. Tendai gakkai. Tokyo: Waseda daigaku shūppanbu, 1973.

———. "Daijō kaidan dokuritsu ni tsuite" in *Kairitsu no sekai*, ed. Mori Shōji. Tokyo: Keisuisha, 1993.

Tamura Yoshirō. *Kamakura shinbukkyō shisō no kenkyu*. Kyoto: Heirakuji shoten, 1965.

Tanaka Fumihide. "Chūsei kenmitsu jiin ni okeru shuho no ichikosatou" in *Chūsei jiinshi no kenkyū*, vol. I, ed. Kurodo Toshio. Tokyo: Hōzōkan, 1988.

Tanaka Takashi, ed. "Gangōji garan *engi* narabi ruki shizaichō" in *Nanto bukkyō* 4 (1957).

Tanaka Tsuguhito. *Shōtoku Taishi shinkō no seiritsu*. Tokyo: Yoshikawa kōbunkan, 1983.

Tasuro Fujishima. "Shōtoku Taishi to Shinran shōnin" in *Nihon bukkyō gakkai nempō* 29 (1963).

Tokura Yoshitaka. "Man'yō Shōtoku Taishi-ka no Hassō o Megutte" in *Nihon bungaku kenkyū shiryō kankōkai*, ed., *Man'yoshū*, III. Tokyo: Yūseidō, 1977.

Tsuchiya Megumi. "Heian zenki sogosei no tenkai" in *Shisō* 24 (1983): 37–76.

Tsuda Sōkichi. *Nihon koten no kenkyū*. Tokyo: Iwanami shoten, 1950.

Tsukuma Sonnō. "Shari-e ni tsuite" in *Eizan gakuin kenkyū kiyo* 3 (1980): 93–108.

Wakaki Yoshihiko. "Shinran Shōnin no jingikan" in *Shinshū kenkyū* 17 (1972).

Yamada Ryūjō and Fukuhara Ryōgen. "Shinran kyōgaku to sono chosakuchū no inyōsho" in *Ryūkoku daigaku ronshū* 365 and 366 (December 1960): 257–309.

Yamagishi Tsuneto. "Tōdaiji nigatsudō no soken to shibi shūdai juichimen kekasho" in *Nanto bukkyō* 52 (1986): 27–49.

Yamasaki Keiki. "Saichō to Shinran" in *Ryūkoku daigaku ronshū* 400–401 (March 1973): 333–351.

Yoshida Kazuhiko. *Nihon kodai shakai to bukkyō.* Tokyo: Yoshikawa kōbunkan, 1995.

———. "Soniryo no un'yo to kōryoku" in *Ronshū nihon bukkyō shi: Nara jidai,* ed. Hayami Tasuku. Tokyo: Yūzankaku, 1986.

———. *Nihon kodai shakai to bukkyō.* Tokyo: Yoshikawa kōbunkan, 1995.

Yuki Yoshifumi. *Shōtoku Taishi shinkō in nihon tendai.* Tokyo: Kōkusho kankōkai, 1986.

Zennosuke Tsuji. *Shōtoku Taishi Eshi Zenshi Koshin-setsu ni kansuru Gi.* Tokyo: Konkodo, 1942.

# Index